DISCARD

The Tragic Vision
and the Christian Faith

The Tragic Vision
and the Christian Faith

EDITED BY

NATHAN A. SCOTT, JR.

A Haddam House Book

ASSOCIATION PRESS · NEW YORK

To

DAVID E. ROBERTS

In Memoriam

Acknowledgments

Indebtedness has been incurred to the following publishers for permission to quote copyrighted material from their publications: Doubleday & Company (Friedrich Nietzsche, *The Birth of Tragedy and the Genealogy of Morals*, trans. by Francis Golffing); Schocken Books (Franz Kafka, *Diaries*, Vols. I and II; *The Great Wall of China*); The Macmillan Co. of England (Volumes 11 and 17 of *The Complete Works of Friedrich Nietzsche*, trans. by Oscar Levy); Random House (Goethe, *Faust*, trans. by Bayard Taylor; *The Philosophy of Nietzsche* [a Modern Library Giant]); New Directions (Franz Kafka, *Amerika*); Alfred A. Knopf (Franz Kafka, *The Castle*; Albert Camus, *The Rebel*); Beacon Press (Karl Jaspers, *Tragedy Is Not Enough*, trans. by H. A. T. Reiche, H. T. Moore, and K. W. Deutsch); Pantheon Books (Denis de Rougemont, *The Devil's Share*); Geoffrey Bles Ltd. (Nicolas Berdyaev, *The Destiny of Man*); Routledge & Kegan Paul Ltd. (R. J. Z. Werblowsky, *Lucifer and Prometheus*); Harvard University Press (Arthur O. Lovejoy, *The Great Chain of Being;* Herman Melville, *Billy Budd*, F. Barron Freeman, ed.); Charles Scribner's Sons (Paul Tillich, *The Shaking of the Foundations*); Grove Press (Edwin Muir, *Prometheus*); Cambridge University Press (A. H. J. Knight, *Some Aspects of the Life and Work of Nietzsche*); Harper & Brothers (Ralph Harper, *The Sleeping Beauty*); The Macmillan Co. (F. Dostoievsky, *The Brothers Karamazov*, trans. by Constance Garnett).

The Sewanee Review also kindly agreed to the use of a passage from an article (J. A. Bryant, Jr., "Shakespeare's Allegory") which appeared in its Spring 1955 number.

Foreword

THE ORGANIZING PRINCIPLE that brings together the twelve essays that make up this book is not simple, and it resists concise summarization. What does it mean to speak of "the tragic vision," and is it a perspective upon the human story that has any relationship at all to the Christian faith? These are the complex questions that bristle intimidatingly before me now, as I cast about for the appropriate prefatory word to this volume. But they are questions that I shall not undertake to resolve here in any systematic way, since that would be presumptuously to bypass the various answers that my collaborators have already proposed in terms of the concrete literary materials with which each has worked. Yet there are a few observations that it occurs to me I should make, by way of putting the reader in mind of certain basic presuppositions to which most of the contributors seem to adhere.

First of all, most of us, as it will doubtless appear with obviousness, do not regard the tragic vision as requiring for its expression that special form of drama of which Aristotle is still the greatest interpreter. Great tragic drama—of which, when one recalls the entire history of the theater in the West from Aeschylus to T. S. Eliot, there seem to be, relatively, only a very few authentic instances—may provide us with the most concentrated expressions in literature of "the tragic sense of life." But, when we speak of "the tragic vision," we are not speaking of something that can only disclose itself in the theater: on the contrary, as Max Scheler reminded us that we must do, "We are speaking of life and history in general without placing ourselves in any particular esthetic circumstances. . . ."[1] We have in mind, that is, *the attitude of attentiveness* to certain types of events, to certain dimensions of human experience—and an attitude that may gain many of its most deeply moving expressions in drama but that may also come to great expression in poetry, in the novel, in philosophy, in history (think of Tacitus or of Spengler), indeed in any of the great literary forms which the humanistic imagination uses to meditate on the mystery of man.

Since my colleagues were willing to consider so many extremely diverse figures under the rubric established by our symposium, I take it that it would also be fair to say that most of them would not contend that the tragic vision postulates any special metaphysic that is in competition with other systems of philosophy. No, they would argue, it is not a metaphysic but an attitude which, as Unamuno says, "does not so much flow from ideas as determine them."[2] It is, as I would put it, an *attitude of attentiveness* to the contingencies and sufferings that it is the lot of man to endure. The man whose vision is of the tragic cast is preoccupied with the inner and outer insecurities of human nature, and the focus is upon the background of danger against which the human drama must be enacted. That which is in view are what philosophers like Jaspers and Tillich call the "boundary situations" of human existence, in which man is nakedly exposed to the primal terrors and threats to which his limited and imperfect creatureliness is subject. But the attitude of attentiveness before the quandaries and ambiguities of life has not, I think, ever been unbroken in Western spiritual history since the advent of Christianity, except in the extremest forms of modern nihilism. That is to say, as one moves about in the literature of tragedy—whether one goes to *Lear* or to *Phaedra* or to *Samson Agonistes* or to *Billy Budd* or to *The Wild Duck* or to *The Sound and the Fury*—one very rarely encounters a presentment of existence as utterly unredeemable or of the human enterprise as fated ultimately to career into a meaningless void: the attention of the tragedian seems never to be *riveted* on the problematical but seems always to some extent to be engaged by at least the dream of some brave new world or country of the spirit wherein the brokenness of man may be repaired and healed. It may be that the true explanation of this is simply that our tragic sense has, in point of fact, been a bequest of Christianity. But however it is to be explained, the fact itself is not, I think, subject to serious disputation. And this is why I say that the special sort of attentiveness to be attributed to the tragedian does not represent an *absolute* or an *unbroken* fixation.

It is by no means improper, though, to postulate (as it seems to me Professor Cherbonnier in effect does in his essay) an ideally *intransitive* attentiveness before the facts of evil, and then to extrapolate from it to the metaphysic that such an attitude would indeed seem to presuppose. And the chief value of such a procedure (again, as Professor Cherbonnier's essay beautifully indicates) is that, in terms of juxtaposition and contrast, it makes possible an even sharper definition of what is radically distinctive in the witness that the Christian faith makes about the human predicament. But, however much a metaphysic alternative to the Christian faith may be a co-implicate of such an attitude, it should be borne in mind that this is an attitude that, on the whole, has not been, fortunately, a decisive force in the last two thousand years of Western spiritual history. And though the tragic vision of the Greeks prevented an Aeschylus or a Sophocles from declaring that "my flesh also shall rest in hope," "our own tragic sense of life," as Mr. Ralph Harper has said, "has come from another source altogether, and is more developed if not more hopeful."[3]

Now this leads me to what I take to be a third presupposition to which my collaborators seem generally to adhere: that the tragic sense of life is not alien to or unassimilable to Christian vision. Even Professor Cherbonnier, who is especially concerned to stress the absolute disjunction between a *metaphysic* of tragedy and the biblical *kerygma*—even he, I suspect, would want to grant that "the tragic vision" (in the more commonly impure mode of it that I am here speaking of) is not something independent of and opposed to the Christian imagination. Indeed, those interpreters of the Christian faith who are discomfited by the testimony of the tragedian are likely to be those who have somehow blunted the full meaning of the Christian faith itself, and of the Cross and God's providence. Surely the penultimate event in the Christian story which took place on Calvary can be made no sense of at all apart from the kinds of perceptions which the tragedian seeks to assist us in attaining. And it is, I feel certain, only those who have accepted a "vocation to tragedy" who can understand the whole point and meaning of Job's declaration, "I know that my redeemer liveth," or who can understand the full poignancy and gloriousness of Paul's word, "If God be for us, who can be against us?" Indeed, the facts of tragedy are never scanted by the profoundest Christian faith: life is not, to be sure, seen as being at cross purposes with itself; but what is recognized is that, when we take account of what we are up against in this world both from within and from without, the ultimate ground of our hope can rest only in a God who himself suffers, who "himself took our infirmities, and bare our sicknesses" and thereby accomplished our deliverance from the woe of being alive. The final accent of Christian proclamation will not be the accent of tragedy; but every expression of ultimate assurance, in the degree to which it springs from a true understanding of our actual human situation, has incorporated into itself a tragic note and will in some way resemble the descrip-

tion of the Christian's situation which Paul offered in his
second letter to the church at Corinth, when he spoke of our
being "troubled on every side, yet not distressed; . . . perplexed, but not in despair; persecuted, but not forsaken; cast
down, but not destroyed; always bearing about in the body
the dying of the Lord Jesus, that the life also of Jesus might be
made manifest in our body."

This alliance between the tragic vision and the Christian
faith has not, it is true, been unceasingly witnessed to in
Christian history. And, indeed, what has been most characteristic of the *avant-garde* movements in Christian thought during the last two decades or so is the reawakening, within the
Christian community itself, of the tragic sense, after a long
period of flirtation with the various gospels of modernity
which promised to resolve all the vast contradictions of life
by means of some simple scheme of science or education. We
are, of course, living today in what many of the European
specialists in *Zeitgeist* tell us is an "extreme situation," and
even to Americans the alarmism which the term connotes no
longer seems excessive. For, as we grope about amidst the
uncharted waters of life in these middle years of the twentieth century, it seems that every step we take must involve
what is called "the calculated risk," and nowhere can we find
guarantees of security or the promise of any immediate renova-
tion of the present disorder. In the last few years there is a
special type of misery that has been the lot of the hordes of
refugees in various parts of the world who, as a result of one
dislocation or another, have found themselves without citizen-
ship and exiled from their native lands: we call them, in the
terrible language of the day, "displaced persons." But there is
surely a deep and melancholy sense in which we are all today
"displaced persons"—persons, that is, who cannot find anywhere a satisfactory dwelling place in the world of our time,

in which, as the French Catholic philosopher Gabriel Marcel says, "the preposition 'with' . . . seems more and more to be losing its meaning."[4] Nor has it been possible to gain any relief from the outer disorder in the world of society and politics by turning back to the inner world of the private self, for there we discover the real costs that contemporary life exacts in nightmare and neurosis, in fear and remorse and hysteria. So it is no wonder that we believe ourselves to be in an "extreme situation" and that we feel the ancient issues of tragedy to have been reinstated with a new kind of urgency.

This, then, is the occasion and the time in which the present generation is turning again to the wisdom of the past for some hint as to where a good counterpoise to chaos may be found. The surface manifestations of this in the emergence of Great Books discussion groups in local communities throughout the land and in the endless tinkering that goes on in the colleges with Great Books courses—the surface manifestations of this new interest are so numerous and noticeable that they need only be mentioned to evoke a familiar image of a characteristic contemporary form of the quest for salvation. But, of course, the Great Books will not save us, and the sooner this is realized the better off we shall be. Yet it is surely a healthy instinct that in our time of perplexity literate people should be seeking out some of the great statements about the human problem that the legacies of literature and philosophy and theology contain, for, when properly used, they cannot but be a profit to the mind. It is not a matter of Matthew Arnold's "touchstones" of greatness nor of Mortimer Adler's salvationism, but rather of the mind's being aided in the search for its own proper order by entering into dialogue with some of the pioneers in the realms of thought and feeling who have shaped the tradition that is today our bright inheritance and our perplexing burden.

So we have come together—the twelve of us—to talk, each in his turn, about some of the great focal versions of the human problem in the literary, philosophic, and religious traditions, and to do so, each in his own way, in terms of his individual understanding of what our common Christian faith is all about. We do not talk about Shakespeare or Milton or Dostoevski or Faulkner as though these were authors whose books afforded any direct guidance as to precisely how we might plunge with a great therapeutic splosh into the maelstrom of contemporary life. Which is to say that we do not ask our authors to be "scriptural." All that the contributors, in each case, have undertaken to do is to suggest a perspective or a strategy of analysis in terms of which the Christian reader may have a profitable transaction with some major anatomist of the human quandary in the intellectual tradition. And everything (with the exception of Professor Cherbonnier's essay in which, in the very nature of the case, rigorous systematization was inevitable) tends to be unsystematic and informal. We do not first present an ordered exegesis of a text or a body of work, then an exposition of the Christian faith, and then a specification of the respects in which the two either collide with or confirm each other. This would make for dull reading and would soon pall intolerably. Instead, each writer presents his subject: in the presentation, exegesis and critical interpretation are intermingled, as they should be: and the reader is generally left to draw his own systematic conclusions.

Nor, within the space deemed manageable by the publisher, has any effort been made to deal with all the figures on whom I should have liked to have had essays. The most grievous omissions are Dante, Corneille and Racine, Ibsen, Conrad, Sartre, and Unamuno; and I should also have liked to have had essays on Hölderlin and Leopardi, on Yeats and Eliot, on

O'Neill and Lorca, and on Tennessee Williams and Arthur
Miller. But all this could not be provided for; the publisher
informed me that so many pages of typescript could be handled at such-and-such a price, with no nonsense about it:
and that was it! So what it was then clearly incumbent upon
us to do was to seek for those bodies of literature apart from
which it seems today impossible for us to do any thinking at
all about the tragic problem. We wanted to concentrate very
largely on the modern period, but it also seemed appropriate
to devote some attention to various phases of the precedent
tradition: so immediately, then, the Greeks and Shakespeare
and Milton pressed themselves upon us as the great unignor-
able figures who simply had to be faced. But since we wanted
to emphasize the collision between the Greek and the Hebraic
perspectives, it seemed feasible to collapse these two problems
into a single chapter—which is what Professor Cherbonnier
has done (though, in the course of his essay, he ranges far
beyond Greek drama in the process of drawing a circle of
definition about his subject). Then, in moving beyond Milton
further into the seventeenth century, we were, of course, faced
with the great tragic literature of French Neo-Classicism; but
bitter choices had to be made, and, since there seemed to be
far more lines connecting Pascal with "the tragic sense of life"
that has been reinstated in our own time, it was to him that we
turned. From there on the selections that were made of sub-
ject-figures were, I believe, the inevitable and the unavoidable
ones: Goethe's is the great looming presence at the threshold
of the modern period, and, in the nineteenth century, it is in
Kierkegaard, Dostoevski, Nietzsche, Hawthorne, and Melville
that "the tragic vision" has its most poignant and memorable
life. And, similarly, if, as it became apparent, there could be
room for only three essays on twentieth-century figures,
Freud, Kafka, and Faulkner enforced themselves upon us as

the three writers we could not possibly ignore. Professor Outler has quoted the fine sentence of Lionel Trilling's in which he tells us that "if we want the sense of the human mystery, of tragedy truly conceived in the great terms of free will, necessity and hope, surely we do far better to seek it directly in Freud himself" than in many of the novelists and dramatists of our day. Professor Miller cites no less an authority than W. H. Auden, as he reminds us (in Auden's words) that "had one to name the artist who comes nearest to bearing the same kind of relation to our age that Dante, Shakespeare, and Goethe bore to theirs, Kafka is the first we would think of." And Professor Waggoner might also have marshaled a very impressive body of contemporary opinion to the effect that in William Faulkner we have the greatest living novelist on the present scene, and one whose account of the human voyage presents us with an authentic instance of "the tragic vision."

These, then, were the considerations that determined the shape of the book.

A foolish criticism of symposium-volumes that I often hear has to do with the multifariousness of literary styles that they generally entail. But how silly! For if it be granted (and on the day when the concession can no longer be made, the intellectual life in this country will really be in jeopardy) that it is a worth-while thing to do to bring together a group of able people to think and write about books and ideas, then it must be granted that each will handle language in the way that his mind and sensibility make necessary and inevitable. So (beyond the usual minor tampering with diction and syntax that the editor of this kind of book must do) I have made no effort to bring the styles of my collaborators into conformity with the canons of anybody's book of rules; and I hope that my refusal to do this will increase the reader's exhilaration in joining a lively company.

This book is dedicated to the memory of David E. Roberts (sometime Marcellus Hartley Professor of the Philosophy of Religion in Union Theological Seminary), whose career, at the time of his death in New York City on the fourth day of January, 1955, was widely regarded as one of the most promising on the theological scene in the English-speaking world. Since these essays are being offered particularly to the student community, this dedication seems especially appropriate, for in the last ten years of his life David Roberts became, in the academic world, one of the most sought-after preachers in America and, from the pulpits of college and university chapels all over the land, helped large numbers of young people to rediscover the relevance of the Christian faith for our time. But those who are familiar with his teaching career will doubtless feel that by far the better reason for this dedication is the seminar on "Christianity and Tragedy" that he and Professor Richard Kroner led together and that was, for several student generations in Union Seminary, one of the most exciting courses in the curriculum. Indeed, I dare say that it was in this seminar that many of the younger teachers on the campuses today got their best clues for dealing with the kinds of questions which their students are asking about the Christian faith and about human existence; and, in fact, they will often be found eager to testify to the fact that the "Tragedy" seminar is one of their brightest memories of Union. "Dave" (as he was affectionately called by both his students and his colleagues) understood, I believe, with a sensitiveness unsurpassed by any other Christian thinker of our time, the terrible profundities implicit in those great sentences of Pascal on "the grandeur" and "the misery" of man. And his friends found in the remarkable gallantry of his own character (as many others are today discovering in his fine books) a kind of proof of the power of the Christian faith to redeem our human nature from the woes of life.

NATHAN A. SCOTT, JR.

NOTES

1. Max Scheler, "On the Tragic," *Cross Currents*, Vol. IV, No. 3 (Winter 1954), p. 178. Translated and taken from *Vom Umsturz der Werte*, Vol. I (Der Neue Geist-Verlag Dr. Peter Reinhold, Leipzig, 1923), by Bernard Stambler.
2. Miguel de Unamuno, *The Tragic Sense of Life*, trans. by J. E. C. Flitch (London: Macmillan and Co., Ltd., 1921), p. 17.
3. Ralph Harper, *Existentialism: A Theory of Man* (Cambridge: Harvard University Press, 1948), p. 8.
4. Gabriel Marcel, *The Mystery of Being*, Vol. I, trans. by G. S. Fraser (Chicago: Henry Regnery Co., 1950), p. 28.

Contents

Foreword   ix

1. BIBLICAL FAITH AND THE IDEA OF TRAGEDY   23
   Edmond LaB. Cherbonnier

2. SHAKESPEAREAN TRAGEDY: A CHRISTIAN
   INTERPRETATION   56
   Roy W. Battenhouse

3. MILTONIC TRAGEDY AND CHRISTIAN VISION   99
   T. S. K. Scott-Craig

4. THE ANGUISH OF PASCAL   123
   Émile Cailliet

5. GOETHE'S FAUST: THE TRAGEDY OF TITANISM   153
   Richard Kroner

6. SÖREN KIERKEGAARD: FAITH IN A TRAGIC WORLD   174
   Paul L. Holmer

7. DOSTOEVSKI—TRAGEDIAN OF THE MODERN
   EXCURSION INTO UNBELIEF   189
   Nathan A. Scott, Jr.

8. NIETZSCHE: THE CONQUEST OF THE TRAGIC
   THROUGH ART   211
   John E. Smith

9. THE VISION OF EVIL IN HAWTHORNE AND
   MELVILLE   238
                              Randall Stewart

10. FREUD AND THE DOMESTICATION OF TRAGEDY   264
                              Albert C. Outler

11. FRANZ KAFKA AND THE METAPHYSICS OF
    ALIENATION   281
                              J. Hillis Miller, Jr.

12. WILLIAM FAULKNER'S PASSION WEEK OF THE
    HEART   306
                              Hyatt H. Waggoner

    About the Contributors   324

    Selected Bibliography   330

Biblical Faith and the
Idea of Tragedy

A BOOK APPEARING fifty years ago under the title *The Tragic Vision and the Christian Faith* is difficult to imagine. Those were the days when men fancied that the last war had been fought, and that mankind was securely aboard the bandwagon of inevitable progress. In such a climate, there was as little place for the idea of tragedy as for the central Christian affirmation that this is the kind of world which, in the name of piety and justice, could send perfect goodness to the Cross. The most common brand of religious thinking accordingly soft-pedaled the historic Christian understanding of human life in favor of the more palatable notion that the kingdom of God was just around the corner.

Such unrealistic optimism could flourish only in the hothouse conditions of the Victorian era. But under the impact of the relentless sequence of ugly events which began in 1914, disillusioned optimists began to search for a more adequate interpretation of human life, one that would make sense of a world in which reason is no match for brutality, and goodness is at the mercy of power. They did not have far to look. They found ready at hand a very ancient and very different creed from the sweetness and light of the nineteenth century, the so-called "tragic view of life." The seriousness with which it was embraced by disenchanted moderns is illustrated by the following words of F. Scott Fitzgerald, in a letter to his daughter:

23

Hemingway "dirty trick"

> Not one person in ten thousand finds time . . . to form what, for lack of a better phrase, I might call the wise and tragic sense of life. By this I mean . . . the sense that life is essentially a cheat and its conditions are . . . those of defeat . . .[1]

The prophets of this sophisticated doctrine sometimes imagined that they were discovering something new, but, actually, the "tragic vision" has recurrently dominated man's spiritual history. In the recent words of a contemporary poet:

> [Tragedy] has been the underlying theme in the work of every poet from Homer to Eliot. It is implicit in any poet's vision of reality. For poetry, like the other arts, gets its meaning from the tragic nature of things, whether as escape from it in play, or celebration of it in the more exalted moments. Against the backdrop of Fate, life shows at its noblest and most endearing. Its glory is in its doom.[2]

Christian thinking over the past fifty years has tended at times to follow the swing of the pendulum. Just as "liberal" Protestants of a generation ago shared the common cultural assumption of an onward and upward march of history, so their present-day successors have echoed the contemporary preoccupation with meaninglessness and despair. Recoiling from the discredited optimism of recent memory, they have sometimes taken up the refrain, so popular with today's intellectuals, that only a pessimist can be truly profound. In their search for a philosophy which could account for the disorders of the twentieth century, they have made common cause with their contemporaries in refurbishing "the tragic view of life," and have sought to incorporate it into Christianity. As one Christian writer recently said:

> There is a . . . tragic law which controls the historical process, the law that ordains that human greatness utterly fall. . . . That is the subject of Greek tragedy. That is the message of the prophet to the nations of the world. They are all subject to the law of tragic self-destruction . . .[3]

Although it will be insisted here that this close correlation of the Christian with the tragic view of life is unwarranted, we must recognize that there is in it a measure of plausibility. The two views are at least united in what they oppose. They both resist the unrealistic assumption that goodness always triumphs, or that it at least will triumph with the aid of more extensive education and a higher standard of living. Both are constrained by the facts of experience to acknowledge that life may confront a person not with a choice between good and evil but with a choice between the lesser of two evils; that to try to put a lofty principle into practice may result in more harm than good; and that in order to preserve one's own integrity one may have to forfeit one's life. Hence believers in the "tragic vision," together with adherents of the Christian faith, have made common cause against the sentimental illusions of a more credulous age. The former complain with Sophocles: "Strange, that impious men, sprung from wicked parents, should prosper, while good men of generous breed should be unfortunate! It is not right that heaven should deal so with men."[4] The latter exclaim with the prophet: "Spoiling and violence are before me, and there are those that raise up strife and contention; therefore the law is slacked and judgment doth never go forth. For the wicked doth compass about the righteous; therefore wrong judgment proceedeth" (Habakkuk 1:3–4).

It is quite possible, however, for two allies to unite for defensive purposes against a mutual foe without necessarily having anything positive in common. Once the enemy has been defeated, erstwhile comrades-in-arms may discover that their respective philosophies of life are incompatible.

During twenty-five years of their joint attack upon a delusive optimism, Christianity and the tragic view of life had little time for critical scrutiny of each other. Now that the battle is over, however, irreducible differences between them are beginning to emerge, and I shall here attempt to show that, although both prophet and tragedian raise a similar, anguished question, their respective answers to it are, for the most part, mutually incompatible.

The tragic view of life derives ultimately from the philosophy known technically as gnosticism or mysticism, often spoken of as typically "Greek," but in fact quite common throughout the world. Its primary premise can be formulated in various ways, but the simplest is probably Hegel's version: "The truth is in the whole." From this quite plausible axiom, the entire theory of tragedy logically evolves. It implies, first, that an adequate philosophy of life must not only include everything, but must also *affirm* everything. It must not suppress any aspect of reality simply because some particular moral code finds it offensive or ignoble; it must not disparage any human emotion or action simply because some find it unpleasant or shocking. Conversely, it must not prefer other aspects of life simply because they are accounted "beautiful" or "good." This would unduly elevate a mere part at the expense of the whole. In short, if the truth is the whole, then reality is neutral, not partisan. It knows no good or evil, for the "good" is always partisan. The "good" will tolerate no opposition: although it may acknowledge the *existence* of evil, it denies to evil the *right* to exist. The distinction between good and evil, consequently, is truth's worst enemy. As an eloquent spokesman for this view has said:

> Only that which is "beyond good and evil" is real. . . . The moral good has a bad origin, and its bad origin pursues it like a curse.[5]

Life as it is actually lived, however, presents a striking contrast to this ideal of neutrality. Flesh-and-blood men are always partisan. The moment they stop speculating about ultimate truth and engage in the business of day-to-day living, they cannot help taking sides. He who attempts to remain neutral simply capitulates by default to one side or the other. In short, life as we know it contradicts the ideal of absolute neutrality. If the truth is the whole, then it is mocked by the rough and tumble of this world, where justice struggles against injustice, good is pitted against evil, and each side insists upon unconditional surrender.

Nor is this active partisanship accidental to human existence, a defect which might conceivably be overcome in the course of time. Rather, life itself appears to *depend* upon the interplay of polar opposites which, though contrary to each other, are equally necessary to earthly existence—light and dark, wet and dry, long and short, male and female, reason and emotion, positive and negative, mind and matter, all the famous "pairs of opposites" by which philosophers describe finite existence. The Chinese group all these warring opposites under the two primary headings *yin* and *yang*, and regard the conflict between them as integral to life itself. The ancient Greek philosopher Heraclitus reached much the same conclusion when he said that the most fundamental law of existence is strife.

This is the lowest common denominator of tragic philosophy, the clash of neutral, irreconcilable opposites which, considered in the light of ultimate truth, are equally valid. As one contemporary writer puts it, "Tragedy occurs wherever the powers that collide are true independently of each other."[6] Or, as another critic says, "The tragic conflict is not merely one of good with evil, but also, and more essentially, of good with good."[7]

Tragic writers differ chiefly in their respective ways of conceiving the clash of antinomies which constitute human life.

To mention one rather surprising example, Sigmund Freud interprets his psychoanalytical data by incorporating them into tragic philosophy. He postulates two co-eternal, equally valid forces, the instinct of life and the instinct of destruction:

> The meaning of evolution . . . must present to us the struggle between . . . the instincts of life and the instincts of destruction, as it works itself out in the human species. This struggle is what all life essentially consists of . . .[8]

And quite consistently with tragic philosophy, Freud often (though not always) refused to take sides with the life instinct against the destructive instinct.

Another common version of tragic philosophy narrows its focus from the cosmic scale to human nature itself and discovers there a bundle of irresolvable contradictions. It finds, for example, that human nature is a composite consisting of "vitality and form"; that is, the rational, structured element which makes for order, restraint, and obedience to law *versus* the dynamic, vital impetus to break out of tedious normality and stultifying convention in the name of creative novelty. The tension between these two aspects of human nature has, as we shall subsequently notice, been a frequent subject of tragic plot.

Still another way of conceiving this built-in dilemma (and one which is much in vogue among contemporary existentialists) sees tragic conflict as a necessary consequence of human freedom. Every exercise of freedom involves the individual in a decision for some particular aspect of reality *at the expense* of another. He cannot help being "for" one facet of reality and against its opposite. Intellectually, he may realize that both sides have a legitimate status in the context of ultimate reality. But his human freedom involves him in the agonizing necessity of choosing between them. As one of the prophets of existentialism, Jean Paul Sartre, puts it, "Man is condemned to be free."

Finally, among the more sophisticated philosophers of the tragic, like Plotinus or Schelling, the very existence of separate, discrete individuals is itself sufficient to set up a tragic conflict. The perfect harmony of ultimate reality is disrupted simply by the emergence of independent entities, each pretending to the perfect unity which properly belongs only to "the whole."

Such are the principal variations on the theme of tragedy as the fatal conflict between incompatible and equally valid forces. As one proponent of tragedy says:

> Tragedy means a conflict between polarities, but it need not necessarily be a conflict between good and evil. . . . True depth of tragedy would become apparent when two equally divine principles come into conflict. . . . the greatest tragedy is suffering caused by the good, not by evil, and consists in our being unable to justify life in terms of the distinction between good and evil. . . . The most tragic situations in life are between values which are equally noble and lofty.[9]

It is now clear why literary critics are so careful to distinguish tragedy from the morality play. A morality play teaches an object lesson by depicting the triumph of goodness and the punishment of evil. Tragedy, however, portrays the downfall of the man who heroically embodies some great (though morally neutral) ideal or power. To view his demise in terms of good and evil is to step outside the tragic frame of reference.

In a morality play, moreover, the villain is wicked because of free choice, not by necessity; it is always possible for him to turn from his evil ways and be saved. The dominant theme of tragedy, however, is that of necessity. The hero marches along a predetermined path to inevitable doom (*nemesis*).

Few tragic authors are willing to draw this logical conclusion from the fatalism inherent in tragic theory, and many actually do borrow, for dramatic purposes, the freedom which their philosophy denies. What this proves is not that tragic theory provides for freedom, but rather that few writers are able to follow the theory with consistency.

Some of Shakespeare's plays, for example, are certainly more tragic than others. *Caesar, Hamlet,* and *Romeo and Juliet* are more consistently tragic, since they minimize the moral element and contain an undercurrent of fatalism. But Othello's jealousy and Lear's blindness are more like avoidable sins which entail the hero's destruction only because he gives in to them. Shakespeare's ambiguity only accentuates that of every tragic writer. Most of them dilute their tragic philosophy with a mixture of common sense. Shakespeare's inconsistency is more pronounced because his common sense was reinforced by his Christian heritage.

The philosophical stage setting for tragic drama is now complete. It consists of two shifting backdrops: the *ultimate perspective* of the detached observer, of the aesthete, in which all differences cancel each other out and in which no discord is possible; and the *finite perspective* of the man of action, in which strife and contradiction are the rule. The poet Hölderlin based his poem "Song of Destiny" *(Schicksalslied)* on this contrast between the imperturbable serenity of the "ideal" world and the intrinsic strife and tension of earthly existence.

Some tragedians, like Aeschylus, appear to believe with Hölderlin that the "ultimate perspective" actually corresponds to another, ideal world with a separate existence of its own. With Sophocles the characters are allowed to question this, though at their peril; by the time of Ibsen the "perfect realm" has become more of an ideal of the mind; and with contemporary existentialists like Kafka or Sartre, it has dwindled to

and culture, which are human consciousness, resourcefulness and power in action, inevitably take on the character of *hybridic* trespass."[16] Or, alternatively, one can conclude that it is man's glorious destiny to go on to the limit of his creative capacities, even though eventually he will bring the whole cultural edifice crashing down around his ears in a cataclysmic *Götterdämmerung*. This is the mood of Blake, Byron, Nietzsche, and the romantic school generally. Their attitude toward human creativity is, "Though this be evil, make the most of it." Their frank advocacy of evil is perfectly illustrated by the following passage:

> The responsibility for evil exalts man instead of humiliating him. . . . The idea . . . of the fall is at bottom a proud idea and through it man escapes from the sense of humiliation.[17]

Since the entire theory of tragedy involves a double perspective, it follows that the tragic effect depends upon the cooperation of the spectator. He must be willing to hold both perspectives before him in a kind of tension. He is asked both to take seriously the hero's prowess and eventual demise, and at the same time to remain aware that all such partial, one-sided concerns are ultimately invalid. He continually teases himself with the common-sense meaning of guilt and goodness, even while he knows them to be ultimately transcended.

The spectator thus becomes part of the act, deliberately maintaining a conscious ambivalence. The moment he relaxes the tension between the two perspectives, the tragic effect dissolves. If he adopts the finite perspective to the exclusion of the ultimate, tragedy becomes either a morality play or a picture of unrelieved frustration. If he relinquishes the finite in favor of the ultimate perspective, and allows himself to view the hero's world *sub specie aeternitatis*, he realizes that the whole play is really "much ado about nothing." Tragedy is thus converted at a stroke into comedy, and the drama becomes a farce.

Perhaps this explains why the great Greek tragedians were expected to follow their serious dramas with a riotous satyr play, which often burlesqued the grave personages of the preceding tragedy. It is therefore not surprising to find Socrates contending at the conclusion of the *Symposium* that comedy and tragedy are based upon the same fundamental principle— a thesis recently taken up again by Richard Kroner. The point is illustrated beautifully, though perhaps not intentionally, by the Spanish philosopher Unamuno in his book *The Tragic Sense of Life*. He begins by ringing the customary changes upon the self-defeating character of all human existence. By the time he has reached his final chapter, however, his earlier, fatalistic mood has undergone a transformation. He concludes:

> The greatest type of heroism to which an individual, like a people, can attain is to know how to face ridicule; better still, to know how to make one's self ridiculous and not to shrink from the ridicule.[18]

There is thus an inner logic which leads directly from the tragic to the comic. The tragic effect requires of the spectator a constant flirtation with two perspectives at once. The person who declines to wear these bifocal lenses may, with Unamuno, discover in even the greatest tragedy a suspicion of the ridiculous.

This consciously induced ambivalence holds the secret to the spellbinding effect which tragedy has exerted upon millions of its adherents. The spectator's mind is brought to a standstill by the constant flickering of perspective, and he watches in helpless fascination as the hero contrives his own doom. Devotees of tragedy are fond of urging the prospective convert to "enter sympathetically into the tragic experience":

"We must respond from the depth of our own soul if we are to feel the enthusiasm of that [tragic] philosophy."[19] What this really constitutes is an invitation to maintain a schizophrenic oscillation between the two perspectives, and thereby to become a party to one's own hypnosis. The following quotation is an example of such an indirect invitation:

> This is the vision of a great and noble life: to endure ambiguity in the movement of truth and to . . . stand fast in uncertainty . . .[20]

Because of its cultivated ambivalence the tragic attitude has been described as a mixture of doubt and "faith":

> Tragedy, therefore, cannot exist where there is no faith; conversely, it cannot exist where there is no doubt; it can exist only in an atmosphere of skeptical faith.[21]

What this writer means by "faith," however, is a far cry from what the Christian means. It is the knowledge, from the ultimate perspective, that everything happens in accord with a universal law of compensation, that the hero's suffering is really only the necessary restoration of the metaphysical balance. This saving knowledge is the basis of the claim by its adherents that tragedy provides them with a kind of religious deliverance. According to one devotee, it

> cleanses us of all that in our everyday experience is petty, bewildering, and trivial—all that narrows us and makes us blind. . . .
>
> This tragic knowledge . . . is also a way for man to transcend his limitations. . . . When man faces the tragic, he liberates himself from it. This is one way of obtaining purification and redemption. . . . Deliverance within the tragic . . . liberated man by letting him see through the tragic as through a glass to the unspoken and unutterable depths of life . . . .

> In and through this knowledge, the whole man is trans-
> formed.[22]

Although this brand of salvation includes the catharsis of
pity and terror, even these emotions depend ultimately upon
knowledge. They are the product of tragic insight, not of
personal involvement. They are emotions of detachment and
aesthetic distance, to be savored by the connoisseur for their
psychological effect. Pity and terror are, as Aristotle observed,
merely purgative, the emotional accompaniment of the knowledge that the hero's suffering and defeat are intrinsic to finite
existence.

The spectator's advantage over the hero consists in this
superior insight, attainable only from the ultimate perspective
and possible only to an *observer*. Conversely, the hero's downfall is due to ignorance, to the one-dimensional point of view
imposed upon him by the necessities of action. Action requires
decision, judgments of good and evil, as though all these
merely finite distinctions had ultimate significance. In taking
them seriously, as he must, the hero loses his grip on the ultimate perspective. As one contemporary writer puts it, "All
life-force stems from blindness."[23]

This inevitable ignorance exposes the hero to frustration and
despair. The observer, however, since he enjoys a vantage
point above the strife, does not share these emotions. He
understands them as the inexorable consequence of life lived
on the finite plane (that is, in action), and this knowledge
gives him immunity to the depths of anguish and defeat
exhibited on the stage:

> When we watch tragedy, we transcend the limits of existence
> and are thereby liberated. Within the knowledge of the tragic
> the striving for deliverance no longer signifies exclusively the
> urge to be saved from anguish and misery. It also signifies our

urge to be delivered from the tragic structure of reality by transcending that reality.[24]

In some cases, like Captain Ahab in *Moby Dick*, the author tries to make his hero play both roles, protagonist and observer, at the same time. Though a fiercely committed man of action, Ahab nevertheless philosophizes about the destiny which has already assigned to every man his appointed end, and which will have its way despite them all.

Moby Dick anticipates the existentialist version of tragedy. Since, according to the existentialist, men are essentially finite and nothing more, he renounces the spectator's role as untrue to the "human predicament." The way to live "authentically" is to plunge into action, while renouncing all illusions that the action has any significance. Whereas, in tragedy of the traditional kind, the spectator is a man of action who is enabled by the theater temporarily to escape his finite conditions, the existentialist is a congenital observer. The harder he plays at being a man of action, the more obvious it becomes that this is strictly a role. He remains his own *voyeur*, saved from the impact of defeat by the knowledge of its ultimate meaninglessness.

Because the heart of "salvation by tragedy" is this special kind of knowledge, it makes no difference that the spectator knows in advance how the tragic narrative will end. In fact, it is preferable that he *should* know it. For knowledge is timeless, and the more thoroughly he knows every step of the plot, the more he acquires the feel of a timeless perspective. The successive stages of dramatic action unfold, not as a surprise, but as the inexorable march of a foregone conclusion.

Although he understands and even appreciates the hero's courageous defiance, he watches with something of the detachment with which he might watch a fly fall prey to the spider.

He does indeed identify with the victim sufficiently to derive a vicarious sense of dangerous living. From his transcendent level of understanding, however, he can afford a sardonic smile at the feverish preoccupations of mortal men, secure in the knowledge that the truth, after all, is the whole.

So much for the analysis of the tragic view of life. The remainder of this chapter will compare it with the biblical. The full development of biblical philosophy has had to wait until recent times, when the contemporary work of such writers as Sir Edwyn Hoskyns, Abraham Heschel, Gregory Dix, Claude Tresmontant, John Bowman, G. Ernest Wright, and others has not only established it as a respectable metaphysical alternative, but has also shown that at nearly every point it stands in flat contradiction to tragedy.

The mainspring of tragic philosophy, for example, is the double perspective. But biblical philosophy acknowledges no such convenient pretext for equivocation. Throughout the Bible there runs a single criterion of both truth and goodness, equally applicable "on earth as it is in heaven." This is the philosophical significance of the concept of God as Creator. It contradicts the tragic notion that the relation of God to the world is properly expressed as that of the infinite to the finite, the absolute to the relative, or the timeless to the temporal. Whereas tragedy regards this present world as the negation of the "divine," the Bible asserts that there is no necessary incompatibility between it and the very nature of God himself. He has upset the calculations of the tragic philosopher by creating the kind of world in which he can be quite at home. Even if the Old Testament accounts of God's walking on the earth are not historically true, the point remains that he is the *kind* of God who *could* do so, if he chose. And in the New Testament, he did so choose. "The Word was made flesh, and dwelt among us" (John 1:14). The spatial, temporal, physical conditions of human existence were proven to be not the negation of the divine but the expression of his will.

Men therefore need not apologize for applying all-too-human conceptions to God. As William Poteat has shown in a penetrating recent essay,[25] the relation between God and the world can be described with a common language and within a single philosophical perspective. The same words which apply peculiarly to human beings, as distinct from the rest of creation, are the very words which provide the clue to the nature of God: will, purpose, responsibility, intelligence, the discrimination of good and evil, forgiveness, love, even chagrin. From a Greek point of view, such a claim would appear as the height of *hybris*, a presumptuous attempt to arrogate divine honors to mere men.[26] Intellectual issues, of course, are never settled by resort to moral epithet. The person who prefers to consider the question on the moral level, however, may well ponder whether it is more "prideful" to allow God the freedom to create the kind of world the Bible describes, or to insist *a priori* that he must not. Within the biblical context, true humility consists not in the indiscriminate depreciation of man and his capacities but in acknowledging that God's mind is unreadable and his actions full of surprises: "How unsearchable are his judgments, and his ways past finding out! For who hath known the mind of the Lord . . . ?" (Romans 11:33–34); "For my thoughts are not your thoughts, neither are your ways my ways, saith the Lord" (Isaiah 55:8).

The Bible does recognize a discrepancy between certain facts of life and the will of God. But this discrepancy is moral, not metaphysical. It is a disparity between life as it often is, and life as it could be and ought to be. The biblical understanding of the conflicts and calamities of existence is therefore completely different from the tragic. Whereas the latter sees them as the inevitable consequence of the clash of equal and

opposite forces, the former regards neither the conflict as inevitable nor the forces as neutral. For the Bible, conflict is not
integral to life, but adventitious to it. The many "pairs of
opposites" are not necessarily at war with one another. While
vitality and form *may* at times be at cross purposes, they do
not *necessarily* conflict. When they do, it is because of the
dislocation of God's plan for the world, and not because of
any inherent necessity. As Reinhold Niebuhr has aptly said,
"Life is thus not at war with itself. Its energy is not in conflict with its order."[27]

In holding that human disaster *need* not happen, the Bible
takes a far more serious view of it than tragedy, which either
capitulates in resignation or exhausts itself in futile protest.
The Bible also takes disaster more seriously in another respect,
in the frank and unequivocal acknowledgment of it as evil.
Where tragedy tends to call one and the same event both
good, from one perspective, and evil, from the other, there is
no trace of such ambivalence in the Bible. Evil is constantly
called by its right name, and is not finally merged with the
good in an alleged ultimate unity of things. In contrast to the
notion that evil is really good in disguise, so common in tragic
philosophy, the Bible's constant refrain is the seriousness and
significance of the choice between them:

> Abhor that which is evil; cleave to that which is good (Ro-
> mans 12:9).

> Seek good, and not evil, that ye may live (Amos 5:14).

> Test all things; hold fast to that which is good (I Thessalonians
> 5:21).

> Follow not that which is evil, but that which is good. He that
> doeth good is of God: but he that doeth evil hath not seen
> God (III John 11).

There is, of course, a certain reserve about men's ability always and accurately to *detect* evil. "Judgment is mine, saith the Lord." There is also an appreciation of the fact that in the complexities of life good and evil may, as Reinhold Niebuhr has repeatedly pointed out, become so intricately intertwined that any given act or situation may be compounded of both. But the Bible never confuses the creative with the destructive. Its retort to tragic ambiguity is, "Woe to them that call good evil and evil good" (Isaiah 5:20).

Since life is a battleground not of equal opposites but of good and evil, salvation is to be found in exactly the kind of life which, on the tragic view, is doomed to folly and defeat. Instead of cultivating the aesthetic insulation of the detached observer, the Christian engages in a life of active partisanship on the finite level. For God himself is decidedly partisan in human history: "I am the Lord . . . that frustrateth the tokens of the liars, and maketh diviners mad; that turneth wise men backward, and maketh their knowledge foolish" (Isaiah 44:24–25). The life-and-death question is, therefore, not *whether* to take sides, but *which* side to join:

> Behold, I have set before thee this day life and good, and death and evil; therefore choose life, that both thou and thy seed may live. . . . But if thine heart turn away, so that thou shalt worship other gods, and serve them, ye shall surely perish (Deuteronomy 30:15, 19, 17, 18).

Life's deepest questions thus find their answer not in speculative theory or aesthetic ecstasy but in allegiance to God and alignment with his purposes. Instead of the splayed consciousness induced by the tension and ambivalence of tragedy, the Christian hopes for a personality unified through its focus upon the only possible source of unity, the will of its Creator.

Thus far the biblical interpretation of life bears a certain resemblance to the morality play. The theme of both is the freedom of men to align themselves with the forces of either good or evil, and the ultimate triumph of good. Within limits, the Bible, like the morality play, sees in the disasters of history a certain degree of poetic justice. For one thing, since all men become involved in the perpetuation of evil, there is none who can claim total innocence: "Whom the Lord loveth, he also chasteneth." In the second place, there will one day be a time of reckoning and a last judgment, when injustice will be redressed. Thirdly, even in the short run, the apparent success of the unrighteous may be accompanied by a gnawing inner anxiety and torment, while the man who fails by worldly standards may still possess those inner resources which are not for sale.

But here the similarity between the Bible and the morality play ends. The Bible does not define goodness in terms of moral "do's" and "don't's," but as allegiance to the Creator. The moralist's rule book is simply an abortive attempt to construct an external facsimile of the quality of life that results from this allegiance. "This is the work of God, that ye believe on him whom he hath sent" (John 6:29). Hence the destruction which the sinner brings upon himself is not meted out with the vindictiveness of a moralistic censor, nor, for that matter, with the dispassionate impartiality of tragic destiny. Rather, heaven itself is grieved at the loss of a single soul: "I am not come to call the righteous, but sinners to repentance" (Matthew 9:13); "More joy shall be in heaven over one sinner that repenteth, than over ninety and nine just persons" (Luke 15:7).

The Bible is able to take the more compassionate attitude toward the sinner because, though he sins voluntarily, he has also been deceived. He allows himself to be hoodwinked by false promises. The classic instance, of course, is Eve's conversation with the serpent. She lets herself be persuaded that the serpent's account of the forbidden fruit is true, rather than God's. Though she is responsible, she has also been victimized. Hence the close correlation between deceit and sin (see Hebrews 3:13; Romans 7:14), and hence the designation of the devil as the "father of lies" (see John 8:44; Revelation 12:9, 20:10). The Bible chronicles the pathetically similar devices by which the devil has repeatedly persuaded mankind to buy the Brooklyn Bridge.

Thanks to this concept of self-induced ignorance, the Bible abounds in scenes of dramatic irony somewhat comparable to those of tragedy. Oedipus ignorantly pronounces a curse upon himself; in the role of judge, he is obliged to condemn himself; his very wisdom leads him into blindness, both figurative and literal. The Bible matches this with the ringing words of Nathan to King David, "Thou art the man!" There is also a poignant irony in the words by which the high priests seek to justify their liquidation of Jesus: "It is expedient for us, that one man should die for the people. . . . If we let him alone . . . the Romans shall come and take away both our place and nation." Of course, one man did die for the people, though not in the sense they intended, and the Romans still came and took away their place and nation.[28] At the trial of Jesus, it is quite clear who is *really* on trial. And when Pilate asks Jesus his famous question, "What is truth?" the truth is standing directly before him, but he cannot recognize it.

There is, however, a significant difference between tragic and biblical irony. In both cases, irony is the result of ignorance. But in tragedy, this ignorance is the inevitable consequence of the human condition, of the hero's involvement in the necessities of action. For the Bible, it is due to willing self-deception, and therefore affects only the person who forsakes the Lord. From the biblical point of view, the crowning irony is reserved for the person who seeks to avoid it through aesthetic detachment.

Perhaps the most basic point at which the Bible differs from both the morality play and from tragedy is its denial that *all* of life's calamities can be given a convenient rationale. As opposed to the morality play, it acknowledges a residue of evil and suffering which cannot be included within the neat scheme of poetic justice. As opposed to tragedy, it does not seek to reconcile the spectator to them by persuading him that they are necessary. All such attempts to explain evil only end by explaining it away.

The Bible therefore goes out of its way to *insist* on the actuality of evil, not in terms of simple blacks and whites, as the morality play tends to conceive it, but of complex shades of gray, as the parable of the wheat and the tares suggests. According to the Bible, once evil obtained a foothold in the world, it mushroomed into a network in which all men become entangled and in which no man escapes complicity. Evil becomes an objective reality, a decisive factor in human affairs. The blows of circumstance begin to fall at random, so that relatively innocent bystanders are often injured, while the unscrupulous manage to beat the game, at least for the time being. The neat poetic justice of a morality play thus gives way to the rough justice, or rough *in*justice, of common experience.

The Christian, therefore, does not expect a magical exemption from the hard knocks of life. In rejecting the role of self-sufficient observer for that of active participant, he becomes vulnerable to the very emotion which tragedy would purge away. He is acquainted with grief at life's injustices, for God himself is grieved at them. The shortest sentence in the Bible is also one of the most significant: "Jesus wept."

Because the Bible's chief concern is not the theoretical question of how to explain these enormities, but the practical question of what to do about them, it replies, not with speculative theory, but with solid facts. It proclaims that the Creator himself is active in his creation to save it from the self-destructive consequences of human waywardness. On men's behalf, at one climactic point in time, he voluntarily endured the worst that history could offer; triumphed over it, physically as well as in every other way; and then offered the fruits of his victory to all who will accept them from him. Precisely because he is able to weep, the Christian avoids the emotional anesthesia which tragedy induces, and is therefore able to respond with another emotion which is even more foreign to tragedy, joy. There is no scene in tragic literature remotely comparable to the elation of the Psalmist at the prospect of God's deliverance; the almost cavalier exuberance of the prophet at the thought of God's invincibility; the jubilation of the apostles on beholding the risen Lord; or the exultation of the redeemed in the apocalyptic vision of the heavenly banquet. These are the affirmations of gratitude and triumph over an adversary whom tragedy never even engages.

Oddly, the mutual incompatibility between biblical and tragic philosophy has sometimes been overlooked. More curiously still, it has been overlooked more often than not by Christians themselves. In their eagerness to do justice to the majesty and sovereignty of God, for example, they have sometimes referred to him as "the Absolute," or "the Infinite." This is done by inference every time a Christian grants that the biblical conception of idolatry may be simply equated with what tragic philosophers call "absolutizing the relative." The application of such terms to the biblical God, however well-intentioned, introduces tragic concepts into Christian thinking. For if God is "the Absolute" or "the Infinite," then he (or, rather, "it") stands in contradiction to everything in this "relative," "finite" world. The biblical metaphysic has thus been exchanged for the tragic. Professor Arthur O. Lovejoy has exposed the co-existence of these two conceptions of God side by side in Christian thought:

> The most extraordinary triumph of self-contradiction, among many such triumphs in the history of human thought, was the fusion of this conception of a self-absorbed and self-contained Perfection—that Eternal Introvert who is the God of Aristotle —at once with the Jewish conception of a temporal Creator and busy interposing Power making for righteousness in the hurly-burly of history, and with primitive Christianity's conception of a God whose essence is forthgoing love and who shares in the grief of His creatures . . . . Most of the religious thought of the West has thus been profoundly at variance with itself.[29]

Since a given conception of God entails a corresponding metaphysic, it is not surprising that historic Christianity has been infiltrated by numerous ideas which belong to the tragic rather than to the biblical philosophy. It is not uncommon, for example, to encounter Christian authors who disparage the natural world (the medieval *contemptus mundi*), who employ the tragic double perspective (Luther's *iustus et peccator simul*), or who hold that the conditions of "finite existence" inevitably oblige men to sin. These three ideas, all imported from tragedy, have occasionally crept into the doctrine of "original sin." As sometimes formulated, this doctrine speaks as though all men were involved in the same hard necessity which obliges Hamlet to incur "tragic guilt." The biblical view, however, while it does acknowledge a web of evil as an objective reality, also insists that evil and guilt, being the consequence of wrong human choice rather than an inevitable constituent of human existence, need never have arisen.

Another tragic concept which has occasionally found its

way into Christianity is the notion that faith must always have doubt as its counterpart. The currency of this idea in contemporary thinking is indicated by the recent publication of a book entitled *Christian Doubt*. While it is of course true that a given Christian person may undergo a siege of doubt, just as he may also steal, it by no means follows that doubting is *normative* for him, any more than dishonesty. Just as the correlation of doubt and faith presupposes the tragic double perspective, so also the Bible's single perspective renders doubt incompatible with trust in God and his promises.

Another point at which Christian writings have sometimes betrayed tragic influence is the conception of life as a perpetual conflict between equal and opposite forces, particularly between creative energy and rational order. One Christian writer, for example, has written, "This dialectical opposition of the vital and the mental is to be seen in every conscious act. It rules the whole process of human life."[30]

Perhaps the most famous example of an ostensibly Christian writing which nevertheless conceives life as a conflict between energy and order is Milton's *Paradise Lost*. Satan represents vigorous, creative energy in rebellion against the constraints of "divine" form and order. As one critic has observed,

> Milton has in fact emasculated his Messianism by unconsciously proceeding from the same assumptions as Blake: that energy and creative vitality are Promethean and thus devilish, whilst Christ is Reason and his lesson is passivity, obedience, and self-restraint.[31]

Though not without a strain of genuinely biblical thinking, Milton never apparently distinguished it from the tragic. The result has been sufficient confusion to keep the critics busy for years to come.

From the conception of life as a tragic collision of equally

valid forces it is but a short step to the further notion, so
heavily dependent on the tragic double perspective, that what
is creative is also destructive, and vice versa. Such a conception may be expressed either by hyphenating the phrase "creative-destructive" or by explicit statements like the following
passage from a contemporary Christian writer:

> The will to create, the need to write, coincide deep down
> with the Luciferian temptation. . . . How are we to eliminate
> the devil's contribution to the sublimest creations of this
> earth? . . . At the sources of our poems and in our inkwells
> . . . the devil is present. . . . Shall we be able to conceive that
> the Devil is in the last analysis a mystery of Good?[32]

These words confuse the biblical conception that creative and
destructive forces may be intricately intertwined, with the
tragic view that evil is a necessary ingredient of good.

Perhaps the furthest penetration by the tragic view of life
into Christian usage, one which goes beyond the hyphenation
of "creative-destructive" and all but capitulates to the equation
of good and evil, is the famous liturgical phrase, *felix culpa*.
Meaning "happy (or fortunate) guilt," it refers to the fall of
Adam as ultimately a fortunate occurrence, on the ground that
otherwise there would have been no need for the incarnation
of Christ, and mankind would consequently never have enjoyed all the benefits of his coming. Perhaps the *locus classicus*
of the idea of *felix culpa* is, again, *Paradise Lost*. In his celebrated article on "Milton and the Paradox of the Fortunate
Fall,"[33] Professor Lovejoy points out that whereas in the early
part of the poem the fall of Adam is deplored as a "ruinous
enormity," by the time the reader arrives at the Twelfth Book,
Adam begins to describe his transgression as a ground for self-
congratulation!

In addition to the numerous illustrations of *felix culpa* ad-
duced by Professor Lovejoy, there is a devotional poem of the

fifteenth century which expresses it perfectly. If Adam had not eaten the forbidden apple, it says, then Our Lady would never have become Queen of Heaven. Therefore blessed be the day that the apple was eaten, and therefore let us sing, "Thanks be to God."[34] Here is full-blown tragic philosophy in the midst of an ostensibly Christian poem: the double perspective, the confusion of the creative with the destructive, the loss of the distinction between good and evil.

Professor Lovejoy has traced the ancestry of *felix culpa* back at least as far as Pope Gregory the Great, and perhaps even to St. Augustine. It is now permanently ensconced in the Roman Catholic liturgy. The *Exultet* of Easter Eve not only contains the phrase, *O felix culpa*, but also addresses Christ as Lucifer. Most significantly, the contemporary Roman Catholic writer, Claude Tresmontant, has identified *felix culpa* as a pagan concept, and observed that, according to the Bible, God's original plan was for men to be completely *felix*, quite apart from any admixture of *culpa*.[35]

Finally, when vitality is opposed to order, when the creative is confused with the destructive, and when guilt is regarded as fortunate, one is not far from another conception which belongs properly to tragedy, the conception of sin as *hybris*. It is sometimes imagined that the idea of sin is peculiar to the Bible. Actually, nearly every philosophy and religion has its own definition of sin. They differ in their respective conceptions of what *constitutes* sin—*hybris*, as tragedy would have it, or misplaced allegiance, as the Bible maintains. In the development of Christian thought, *hybris*, under the name of pride, has sometimes displaced the biblical view of sin as misplaced allegiance. A contemporary non-Christian author, who is completely impartial where the present issue is concerned, has made this point so clearly that his testimony must be reproduced at length:

The sense of trespass and sin inherent in the dynamism of human life, which, to our modern consciousness is typically "Christian," is in fact essentially Greek. This sense, unrelieved by a sense of calling (for that was a Jewish discovery), is expressed in the myth of Prometheus. . . . Prometheus is not only a hero, he is in the first place a sinner. We have here an attitude whose parallel is not the Old Testament. . . . Pride, the Greek original sin of *hybris* . . . we find as an almost ever-present nightmare in Greek culture, as *the* interpretation of the Biblical fall-myth, gaining ground since Apocryphal times, and becoming classic since Augustine and Gregory. . . .

The initial development depends upon the sort of "fatherhood" ascribed to God. It can be that of Zeus . . . but it can also be that of the Biblical God. . . . Historical Christianity, one must conclude, has chosen the former. The Christian acceptance of the ambivalent Greek-*hybris* complex, combined with a Hebrew sense of calling by and relation to a personal God, could easily create a situation where every human act must be a sinful trespass, and where in fact there can be no escape, except with the intervention of divine grace. Not only is this very different from the old Jewish idea of God, to whom people have direct and immediate contact, and who, in spite of occasional outbursts, nevertheless loves his people and yearns for them. It is tantamount to saying that every human act, as long as it is merely *human*, is *hybridic*, Promethean, and of the devil. In other words, every human act is condemned. The only thing that matters is Christ's move toward us, and (possibly) our response. Implicitly, this contains a condemnation of civilization of which the Greek myth in itself can hardly be said to be guilty in this form. . . . Professor Grierson is certainly right in saying that the "pessimism" ascribed by Dr. Tillyard to Milton personally is actually inherent in the Evangelicism of Milton's time, and "indeed . . . in Christianity in any form that is historical!" The other possibility is illustrated by Jewish experience. The fundamental danger as presented in the books of the Old Testament is not that of aspiring too high, but of not aspiring high enough; that is, of infidelity to a spiritual calling by harking back to the eternal rhythms of nature: "Let us serve the Baalim." But they were fighting a hopeless battle against a God who would not let them sink back to a level of existence from which he had called them of all the families of the earth to a destiny of their own. . . .

In a *hybris*-possessed culture, man's equality with God can only be viewed with horror and recoiling. As Miss Harrison has put it, ". . . [in Greece] there grew up the disastrous notion that between God and man, there was a great gulf fixed, that communion was not possible. To attempt to pass this gulf was *hybris*, it was *the* sin against the gods." In the comparatively *hybris*-free Biblical world, the idea could be born of man as called to an *imitatio Dei:* "Be ye holy even as your father which is in heaven is holy.". . . This difference between Biblical and Greek *prise de conscience* can hardly be overrated from a phenomenological point of view.[36]

Although these statements may underestimate the extent to which historical Christianity has, however inconsistently, remained faithful to the biblical view, they do confront contemporary Christians with Elijah's question, "How long will ye go limping between two opinions?" It has often remained to non-Christians to perceive more clearly the irreconcilable difference between these two allegiances. As one contemporary philosopher declares:

The chance of being saved destroys the tragic sense of being trapped without chance of escape. Therefore no genuinely Christian tragedy can exist. . . . Christian salvation opposes tragic knowledge. . . . What is essential to the Christian cannot even emerge in tragedy. . . . Every one of man's basic experiences ceases to be tragic in a Christian context. . .[37]

Tragedy offers "salvation by knowledge," an explanation of why catastrophe is built into human existence. The Christian rejoices to find himself in the kind of world where goodness is not only possible, but where it coincides, in principle, with his own beatitude. Precisely on that account he is the more acutely sensitive to the devil's successes. Instead of making his peace with them, or of merely railing at them, he casts his lot with One who has overthrown the powers of darkness in a mighty act of deliverance. Where the disciple of tragedy, breathing a sigh of mingled despair and defiance, utters the cry, "Such is life! What a relief to have understood it!" the Christian replies, "Nay, in all these things we are more than conquerors through him that loved us."

NOTES: Chapter 1

1. Cited by Robert Clurman in *The New York Times Book Review*, August 5, 1956, p. 8.
2. John H. Wheelock, "A True Poem Is a Way of Knowing," *The New York Times Book Review*, May 23, 1954, p. 27.
3. Paul Tillich, *The Shaking of the Foundations* (New York: Charles Scribner's Sons, 1948), pp. 19–20.
4. Sophocles, Fragment 107; trans. by F. M. Cornford.
5. Nicolas Berdyaev, *The Destiny of Man*, trans. by N. Duddington (London: Geoffrey Bles, 1948), pp. 18, 84.
6. Karl Jaspers, *Tragedy Is Not Enough*, trans. by H. A. T. Reiche, H. T. Moore, K. W. Deutsch (Boston: Beacon Press, 1952), p. 57.
7. A. C. Bradley, *Oxford Lectures on Poetry* (London: The Macmillan Co., 1950), p. 91.
8. Sigmund Freud, *Civilization and Its Discontents*, trans. by Joan Riviere (London: Hogarth Press, 1953), p. 103.
9. Nicolas Berdyaev, *op. cit.*, pp. 31–32.
10. Reinhold Niebuhr, *Beyond Tragedy* (New York: Charles Scribner's Sons, 1938), p. 164.
11. Karl Jaspers, *op. cit.*, pp. 53–54.
12. Nicolas Berdyaev, *op. cit.*, p. 32.
13. Karl Jaspers, *op. cit.*, pp. 104, 55–56.
14. Paul Tillich, *The Interpretation of History*, trans. by N. A. Rasetzki and E. L. Talmey (New York: Charles Scribner's Sons, 1936), p. 120 *et passim;* my italics.
15. R. J. Z. Werblowsky, *Lucifer and Prometheus* (London: Routledge & Kegan Paul, 1952), pp. 59, 60, 61.
16. *Ibid.*, p. 61.

17. Nicolas Berdyaev, *op. cit.*, p. 26.
18. Miguel de Unamuno, *The Tragic Sense of Life*, trans. by J. E. C. Flitch (New York: Dover Publications, 1954), p. 315.
19. Karl Jaspers, *op. cit.*, p. 86.
20. *Ibid.*, p. 105.
21. Herbert Weisinger, *Tragedy and the Paradox of the Fortunate Fall* (London: Routledge & Kegan Paul, 1953), pp. 227–228.
22. Karl Jaspers, *op. cit.*, pp. 36, 39, 41, 89, 72.
23. *Ibid.*, p. 70.
24. *Ibid.*, pp. 75–76.
25. William H. Poteat, "The Incarnate Word and the Language of Culture," *The Christian Scholar*, Vol. XXXIX, No. 2 (June, 1956).
26. The point has been made by Claude Tresmontant, *Essai sur la Pensée Hébraique* (Paris: Éditions du Cerf, 1953), p. 141.
27. Reinhold Niebuhr, *op. cit.*, p. 168.
28. I am indebted to Canon Edward N. West, *Meditations on the Gospel of St. John* (New York: Harper & Brothers, 1955), pp. 133–136, for his beautiful exposition of this point.
29. Arthur O. Lovejoy, *The Great Chain of Being* (Cambridge: Harvard University Press, 1948), pp. 157, vii.
30. Paul Tillich, *op. cit.*, p. 90.
31. R. J. Z. Werblowsky, *op. cit.*, p. 110.
32. Denis de Rougemont, *The Devil's Share*, trans. by Haakon Chevalier (New York: Pantheon Books, 1952), pp. 132, 133, 134.
33. First published in *ELH, A Journal of English Literary History*, IV, 1937.
34. The paraphrased poem is contained in Carleton Brown, ed., *Religious Lyrics of the Fifteenth Century* (London and New York: Oxford University Press, 1939), p. 120. I am indebted for this and other references, as well as for stimulating thought on the subject, to my colleague Professor Richard Benton.
35. *Vide* Claude Tresmontant, *op. cit.*, pp. 23, 24, 93; also *Études de Métaphysique Biblique* (Paris: J. Gabalda, 1955), p. 66.
36. R. J. Z. Werblowsky, *op. cit.*, pp. xviii, 28, 29, 64, 65, 32, 32.
37. Karl Jaspers, *op. cit.*, pp. 38, 39, 40.

Shakespearean Tragedy:
A Christian Interpretation

THERE HAVE BEEN COUNTLESS readings of Shakespeare, each depending not solely on the text but equally on the perspective of the viewer. Each new student inevitably brings with him to the world of the dramas some firmament of values of his own. He brings premises, explicitly or implicitly, as regards the nature of drama, and more ultimately as regards the nature of man and of history. These furnish at one level or another his stance for viewing. Whether as inklings or as articulated beliefs, they are a working creed of sorts, by which the reader's ear is attuned or his eye enlightened to listen and observe. If his resulting judgments are in clash with those of some other reader, as frequently happens, we need not infer that all interpretation is a hopeless muddle. Opinion is not relative to irreducible taste; for taste is itself relative to perspective and to its conditioning of the sensibilities. Hence the search for an adequate reading goes on, turning about the testing of various perspectives through a comparing of their success in discriminating grain and texture in the logic of the plays. The world of Shakespeare's drama constantly challenges us to revise our vision, both that we may come to a better understanding of his meanings and that in them we may come to a renewed understanding of ourselves.

It will be enough if in the present essay we can explore some of the dimensions of the challenge. These can best be highlighted by a selective review of representative perspectives on

Shakespearean tragedy. As we attempt criticism of their limits we will be feeling our way toward more adequate readings. My own interpretation will emerge, particularly toward the end of the essay, in terms of keys to meaning which are beginning to be discovered with the aid of Christian resources. The suggestive possibilities from this ground of vision I shall then venture to elaborate.

I
SOME ASSORTED READINGS

George Bernard Shaw's judgments on Shakespeare may serve us as a convenient starting point. Shaw himself is a kind of mystical Positivist who regards it his mission as poet to take life "a step forward on its way to positive science from its present metaphysical stage."[1] He has a belief in Creative Evolution, by the light of which he approaches Shakespeare. Understandably, he is disappointed when he finds little awareness in Shakespeare of any such philosophy. There is a moment in *Hamlet*, he thinks, when the hero shows signs of evolving out of a Mosaic morality of revenge into a Christian perception of the futility of punishment; but because Shakespeare had not "plumbed his play to the bottom" the perception slips away when Hamlet sends Rosencrantz and Guildenstern to their death. All told, Shakespeare failed to advance in his evolution beyond "moral bewilderment" and a vulgar contentment with potboilers. His characters weakly collapse into false ideas or dreary platitudes; we are not challenged to triumph with new concepts; we are left with the stultifying pessimism of Ecclesiastes. That there was "magic" in Shakespeare's use of language, Shaw grants, but judges him a less than truly great artist because lacking an adequate view of man. He considers John Bunyan a better artist-philosopher because aware of being moved by a power tending toward a goal beyond pessimism, a "purpose of the world" with which Bunyan identified himself. On the other hand, Shakespeare leaves us as the moral of his plays merely Macbeth's despairing cry, "Out, out brief candle," or Lear's pronouncement that we are to the gods as flies to wanton boys. Shaw's conclusion is that "we are growing out of Shakespeare" and have "nothing to hope from him and nothing to learn from him."[2]

Few readers are likely to accept such a total bundle of judgments. It is too unconventional. Conceivably some readers, in fact, may react by resolving to take a second look at the very resources Shaw would write off—metaphysics, for example, or Ecclesiastes. Is Ecclesiastes all pessimism? It can be read as a sermon on "Remember thy Creator" preached paradoxically through a dramatizing of what life is like when the Creator is forgotten. May not this art of the Bible in the picturing of man's tragedy—especially if we reinforce the picture by drawing on such understanding of evil as Scholastic metaphysics could give Shakespeare—may it not help us appreciate the meaning of the evil depicted in Shakespeare's tragedies? But Shaw, it can be noted, seems singularly uninterested in tragedy as a form of drama. He has cited individual speeches from *Lear* and *Macbeth* as if Shakespeare had been composing not a tragedy but a piece of rhetoric or of moral philosophy. Dare we read Shakespeare in this way? Dare we regard his characters in tragedy as mouthpieces for the dramatist's personal creed? On the other hand, are Shakespeare's plots the shabby potboilers Shaw supposes them to be? And is the language mere "magic," charming us quite without reference to its image of man?

Yet certain aspects of Shaw's perspective, we must admit, have an oddly familiar ring as if we had heard views rather like them from more conventional quarters. Among Puritan Protestants, for example, there still lurks a suspicion of Shakespeare and a preference for Bunyan. Not that these people would interpret Bunyan, or Jesus, as Shaw sees them as Creative Evolutionists; but like Shaw these religionists wish literature to be didactic with their own insights, and Shakespeare seems to thwart their hope. They find him too secular. I have even heard an Episcopalian bishop confess he had not read Shakespeare since college days—though he attributed his loss of interest chiefly to Harvard's method of teaching him the plays. Among Roman Catholics, too, so eminent a mystic as E. I. Watkin can say that Shakespeare, though occasionally supreme as an artist when inspired by a poetic *anima*, was yet as a man "mediocre, commonplace in outlook," a bourgeois "Forsyte Shakespeare" concerned only with commercial success, and less noble in stature than Blake or Milton. Behind Watkin's disappointment lies his belief that there is an "essential incompatibility between drama and religion," because tragedy, the supreme form of drama, "cannot subsist together" with faith. "Either the faith will kill tragedy," he says, "or the tragedy will banish the faith," for religion is optimistic while tragedy rests in pessimism.[3] Whether or not Watkin is right in his contention, who of us has not encountered it in theological circles and elsewhere?

Views at other points like Shaw's can be found among professors of English literature. E. E. Stoll, for example, argues persistently that only "the magic of the poetry," along with Shakespeare's skill in playing on the psychology of the audience to enthrall them by artificial devices, makes effective his otherwise improbable stories. Certainly these stories are not, says Stoll, "the image of life." Moreover, they carry "no message." Indeed, "notions not only of the benevolence of Heaven or Nature, but of the responsibility of man, are undermined" by Shakespeare's lack of a religious philosophy.[4] Where Stoll would see "no message," other professors have seen the speci-

fically pessimistic message Shaw sees. A recent school text of
Lear, for example, quotes the lines

> As flies to the wanton boys are we to the Gods,
> They kill us for their sport

and, without stopping to observe that in context these are the
words of a blind man suffering as the consequence of his own
sport, calls them "the most fitting motto" of the play and uses
them to point out Shakespeare's pessimism.[5] Even in a book
with the promising title *Shakespeare and the Nature of Man,*
we find it said of this same passage that it "apparently expresses the final truth" for Shakespeare "about the relation
between man's fate and the forces which control it."[6] But
have not these eminent judges missed somehow the full orbit
of the play's logic? And if so, why?

Can it be because in the deaths of Cordelia and Lear at the
end of the story they see only this natural fact and nothing
else? We know this to have been Dr. Johnson's difficulty. He
roundly declared:

> A play in which the wicked prosper, and the virtuous mis-
> carry, may be good, because it is a just representation of the
> common events of life: but since all reasonable beings naturally
> love justice, I cannot be pursuaded that the observation of
> justice makes a play worse.[7]

And elsewhere he goes on to find fault with Shakespeare's
plays in general for making "no just distribution of good and
evil," and for being carelessly written "without any moral
purpose"—a fault which he believes the "barbarity" of Shakespeare's age "cannot extenuate; for it is always a writer's duty
to make the world better, and justice is a virtue independent
of time and place." This is high-sounding complaint from an
obvious moralist. But let us note, in addition to Johnson's as-

sumption that his own age is less barbarous, certain other features which his outlook shares with Shaw's. Johnson seems oblivious of the fact that Shakespeare is writing a tragedy; like Shaw, he simply expects all art to be didactic, to "better the world." Moreover, in championing moral justice (the virtue which "all reasonable beings naturally love") as against the justice of nature ("the common events of life"), Johnson would nevertheless like the former taught in terms of a very common standard indeed: natural rewards of prosperity or punishment. Johnson's perspective, in other words, is that of a naturalistic idealism; he wants a man-made world of justice according to man's reason, and is discontented with Shakespeare for withholding this hope.

At the same time Johnson has quite failed to see the very real ground for hope which is given in the play. "See better, Lear" is a wish expressed in the play's first scene by Kent who is being banished; and by the end of the play is not this wish fulfilled when Lear cries:

> Do you not see this? Look on her, look, her lips,
> Look there, look there!

The cry marks a complete about-face from Lear's disapproval of Cordelia's lips in the play's first scene. We may choose to call the new vision either a supernormal or a supernatural change, but toward it the play has been growing through storms and lightning flashes. The Lear who by Act IV awakes in Cordelia's arms to say to her

> When thou dost ask me blessing, I'll kneel down,
> And ask of thee forgiveness. So we'll live
> And pray, and sing . . .

is a transformed Lear from the self-centered father of Act I, who would test gratitude but knew not its meaning. Is the discovery of gratitude not a prosperity? Is the finding of true love not a reward, even in the present life? Lear's perspective has been newly oriented, his vision purged. In fact, may we not say that his old self has been exchanged for a new? With the putting off of the "old man" through a process of unclothing he has been brought to a virtual "nothing," from which he is awakened to find himself a child in a new order. The England over which he ruled has undergone likewise an undoing of its old state, but has emerged purged of its evil at the gates of a new era. Even the bastard Edmund is seen touching the ground of a new self:

> I pant for life. Some good I mean to do
> Despite of mine own nature.

This underground optimism in the play's logic is not seen by Johnson because his perspective has not been adapted to reading it. But with a different perspective a student in our own day can see in *Lear* "a miracle play" in which Shakespeare reveals our world as "a miraculous world."[8]

At a technical level, Dr. Johnson's fault can be seen in his regarding of plot as a mere convention, useful for moralizing, rather than as a rehearsal of a community's significant journey toward self-realization. Johnson has failed to see plot as the imitation of an action of history. This neglect of plot's true significance seems characteristic of other critics already mentioned who, as it were, have plucked Gloucester's eyes out of the body of Shakespeare's work and held up those eyes as Shakespeare's. But the tendency to underrate plot may also be seen conspicuously in Coleridge, though on somewhat different grounds from Johnson's, and through Coleridge it has had a vast influence. As a fountainhead of Romantic criticism, Coleridge warrants at least our brief review.

According to Coleridge the whole focus of drama is on

character.[9] Plot, he tells us, was for Shakespeare "a mere canvas and no more." It was of no dramatic interest except on account of the characters. We may therefore say that Shakespeare "never took trouble in inventing stories" but contented himself with borrowing suitable ones, while directing his whole imagination to bringing before us a gallery of richly individualized persons—in short, giving us the pleasure of beholding "just the man himself." That this view overlooks innumerable subtle changes made by Shakespeare as he reformulated borrowed stories—at times striking changes—I think we need not here pause to argue. What is more significant are the consequences of the view. It entails, for one thing, a lack of interest in genre. Coleridge takes no care to distinguish tragedy as a particular form of the human story, one in which the action is that of man's downfall. Instead, he talks broadly of "dramatic interest," which artistic genius accomplishes by producing forms of conscious experience illustrative of man's moral being. Coleridge redefines "unity of action" to mean the artist's genius for developing "homogeneity, proportionateness, and totality of interest" in all the parts which make up the landscape of character. Thus "action" tends to be seen not as emergent event but as inspired self-expression, both on the part of the artist and his characters. Not man's deeds as related to his destiny, but man's powers of heart and mind as exhibited in moral and imaginative experience, become Coleridge's focus. Shakespeare is hailed as "the pioneer of true philosophy" for presenting to the spectator "the great component powers and impulses of human nature" individualized in "their different combinations and subordinations."

But are not man's powers dependent on powers around him and above? Has he not a destiny governed by laws not of his own making? These are questions Coleridge evades. He returns us to the poet and his laws of composition. Shakespeare, we are told, merely "followed the main march of the human affections." As a man he was of no "religion, or party, or profession" but simply a genius of oceanic mind. "He entered into no analysis of the passions or faiths of men, but assured himself that such and such passions and faiths were grounded in our common nature, and not in the mere accidents of ignorance or disease." But here we might ask: Do not ignorance and disease sometimes condition a man's passion and qualify his faith? May not the prince Hamlet, for example, be taken as a case in point? Are not his passions and faith grounded in a human nature that is heartsick and also ignorant regarding life after death? Furthermore, in patterning the progress and outcome of Hamlet's passion and faith, may not Shakespeare be implying an understanding, taken from his own religion, as to the laws of God and nature which operate under these conditions to give judgment and justice? In that case the logic of the play's action (as something other than the logic of Hamlet's creed) could depend on Shakespeare's creed. But Coleridge reads Hamlet otherwise. Focusing on character, he reads the prince not as acting tragically, but as failing to act. The tragedy then is that one of man's powers, his power for action, has been overbalanced by another of his powers, the speculative faculty. The downfall is a fall from psychological equipoise.

Of Victorian criticism we need only remark that it largely follows Coleridge in the portrait-gallery approach. Generally it focuses on the characters, examined individually for their passions, traits, and sentiments, with the critic judging their relative good or evil in the light of his own native idealism. In so far as the whole play is considered it is read impressionistically in terms of atmosphere and tone. And when these are taken as the key to the playwright's philosophy of life, it is not difficult to arrive at Dowden's theory that Shakespeare while writing the tragedies was "in the depths" of despair. Swinburne, with his own creed of "Glory to man in the highest" finds in *Lear*, quite understandably, a "darkness of revelation" and cites the words of blind Gloucester as striking "the keynote of the whole poem."[10]

A. C. Bradley is the first critic effectively to oppose this reading in his *Shakespearean Tragedy* (1904). Bradley argues that neither Gloucester's words nor Edgar's statement that "the gods are just" accords with our final impression of *Lear*. He believes that "we feel at last, not depression and much less despair, but a consciousness of greatness in pain, and of solemnity in the mystery we cannot fathom." What impresses him is a sense of "law and beauty" in the play's whole action.[11] Thus with Bradley an attention to the logic of action comes to the fore. Yet we may continue to see Coleridge's influence in Bradley's appeal to imaginative impressionism, as well as in Bradley's interpretation of action as "the translation of thought into reality."[12] A metaphysic of nineteenth-century Idealism still pervades the perspective.

II
BRADLEY'S READING

Bradley's book, however, deserves careful study as a landmark in the history of criticism. It is the first systematic, analytic, and detailed examination of its topic; and it contains along with a painstaking reading of the four chief tragedies of Shakespeare a notable chapter on "The Substance of Tragedy." Its viewpoint has dominated a whole generation of readers. Bradley has indeed a scrupulous sensitivity of taste, but also notable limitations consequent upon his initial perspective. The chief source of that perspective we can easily identify, for Bradley several times refers us to his essay of 1902 on "Hegel's Theory of Tragedy."[13] It is true that in that essay he offers some amendments of his own after first summarizing Hegel's theory. But he calls his own supplements "trifling" in importance when compared with "the theory which they attempt to strengthen and to which they owe their existence." His later book is substantially a neo-Hegelian reading.

In it he describes tragedy as a story of calamity involving spiritual conflict and waste. The conflict is that of "forces" acting within the characters to generate strife between them, and acting also within the soul of the hero to generate conflict there. These forces consist of "whatever can animate, shake, possess, and drive a man's soul"—doubts, desires, scruples, ideas —whether good or evil. Bradley's "forces," let us note, are remarkably like Coleridge's "powers" of the psychic life, only now they have a cosmic ground. Bradley sees them as parts of "a moral order and its necessity" which seems to "determine," far more than the individuals caught up in it, "their native dispositions and circumstances and, through these, their action." This moral order, as Bradley describes it, "poisons itself" in producing evil; it also reacts "from the necessity of its nature" against attacks made on it by persons whom "evil inhabits." Yet these very persons are within it and produced by it. It "produces Iago as well as Desdemona, Iago's cruelty as well as Iago's courage." Hamlet or Antony or Macbeth are the "parts, expressions, products" of this order; "in their defect or evil *it* is untrue to its soul of goodness and falls into conflict and collision with itself"; and when in order to "save its life and regain peace from this intestinal struggle it casts them out it has lost a part of its own substance." Or again:

> The whole order against which the individual part shows itself powerless seems to be animated by a passion for perfection; we cannot otherwise explain its behavior towards evil. Yet it appears to engender this evil within itself, and in its effort to overcome and expel it, it is agonized with pain and driven to

mutilate its own substance and to lose not only evil but priceless good. That this idea, though very different from the idea of a blank fate, is no solution to the riddle of the universe is obvious; but why should we expect it to be such a solution? Shakespeare was not attempting to justify the ways of God to men, or to show the universe a Divine Comedy. He was writing tragedy, and tragedy would not be tragedy if it were not a painful mystery. Nor can it be said even to point distinctly, like some writers of tragedy, in any direction where a solution might be.[14]

If we ask what this good "substance" is that is wasted, it turns out in Bradley's later explanation to be, for example, Macbeth's courage and imagination, Othello's innocence and romantic love, Hamlet's speculative genius and his exquisite moral sensibility—in other words, we may say, pretty much the powers and passions and faiths of Coleridge's psychology of character. Coleridge saw these powers of the soul as tragic when out of "equipoise." Bradley sees them as fatal goods when obsessed, respectively, by such powerful evils as Macbeth's thoughts of murder, Iago's deceptiveness, or Gertrude's depravity. These poison or drive an initially healthy hero into treachery, or jealousy, or melancholy, with consequent calamity.

In the case of Hamlet, Bradley attempts to read from the play what the hero was like "just before his father's death." His nature then, we are told, was not "one-sidedly intellectual" but was "healthily active"; he was a man who "in any *other* circumstances than those presented [in the play] would have been perfectly equal to his task." But the "moral shock of the sudden ghastly disclosure of his mother's true nature" poisoned his mind with a loathing of her coarse sensuality and forced Hamlet into melancholy. Bradley holds that in conflict with this morbid state there continue to persist "healthy" feelings and motives (such as "love of his father, loathing of his uncle, desire of revenge"), but that these healthy impulses "emerge with difficulty from the central mass of diseased feeling" and rapidly sink back into it, losing the name of action.[15] In the case of Macbeth, Bradley sees the hero's initial "good" in his courage and imagination. But in conflict with these is a treasonous ambition, beginning with some half-formed guilty idea "floating in the mind" of Macbeth and his Lady even before the play opens, and perhaps already given voice in some "ambitious conversations" between them. Thus the thought of murdering Duncan, already present in Macbeth's soul in a slumbering form, rises to confront him when the witches speak, and gains from these witches a support and aid which "assures the effect" of the evil power working in the soul. In the case of Othello, Bradley sees an unusual instance of initial innocence and love maintained for half the play, almost to the detriment of dramatic interest, for the main conflict is "merely incubating." Iago "does not even begin to poison" Othello's mind until the third scene of the Third Act. There is "not a syllable to be said against" Othello, in Bradley's view, up to the point where Iago is dismissed (III.iii.238); but only two lines later we see in Othello's sudden jealousy that "the poison has been at work."[16]

Let us now test Bradley's view with some questions. How "good," let us ask, is Othello's love before Iago starts working on it with his deceptiveness? Is not that love, from the very start, jealous of any threat to its own good name? Why must Othello humiliate Brabantio? Why, later, dismiss Cassio, unless out of jealous love for the good name of command? By standards of natural reason these actions may not seem those of an inordinate love (though I doubt our natural reason would approve if uninfluenced by night and the magic of Othello's language), yet certainly by standards of charity they are inordinate. Iago's tempting then follows. And does it not consist of a taking advantage of this already inordinate love by presenting new threats to good name, in terms of evil names imagined for Othello's detestation, thus luring him more and more into a world of names divorced from reality, until his jealous love is so cut off from natural reason as to reason the unnatural act of his wife's murder? Thus read, what we have is not an illogical collapse into jealousy but a progressively prepared one, finally lured to disaster by Iago's solicitous talk. From beginning to end Othello's romantic love has been subjectively conscientious and in that sense morally "good"; but objectively considered, it has become increasingly evil.

And similarly Macbeth and Hamlet. We need not suppose with Bradley that Macbeth begins already guilty of latent thoughts of Duncan's murder. But how "good" exactly is the savage courage of "valour's minion" with which he does begin? This inordinate courage, though restrained by reason, is already "Bellona's bridegroom," memorizing "another Golgotha." How good is a courage "Nothing afeard of what thyself did make/Strange images of death" (I.iii.96–97)? Thus conditioned, the self can be tempted by the name of king and by what Lady Macbeth names courage. Is it by "thoughts of murder" that Macbeth is poisoned, as Bradley supposes? Is it not rather that his own will's inclination to violence is already an inordinate love of death, preparing him to respond inordinately to the tempting scriptures of the witches? Or, finally, Hamlet. Can we say of his moral sensibility, in which Bradley sees a "good" force, that it has been at any time "healthily active"? Does it not incline to idolize the elder Hamlet and judge all excellence in terms of devotion to his image? And is such an inclination healthy? Is it not a disorder of love, and itself a cause of melancholy, being the disposition responsible for Hamlet's viewing Gertrude's behavior as loathsome depravity? How does the Ghost later tempt Hamlet into wild and whirling words, if not by appealing to Hamlet's initial idolatry of his father? Bradley would seem to be on dubious ground when he calls "healthy" Hamlet's love of his father, loathing of his uncle, and desire for revenge.

Having thus questioned Bradley's particular readings, what can we say of the general theory underlying them? We may observe that it assumes an impersonal dialectic of forces rather than a drama of persons engaged in opportunities. Also, there is a strange silence about the nature of the will and of choice.[17] It becomes impossible to conceive of genuine temptation, in the sense of enticement to an inordinate purpose (either through something external or through a man's natural inclination); for in Bradley's perspective the self is seen as the "product" of forces generated in it rather than itself generating its own purposing. We will have noted that Bradley ascribes purpose not to individual selves nor, of course, to any Creator of selves, but to a cosmic "moral order" or "soul of goodness" which has a "passion for perfection" as its purpose. This impersonal purpose is seen as achieved dialectically by a wasteful poisoning and purging of the characters who are its "parts" or "expressions." A major limitation in the picture Bradley gives is that it reduces the human self to "character," omitting the will's role in shaping character. Nor is character seen as an emergent pattern of relationships developed by the will. Instead, character is seen as a kind of moral substance translating itself into deeds. When Bradley, at another point in his discussion,[18] inquires as to what the "action" of a Shakespearean tragedy consists of, he does not mention the self's engagement in purpose. He mentions "character issuing into action" as constituting the "centre of the tragedy." Around this center he sees moving various peripheral factors: namely, circumstances (which provide "ingenious complication" but were of little interest to Shakespeare); chance (introduced to make us feel man's inability to control what he starts); abnormal conditions of the mind ("never introduced as the origin of deeds of any dramatic moment"); and the supernatural, such as ghosts (used merely to confirm movements within character). Would it not be possible, however, from another point of view, to consider "abnormal conditions of the mind" as states of purpose, and to consider chance, the supernatural, and circumstances as together constituting the providential conditions of purpose? But this would mean that Bradley's "sense of the causal connection of character, deed, and catastrophe" would need to be reset within an awareness of the total action of the self under providence.

Finally, it is of some interest to note Bradley's lack of awareness that his own reading has been limited by his Hegelian creed. He begins his book by proposing to the reader to collect "directly from the facts" an idea of Shakespearean tragedy, based on nothing more than "native strength and justice of perception" aided by "concurrent use of analysis and poetic perception."[19] Likewise he thinks that Shakespeare's personal creed, whatever it may have been, was of no "material influence" on the dramatist's representation of life. Shakespeare simply "painted" the world "without regard to anyone's hopes, fears, or beliefs" and did not use religious ideas "to throw any light on the mystery of its tragedy."[20] But if we turn to a later essay of Bradley's on "Shakespeare the Man"[21] we come across a curious fact: Bradley there does attempt to infer Shakespeare's beliefs from the plays. He tells us that Shakespeare's religious position in middle life seems to be "much like Hamlet's." And he goes on to characterize Shakespeare as having a lively sense of "conscience," which he thought of "as connected with the power that rules the world and is not escapable by man." Shakespeare never doubted that "to be good is to be at peace with that inescapable power." To this "natural piety" he may have added as he grew older some approximation to conventional Christian ideas. It is plain, I think, that Bradley has found in Shakespeare just such belief as Bradley's own neo-Hegelianism permitted him to find. The dramatist's work was, after all, influenced by *that* belief. Bradley's good fortune, I suggest, was that he wrote at a time when the intellectual public was attuned to his belief—so much so, in fact, that Hegelianism had captured even some practicing Christian theologians. That vogue, so central to Liberal humanism and naturalistic idealism, has now waned, yet some very recent books on Shakespeare sound the call for a return to Bradley, or elaborate essentially his basic reading.[22]

III
HISTORICAL APPROACHES

Attacks on Bradley have come from the "historical" critics. Commonly they have set out to rescue Shakespeare from modern impressionism by a scholarly study of Elizabethan backgrounds. With these they undertake to show how an Elizabethan climate of ideas guided both Shakespeare's vision and his audience's responses. But inevitably they have differed in their own visions of this Elizabethan background, depending on what feature is selected.

In the 1920's it was fashionable to center on Machiavelli, or on Montaigne, or on Seneca. Then T. S. Eliot countered with the view that at the end of the sixteenth century "the world was filled with broken fragments of systems," Senecanism no doubt being "the most diffused throughout Shakespeare's world" and the most conspicuous in his dramas; but that we "can hardly say that Shakespeare believed, or did not believe, the mixed and muddled scepticism of the Renaissance," since this was but the material enforced upon him "to use as the vehicle of his feeling" in writing himself and writing his time. Thus Shakespeare had an inferior philosophy to Dante's, but "I doubt whether belief enters into the activity of a great poet *qua* poet," it being a poet's job to start from his own emotions and the "emotional quality of believing" according to the philosophies provided him.[23]

Eliot's view here that the ideas or beliefs of an age are for the poet materials he works with, working them up into art quite independently of a personal commitment to their philosophies, is salutary in its emphasis on the poet as craftsman. But if the poet *qua* poet is a fabricator, is he nothing else—or, at best, nothing else than a provider of feeling or emotion with which to empower the "vehicles" of his expression? May he not also provide a placing of each of these felt-vehicles relative to each other in an ordered vision of life which reflects, by its order, the poet's personal belief? Dante, for example, provided for the ideas of Farinata and Cavalcante, two of his contemporaries, an emotional quality of believing on their part; but he also placed their beliefs in the circle of the heretics. In doing so he provides us a clarification of their respective philosophies in the light of a superior philosophy. Was this clarification not part of Dante's total activity as poet? Can we really suppose that any poet's faith is not at work as he goes about the intricate task of selecting significant detail and shaping its order of story?

Eliot's stand here is a curious one, considering his own Christian orientation amid our equally muddled world, and his insistence on every poet's need for a "historical sense."[24] It seems to ignore the Christian doctrine of man's potential membership in a mystical community which transcends the community of his "age" and provides him a ground for viewing that age and the logic of its philosophies and feelings. It also ignores the possibility of a medieval spiritual heritage, even a Dantean one perhaps, continuing slenderly into the Elizabethan period. Why hypostasize Shakespeare's "age," binding it to its skeptical intellectual atmosphere, as if the muddle were the poet's whole world devoid of any vantage ground for seeing it as muddle? Perhaps significantly, Eliot has not included this early essay in his latest collection.

Meanwhile other "historical" critics seem to have followed Eliot in regarding thought-forms as "conventions" into which passion is poured. L. L. Schücking, for example, has implied this in his interpretation of Shakespeare as a "baroque" artist. He explains Hamlet's reasoning on refusing to kill the King at prayer by saying that it is "nothing more than a typically baroque exaggeration of the lust for revenge," an attitude already conventional with other dramatists in even more grotesque forms. Or again, he explains that Lear's outburst against the chastity of woman is accountable if we but remember the aim of all drama of the time to "depict eccentricities." Shakespeare, caught in a vogue of his age, gave his audience "victims of passion" by developing Elizabethan ideas of melancholy and depravity. Nevertheless this critic believes we can infer Shakespeare's own faith: it must have been the Stoic ideal, inasmuch as the characters who are victims of passion so often admire the ideal of life governed by reason.[25]

A reading of Shakespeare in the light of Stoicism has, in fact, appealed to many scholars for still another reason. The more widely they read in the literature of Tudor England the more "godly and learned" treatises they encounter, and many of these writings on moral philosophy contain an amalgam of Stoic-Platonic-Christian humanism. They are weak, however, in discriminating Stoic from Christian premises. As a consequence, when these best sellers are conned as presumably measuring the stock of Shakespeare's "ideas" and, going a

step further, as measuring the meaning of the tragedies, it is
possible to arrive at the view well stated by Lily B. Campbell:
"Shakespearean tragedy made concrete Elizabethan moral
teaching, and that teaching was centered about the conflict of
passion and reason in man's soul. When passion rather than
reason controls his will, man sins or errs."[26] Thus stated, the
teaching is Stoic.

But how exactly will this theory fit what Shakespeare says
in Sonnet 151? Stating there that "conscience is born of love,"
the poet complains to his inconstant Lady:

> Thou betraying me, I do betray
> My nobler part to my gross body's treason.
> My soul doth tell my body that he may
> Triumph in love, flesh stays no farther reason . . .

Here we see disaster as stemming, first of all, from the lover's
adherence to a mutable good that betrays him by its false
beauty. Loving this false-fair, he betrays his nobler part (his
reason) to his body's desire. His soul furnishes his flesh a practical application of reason, which is as much reason as is needed
to raise an action. Now this theory, obviously, is subtler than
the Stoic one. It seems, rather, to parallel that of Aquinas, who
carefully distinguishes his own view from Stoic theory by
tracing sin to an act of reason itself, which becomes corrupted
by inordinate love of a temporal good, and then in its corruption applies reason defectively in counseling appetite.[27]
Moreover, this more complex theory accords well with the
logic of downfall we can see in Macbeth. Does not his inordinate love of a temporal good lead him to betray his "eye" of
reason to "wink at the hand"? And, becoming further corrupted
by love of Lady Macbeth's picture of success, does not his
reason tell his hand how it may triumph—by marking with
blood the sleepy grooms and laying the guilt on them? Thus

blind love and crippled reason alike collaborate in the downfall.
W. C. Curry, in a notable essay some years ago, was able to
trace the progressive disintegration of Macbeth's humanity in
terms not of Stoic but of medieval logic.[28]

It would seem that the historical critics have sometimes
been insufficiently historical in neglecting the medieval world-
picture underneath the Elizabethan one, or in too easily
equating the two. They have been prone to assume that Shakespeare's horizons were defined merely by the popular spokes-
men of his day. Secondly, historical critics have commonly
slighted the dramatic mode. They have not taken sufficient
care to distinguish between "ideas" used by Shakespeare to
characterize the thought of his persons and other ideas guiding him as dramatist in plotting what happens to those persons.
Can the ideas of persons set in a tragedy be excepted from
contributing somehow to the disaster they undergo? How is
Shakespeare to show the inadequacy of certain ideas unless by
showing the muddles of self-defeat which are their historical
consequence? Here is where plot, as revealing by its logic an
imitation of the logic of history, has such principal importance.
Properly it overarches thought and character, putting these
under judgment. But frequently those who approach Shakespeare "historically" have narrowed their concern to finding
sources for the thought voiced by characters and then reading
the tragedy in the light of such thought.[29]

A good illustration is the handling of the speech on "degree"
in *Troilus and Cressida* (I.iii):

> The heavens themselves, the planets, and this centre
> Observe degree, priority, and place
> . . . O, when degree is shaked
> Which is the ladder to all high designs,
> The enterprise is sick! How could communities
> But by degree, stand in authentic place?

At great length Ulysses goes on to attribute all the ills of the Greek camp to insubordination. The main idea of the passage, a plea for the observance of hierarchy, has been traced to such sources as Sir Thomas Elyot, the Elizabethan Homilies, and Richard Hooker. From this fact various historical critics have inferred that Shakespeare was voicing through Ulysses both the doctrine of his own age and his own philosophy. But was he? L. C. Knights has objected that "the play as a whole certainly does not endorse Ulysses";[30] and H. C. Goddard has commented that Ulysses does not see "that the extreme he defends is as far from freedom—or nearly so—as the one he quite rightly denounces." The devastating irony of Shakespeare, says Goddard, is evident when he shows Ulysses turning next to the hatching of a plot for pulling Achilles out of his place by overelevating the stupid Ajax, thus fomenting the very "shaking of degree" he has pretended to hate.[31]

Dare we say, then, that the doctrine of Ulysses is Shakespeare's own belief? In fact let us push the question a bit further and ask: What alternative doctrine might Shakespeare hold—and which perhaps *we* ought to hold in our own present experience of life? If the health of a community does not stand in "degree," in what does it stand? Here is a question of postulates, which every literary critic needs to answer, not merely to understand plays but to understand life itself. It is also a question every historian needs to answer, not only in order to account for the rise and decline of communities in the past but also in order to understand those of his own present. It involves finding a theory which will be adequate to the real logic of "what happens." In this respect the task of the "historian" is identical with that of every "interpreter" of literature.[32] Scholarship can help if, among the doctrines it recalls, it finds one that "fits" the real story of a community— whether that doctrine be Elizabethan or not.

And in this instance the doctrine I would suggest as out-
moding that of Ulysses is one which scholarship can find in
St. Augustine's *City of God*, but which a Christian playwright
or his audience could have known from church tradition. I
mean the doctrine that the health of a community stands principally in the "order of love," in *caritas* as against *cupiditas*.[33]
This order of charity does not invalidate "degree," but it does
provide an object of obedience other than degree. It accords
to the "order of natures" established by God just as much
attention as each deserves. Thus the classical doctrine of
hierarchy in nature is absorbed but transcended; for beyond
that ladder whose top is the sun, there is (in Dante's phrase)
"the love that moves the sun and all the stars." Taken alone
the classical view is static, with no place for creatures in their
several degrees to go. The Christian view provides a goal for
each member of the whole community, including its king.
With no place to go, the classical community inevitably turns
around itself in actions of self-contradiction in which each
member is caught. This is the plight of the "earthly" community—of the community which has its agreement in a common
cupiditas. Such a community, says Augustine, is fundamentally
at war with itself like Romulus and Remus, those two sons-
of-the-wolf. It is betrayed by its own ill-directed love. Its
history is best illustrated, Augustine thinks, by taking his
readers back to Troy, then for further explanation back to
Cain. If Shakespeare takes his Elizabethan readers, and us, back
to Troy, may it not be with a similar vision of history to
impart?

Let us glance at *Troilus and Cressida* from this approach.
Do not all the major characters participate, in various analogous ways, in the one basic action of pursuit of an inordinate
love of self? A cupidity for self-pleasing unites these Greeks
and Trojans in one common struggle. Achilles lolling on his

bed with Patroclus is symbolic of this fact in the Greek camp; but equally symbolic of it is the situation with which the play opens, a Troilus swooning with love, not so much for Cressida as for the self-exaltation of being in love—a yearning for "waftage" to fields where he may "wallow in lily beds." If the older warrior is pleasing himself by sulking, the younger one is mooning. Achilles, as it turns out, loves Patroclus only to enjoy his services, and not as a person whom he might follow to the field to protect. Nor does Troilus at any time bestir himself to protect Cressida; he consents to her being handed over to the enemy, because basically what he cares for is not her welfare but his picture of her as ever "constant" to him. When he loses this picture of her he becomes a savage revenger, as does Achilles similarly on losing Patroclus. But in both cases this latter turn of the action arises from the hero's love of his own love. He fights with no purpose but to avenge an indignity to his self-centered love.

And has that not been Menelaus' purpose too—against which background the play opens? The story of Menelaus and Helen is simply recapitulated in another mode in the circuit of action of Troilus and Cressida: beginning in fondness it moves through betrayal and ends in reckless war. But Troilus and Cressida, as Shakespeare sees them, are both self-betrayed. And the same is true of other characters, who variously are betrayed by the self-centeredness of the "order" or "honor" they champion. Turnings of contradiction are a logical result. Ulysses, for example, claiming to love "order," flatters Ajax and snubs Achilles; pushes forward the whole ritual of war for Helen yet refuses the ritual of peace to Cressida, scorning the kiss of welcome. And Hector, claiming to love "honor," votes for the retention of dishonorable Helen but the deportation of honorable Cressida; wastes sympathy on the enemy Ajax and denies it to his own wife. Such are the representative ironies of "constancy" and "perseverance" when these are made gods to the glory of none other than the worshiper himself. Armed with these, the self undoes itself and decomposes. Symbolic of this fact is the anonymous "one in sumptuous armor" who dies in the battle that ends the play and is accorded this epitaph:

> Most putrefied core, so fair without,
> Thy goodly armour thus hath cost thy life.
> Now is my day's work done. (V.viii.1–3)

His day's work being done, Hector too presently falls and Troy with him—its desolation now epitomized by a lonely Troilus, shouting to the wind-swept plains a futile hatred as night falls, and comforting himself with the final line: "Hope of revenge shall hide our inward woe."

What benefit can there be in such a drama? Profit can come, can it not, in seeing this whole circuit as a day that is done— as a past which, when it is clearly rehearsed, can be viewed as over and ended, ended in a present self-understanding which the spectator reaps as a fruit of a past that is now his past but buried. The rehearsal is a ritual means to our purgation. By imaginatively suffering through it to its end we accept its end, and await life of another order.

Dante had some such concept of tragedy's utility when he placed on the first ledge of the mountain of purgatory, cut into the stone beneath his feet, thirteen images of the fallen proud, from Satan to Troy.[34] Dante's pilgrim, raising his eyes from this floor, sees cut into the rock wall at his side the images of the Virgin Mary, David, and Trajan. His liberation consists in his painful climb from the old order of motivation toward the new dawning one. He must go through the first in review, that the imagination may suffer and see the evil motive as it is, and thus be free to take a new direction. Dante's pilgrim is thus like the spectator of a tragedy, while Dante the author is like a playwright, well aware of the goal which tragedies serve.[35] Somewhat similarly, St. Augustine, in his *City of God* reviews the tragedy of old Rome (from Aeneas to Alaric), that his readers may reperceive it as deadly and past, and step from that past into the new Rome which a Christian perspective can declare. As tragedy in life is a kind of scourge we providentially undergo in our love-driven search for happiness, so tragedy in art is a ritual-scourging of the imagination, a kind of medicinal bloodletting for overburdened and sick hearts, in their love-driven search for the health of truth. An authentic Christian dramatist, we may say, is one who glimpses that the ultimate key to the health of truth resides in the Christian creed. Therefore, like Augustine, he believes in order that he may understand, and reviews segments of human experience in the light of such understanding. His method, however, is not that of philosophic analysis but the more primitive method of rehearsing the mode of the concrete experience.

IV

A Christian Approach

In recent years a turning to Christian sources for perspective in reading Shakespeare has been developing markedly. Students of medieval thought, whether historical critics or followers of the so-called New Criticism, seem to be converging attention on patterns of Christian metaphysics and idiom imbedded in Shakespeare's logic and language. It has been argued, for example, that a profound Christian metaphysic is at work in Shakespeare's vision of justice;[36] that his whole theory of comedy is implicitly medieval in contrast to the neoclassical theory of his major contemporaries;[37] that several of the late comedies are parables of Christian doctrine;[38] that various of the major tragedies depend on the light of a Christian world-

order for their delineation of the action;[39] and that Shakespeare's doctrine of love as set forth in his nondramatic *The
Phoenix and the Turtle* mystically describes a love based on
the analogy of the Persons of the Trinity.[40] So far these
studies have been piecemeal in application, leaving much
unexplored terrain and a good many unfinished edges. But together they reinforce the pertinence of the perspective they
employ. The Christian perspective, moreover, being grounded
initially in history and ritual rather than first of all in philosophy, is proving unusually congenial to our contemporary
interest in anthropology on the one hand and the language of
symbolism on the other. "Shakespeare's world," writes S. L.
Bethell, "is the world of folk legend more profoundly understood—a development, in fact, of medieval Christianity"; and
he goes on to point out that folk legend lies "beyond the neat
categories of psychological motivation, in a world of signs
and portents" in which the supernatural plays a controlling
role.[41]

Critics such as Bethell are much indebted, of course, to the
various books of G. Wilson Knight, who was the first to view
drama as an expanded metaphor and to read Shakespeare in
terms of a logic of symbol-patterns. Knight's own readings
have been frequently brilliant. At other times his intuitional-
ism, while eclectically Christian, has seemed to lack discipline.
Yet it is under his stimulus that studies in Shakespeare's
imagery have taken hold and progressed beyond the tech-
niques of counting and cataloguing to a search for thematic
patterns as carriers of unrationalized yet logically shaped
meanings. Knight is at his most challenging when he asserts
that "each of Shakespeare's tragic heroes is a miniature Christ";
or, again, that since the Christian Mass is "at once a consummation and transcending of pagan ritual," the unique act
of the Christian sacrifice "can, if we like, be felt as central"

to the world of Shakespearean tragedy.[42] The danger I sense in a phrase such as "miniature Christ" is that the discontinuity of ethical dimension between pagan and Christian ritual, or between the tragic man's self-sacrifice and Christ's, may be blurred. Would not "miniature Adam" be a better phrase— especially if we add that Adam is related to Christ by inverse analogy, even as the Old Adam is related to the New Adam? Let us grant the insight of the Cambridge anthropologists that tragedy is related to ritual sacrifice; yet is not tragedy asso- ciated with a scapegoat-sacrifice, whereas the Mass substitutes for the scapegoat the lamb of God? If so, the Mass is a trans- figured "fulfillment" of the tragedy, related to tragedy as type is related to antitype—by analogy but across a gulf of deadly irony. Or, to put the matter another way, the Mass is related to tragedy as Oblation is related to holocaust, both being a kind of pyre—as T. S. Eliot has so memorably written in *Little Gidding:*

> The only hope, or else despair
> Lies in the choice of pyre or pyre—
> To be redeemed from fire by fire.

For the fire of *cupiditas* which leads to destructive death (tragedy) is the antitype of the fire of *caritas* which leads to rebirth (comedy). They are analogous, but the transcendence of the latter may be said to "continue" the former by way of discontinuity: it fulfills love of self by recapitulating it under a higher principle. In this way tragedy can also prefigure comedy as its counterpart.

More recently it has been suggested by J. A. Bryant that any segment of story can be "placed" in relation to Christian story, finding there a center for the meaning of the located segment. He believes Shakespeare knew this—as, of course, Dante knew it and raised his *Divine Comedy* on this premise.

> Fundamentally Shakespeare's plays are explorations of mythic fragments, whereby the movement of the fable at hand, whether from English history, Roman history, Italian novella, or English fabliau, is revealed as participating by analogy in an action which, from the poet's point of view, is Christian, divine, and eternal. *The Winter's Tale* is a case in point.[43]

This is a promising suggestion, worth pursuing. However, I should think we might expect *The Winter's Tale*, since it is a comedy or at least a tragicomedy, to carry an analogue somewhat differently placed from that of a play which is a tragedy principally. If the divine action of providence may be said to have in history its obverse and reverse turnings, its dispensations of death through the Old Adam and of life through the New, then tragedy might be said to be a segment of story related focally to the first of these two aspects.

There is space in the present essay only for trying out very briefly the kind of reading I believe this perspective can yield if elaborated. My efforts at illustration will necessarily be partial and tentative. I would suggest that in general Shakespeare's tragedies rehearse various segments of the Old Adam analogue. The segments can vary, according as particular historic cultures furnish us particular epochs in the analogue. But in each tragedy the hero of the action inclines toward some form of inordinate self-interest, an idolatry of some aspect of himself, and accordingly spends himself in destructive passion which ends in his own spiritual death, often concurrent with physical death. This is the essential tragic cycle, though Lear must represent somehow tragedy's extreme verge—an Old Adam in his old age, so to speak, who goes so far into and through death as to dream at the end of being taken "out of the grave" and beginning another life in a new order.

Lear's story seems to define an epoch in primitive paganism analogous to late Old Testament experience. That is, it is the tragedy of a trial-of-love adulterated by self-seeking, which betrays king and kingdom alike into self-division, with consequent alienations of affection and exiles of various kinds. At the same time the disastrous consequences of the king-father's self-centered love call forth a redemptive counteraction, stemming from his disinherited child. The kingdom's "saving remnant" is figured in Cordelia, the one righteous shoot of the family stock, who, beginning with a Mosaic devotion to natural justice, develops into the gracious suffering servant of Isaiah and Jeremiah. Through her a divine comedy is progressively prepared for Lear and offered to him in foretaste by the end of Shakespeare's play. But first Lear's willful self must decompose (like Jonah's) in a whirlpool of thwarted endeavor, and the tragedy is a rehearsal of this discomposure. The fall is from willfulness to resignation, aided by self-mockery. Then to this wasteland of the self comes a visitation as by miracle, and Lear can depart in peace (like old Simeon of Luke 2), having caught a glimpse of the child who is to enlighten the Gentiles. This experience marks tragedy's utmost limit, at the very gates of comedy.

Or another way of viewing the logic of *Lear* would be to say that its hero is analogous to the prodigal son. He wastes his portion on harlots (which Goneril and Regan literally are in the play) and riotous living, until he is driven to eating husks with swine (as Lear does in feeding on empty memories in his hovel on the heath). As this prodigal begins to come to himself and look homeward, the father who comes out to meet and embrace him is, paradoxically, a daughter, Cordelia, who asks, "And wast thou fain, poor father, To hovel thee with swine" (IV.vii) and who says, "O dear father, It is thy business that I go about" (IV.iv). The latter statement allies her with the wise child of Luke 2:49, a status to which she has arrived after beginning the play with only a Mosaic bond of rational justice. Having begun with an initial attitude like that of the older brother in the prodigal son story, she has grown into the father of that story. Essentially, I suggest, her spiritual evolution is like that of the "younger" branch of the Bible's Old Adam (the branch whose mystical history unfolds from Abel to the child Jesus), providing at last a hinted redemption for the "abused nature" of Old Adam. In other words, *Lear* is an analogue of the Bible's story of mankind's journey toward revelation to a point as far as that journey can go short of the emergence of an adult New Adam.

Troilus and Cressida, by contrast, is a shorter segment. Its action carries us no further than a rehearsal of the logic of "vanity" spoken of in *Ecclesiastes*, culminating in evil days which have no pleasure in them. The golden bowl is broken and mourners go about the streets, as the curtain falls on Troy. The only comedy in this play is in the action of uncle Pandarus and his Greek complement Thersites; and their comic action is less a counteraction to the tragedy than a corroborative one, serving both to elicit and to scoff at the tragic action. Comedy here is related to the tragedy as a doubling of it rather than as a reversing of it. The comedy takes the form either of comedy-of-intrigue (typically Latin) or of satire (typically Greek); it is not romance comedy. Pandarus and Thersites are thus a saving-remnant only in the negative sense of dissolving by their cynicism of love-and-reason the hyphen-ated community of rationalism-and-chivalry which constitutes their civilization. A civilization whose official religion was humanism, a worship of man-made projections of reason and passion as if these were life's final order, directed its most characteristic action to winning or defending a supposed "immutability" of nature, only to find itself vanquished by mutability. Pandarus and Thersites are advance agents of this conclusion. All the characters in *Troilus and Cressida*, and especially its hero and heroine, come to rest in the vanity of human wishes.

Othello comes to an end in the suicide of its hero. This act exactly fulfills the merciless justice which has been Othello's trademark throughout the play. Toward flesh and blood he has no pity when an ideal of moral deserving is to be served. From the outset this has been so. When first he meets his own emotionally upset father-in-law, he shows him no pity or gratitude for past favors. Others with even closer bonds to Othello next come under his righteous indignation—Cassio for being tipsy, Desdemona for being forgetful—and finally his own flesh. He slays himself to vindicate his own sense of rectitude, which has been his particular idol since the play began. We are made aware of this idol in the first scene in which Othello appears, when he refers to "my perfect soul." His is a serene self-righteousness. By what analogue has Shakespeare patterned Othello's destiny? I have several to suggest, all of them perhaps cohering in the concept of "base Judean" (the F^1 reading of V.ii.347).

Let us look at the very center of Othello's first scene on stage. It is night, and Brabantio has come with armed men to seize Othello. Othello says, "Put up your bright swords, for the dew will rust them," and adds a word of rebuke to Brabantio. Recall now, for a moment, Christ at Gethsemane and his words to Peter in John 18: "Put up your sword into the sheath; the cup which the Father hath given me, shall I not drink it?" The two scenes have a strange affinity, as if Othello were revealing to us a grotesque version of the biblical Christ: master of the night by scorn and rebuke instead of by humility and counsel. Another analogue is suggested in Act III, scene iii, when Desdemona, like Veronica of Christian legend, would soothe her lord's anguished face with a handkerchief. Othello brushes her off and the handkerchief is dropped and lost. Thus the episode is both like and unlike the Christian legend, a kind of antitype of it. Still another analogue, this time to Job, is apparent in Act IV, scene ii. Othello protests he could have had patience, had it pleased Heaven "To try me with affliction" and "all kinds of sores," but that he cannot bear to be discarded from "where I have garnered up my heart." But what an ironical version of Job we have here: Othello is suffering no sores other than of his own making; he is not disproving Satan's cynicism but getting his whole vision of life from a Satan-like Iago; he has garnered up his heart not in a trust in God's righteousness but in his own righteousness substituting as god. It is to this substitute god that Othello seems to cry out Job's celebrated words: "Though he slay me, yet will I trust him." Thus we have, as in the two examples above, an upside-down parallel of Christian story.

An analogue of another kind, however, comes at the play's end. Othello's words, "I kissed thee ere I killed thee," bring to mind Judas, as does also Othello's remorseful cry that "like the base Judean" he has thrown "a pearl away/Richer than all his tribe." Here we have a true parallel. Judas was the Judean who threw away the pearl-of-great-price (charity or Christ), and then committed suicide. Judas was the one disciple who was covetous and lacked charity.[44] He seems to have shared the idealism of the Pharisees for a religion of moral code rather than of forgiveness, for it was to these high priests of exterior righteousness that he betrayed Christ. Compare Othello's exterior righteousness, his confidence in his own "perfect soul," his inability to think of Heaven as forgiving (it is "yon marble heaven"), the oath he swears "by the worth of man's eternal soul," and the prayer he addressed to this soul of his (like the Pharisee praying to himself in Luke 18): "It is the cause, it is the cause, my soul." For this "cause," Othello must "Put out the light, and then put out the light," enacting unwittingly a kind of *tenebrae* service. No wonder Othello slays himself at the end: he has had no god other than his own soul or conscience, which is unable to forgive itself. So despair leads to suicide. Is it true that he has "loved not wisely but too well"? Yes; but what he has loved too well is his own will and judgment. Augustine would call such a love a self-pleasing love (*cupiditas*), whose final heroism (as in Cato) is suicide, a violence against self in order to please the self-centered will. It is a pagan "sacrifice"—related to Christian sacrifice in the way in which Dante's bleeding wood-of-the-suicides is related to the sacred wood of Calvary, by disjunctive analogy.

Finally, let us glance at a much earlier play of suicide, *Romeo and Juliet*. A recent editor of this play, after debating whether the lovers are "in any way responsible for their doom," concludes that it is "not part of the basic design" that we should regard their fate "as directly caused, even partly, by their own character flaws." He believes there is "nothing we can hold against" Romeo, unless we insist on "the (admitted) validity of moral conceptions that have no meaning for Shakespeare in this play." How can we blame Romeo, he asks, for killing himself on believing Juliet dead, "since he has, from his first view of her, regarded her as his whole life"?[45]

But perhaps this critic's own final clause can help us to an answer. Romeo does indeed imagine Juliet as his "whole life": he imagines her as the light of his Heaven. Her lips, he says, bestow an "immortal blessing" (as Helen's do for Faustus in Marlowe's tragedy). To Romeo in the dark orchard, Juliet's beauty is his "sun" in the East. To Romeo at the tomb, it is a "lanthorn" which makes that vault a feast of light. Such language is glorious poetry; but does it not imply an idolatry of the shadow-beauty of the creature and thus an inordinate love?[46] In Sonnet 130, Shakespeare says, "My mistress' eyes are nothing like the sun," and she is not a goddess. But in Romeo we have a lover whose mistress is imagined as hardly walking the ground at all; she is a "bright angel" ministering to Romeo's passion for transcendence. The drama, of course, does not call on us to "blame" Romeo for his passion but simply to see it in its tragic potentialities, as we follow with pity and fear[47] the fate which that passion involves. It leads to violence toward neighbor and self, which we as spectators can recognize as moral disorder. But the essential flaw is anterior, a religious disorder. For does not Romeo have his religious stars crossed or confused when he makes of Juliet his dayspring from on high? His final visit to the churchyard with crowbar to force open the "jaws" of death is an action whose very shape makes it an antitype of the Bible's Easter story.

Let us note that Romeo speaks of "the devout religion of mine eye" as early as I.ii.91; the phrase perhaps signalizes his tragic flaw. He worships the idol of his eye—first Rosaline, whom he idealizes in the conventional language of the Petrarchan lover, and then Juliet, whom he hails as "true beauty," a jewel "too rich for use, for earth too dear." In the darkness of night (and night for Shakespeare is generally symbolic of a spiritual condition), Juliet is imagined as a "saint" and Romeo himself as a "pilgrim" to her "holy shrine," where "sin is purged" by a "faith" which her lips seal in answer to his "prayer."[48] Later he swears his love "by yonder moon," while Juliet asks him to swear rather by his "gracious self, the god of my idolatry." In the broad daylight of Verona's streets this religion of Romeo's wavers when tested against another idol of his heart, his reputation, and he gives way to fire-eyed fury. Juliet too, for the moment, calls her idol a "fiend angelical" and "damned saint." But neither lover can endure the thought of banishment from the other. For Romeo, "Heaven is here where Juliet lives" and

> There is no world without Verona's walls
> But purgatory, torture, hell itself.

Note that the earthly city is thus equated with paradise.

Both lovers now evidence a passion for death, which temporarily the Friar restrains by his rational counsels and plans. But the passion breaks out again in Juliet when confronted by her father's edict. She is but distracted from her distraction by the Friar's expedient for a mock-death. When that evasion fails, her passion fulfills itself in final self-slaying. Romeo, likewise, when again he thinks Juliet lost, can dream only of self-immolation at her tomb. There he drinks his cup of poison in a kind of *figura* of the Christian Mass. But his "obsequies and true love's rite," as he calls it, are a dark figure indeed of the Christian rite; his is a Thursday night last-supper, but the obverse of the Bible's. For Romeo it climaxes a religion of love which has transcended reason, only to lose itself not in God-the-Creator but in the creature and the creature's dream of self-transcendence. It is a religion of *eros* devoid of *agape*, like that of Dido or Cleopatra. It is natural love's dark analogue of a supernatural love—what Augustine would call the earthly city's highest glory. It is fittingly memorialized at the end by erecting a "statute in pure gold" to Juliet and also to Romeo. Verona's religion-of-the-eye now has its canonized household gods, potent images for resolving civil feuds and achieving a peace based on what Augustine would call concord or mutual agreement. This is the earthly city's highest peace.

A natural providence has been at work for the city, humbling hate by laying a "scourge" on it. Yet it is part of the tragedy of the story that the Friar's special providence for the lovers has miscarried. In them "grace" has not outgrown "rude will," but instead rude will has turned upon itself to devour the plant in death. As a gardener of his parish he has failed. Why? His natural fear for earthly reputation and safety is partly responsible. Like a hireling shepherd he flees. But also responsible is his reliance on nature's resources only— on moral philosophy and the natural magic of a drug. These are poor substitutes for grace and charity. He would correct Romeo's love-sickness with disputation ("Let me dispute with thee of thy estate") accompanied by exhortations to play the man. He would help Juliet evade suffering by giving her a cup analogous to Calvary's vinegar sponge. He is a kindly brother, who would restrain evil by natural means but has lost the secret of St. Francis for curing it. In this respect Brother Lawrence is a poor apothecary, related by polarity to the Mantuan apothecary of the play. Romeo receives from the Friar advice to "love moderately," whereas Romeo's basic need is to learn to love ordinately, giving to each object of his love its proper due. Again, Romeo is counseled to be "grateful" for the "mercy" of Verona's prince, but the Friar himself neglects the way of gratitude to which he has been ordained by his Savior-prince. Thus the star-crossed authority of the state, and nothing higher, opens and closes the play. Symbolically, perhaps, we are told it is not yet Lammastide, the time of St. Peter's release from prison. This spiritual situation is the fate which conditions the play's tragedy.

Verona's spiritual situation is defined in other ways too. The play opens, for example, with a servant Sampson saying: "Gregory, on my word we'll not carry coals." And presently we see that this Sampson is a firebrand, given to harlotry and feuding—in this respect like the biblical Samson during his unregenerate days. He and Gregory are interested, they tell us, in "flesh," not "fish." And Gregory, of course, is a delightful parody of the ideal his name connotes in Christian lore ("servant of the servants of God"). Such an opening scene is comedy, of course; but Shakespeare's comic scenes have a way of being integral with the theme of the play in which they are used. If read analogically, is not the play full of various Samsons feuding or marrying with their Philistine neighbors? Another passage integral to the play's theme, we may believe, is the set speech on Queen Mab, which Shakespeare assigns Mercutio in Scene iv. Surely it is more than decorative. It serves to define Verona's "courtly" atmosphere by telling us the nature of the "fairy" who captivates human beings to the service of *eros* in its many forms. She is a "hag," the midwife of earthly dreams. She elicits these dreams by a touch of moonshine, spider web, and film. Further interpretation is provided by the Chorus to Act II, which describes Romeo as "bewitched by the charm of looks" and Juliet as a stealer of "love's sweet bait from fearful hooks." Thus guidance for our understanding the tragedy has been given partly by folklore associations and partly by biblical ones.

Scholars have long been aware that Shakespeare's knowledge of the Bible was unusually extensive. From his plays have been garnered, at various times, hundreds of allusions or verbal echoes to "at least 42 books of the Bible"[49] and a tabulation of the 35 biblical characters whom Shakespeare names. But criticism has been slow to assimilate these facts to an over-all perspective on the plays. While the explication of individual passages has profited, the relation of these to the total action of a given play has scarcely begun. And the delay is understandable when the difficulty is considered. To begin with, there is the notable fact that where biblical reference is overt and on the surface, it comes generally from speakers who, like Satan, are citing Scripture for their own purposes—characters such as Shylock, Falstaff, Richard III, or Richard II. Is Shakespeare then using Scripture merely decoratively? Biblical echoes obviously lend poetic power to the talk of a given character. But how do they bear a relation to his action, or to the action of the play as a whole?

What I have suggested in my last few pages is that biblical allusion is less significant than biblical analogue. Analogue may be operating when allusion is not evident; and even when allusion is evident, it may be more important as signaling a dimension by which to read the play than it is as providing "thought" for the character whose speech contains it. A character in tragedy is, among other things, a victim of dramatic irony: his words and actions can mean something else to the spectator than they do to the character himself. Part of the artist's task is to implant this irony. It can be done by shaping an Othello who unwittingly parodies Job and resembles Judas; a Lear who unwittingly enacts the role of a prodigal son; a Romeo who unconsciously blasphemes Christian rites of pilgrimage and adoration of saints. Though few readers may at first discern this irony, dependent as it is on a theological order of fact in the drama, it would seem to be implicit in the shape of the tragic action and potentially apprehendable. In any case, when a perspective grounded in Christian lore is brought to bear on a Shakespearean tragedy, meanings of a kind I have tried to sketch can arise. Their validity must be judged finally by their over-all fruitfulness in revealing the shaped logic of Shakespeare's art. We have, so far, only some first-fruits to judge by, yet enough to challenge further investigation.

NOTES: Chapter 2

1. Postscript (1944) to *Back to Methuselah* (New York: Oxford University Press ["World's Classics" edition], 1947), p. 250.
2. The quotation is from Shaw's *Our Theatre in the Nineties* (1932), II, p. 184, as cited by Sylvan Barnet in a synoptic article, "Bernard

Shaw on Tragedy," *PMLA, Publications of the Modern Language Association of America*, LXXI (December, 1956), to which I am indebted for certain other details in my paragraph.

3. E. I. Watkin, *Poetry and Mysticism* (New York: Sheed & Ward, 1953), chaps. II–III.

4. E. E. Stoll, *Art and Artifice in Shakespeare* (Cambridge, Eng.: The University Press, 1933), vide esp. pp. 8, 26, 163.

5. G. B. Harrison, *Shakespeare: The Complete Works* (New York: Harcourt, Brace & Co., 1948), p. 1137.

6. Theodore Spencer, *Shakespeare and the Nature of Man* (New York: The Macmillan Co., 1942), p. 148.

7. *Shakespeare Criticism*, D. N. Smith, ed. (London: Oxford University Press, 1934), p. 137.

8. H. C. Goddard, *The Meaning of Shakespeare* (Chicago: University of Chicago Press, 1951), p. 557.

9. For the views I shall cite from Coleridge, vide *Shakespeare Criticism*, D. N. Smith, ed., esp. pp. 258, 270, 272, and 324.

10. Algernon C. Swinburne, *A Study of Shakespeare* (New York: R. Worthington, 1880), p. 172.

11. A. C. Bradley, *Shakespearean Tragedy* (New York: The Macmillan Co., 1904), p. 279.

12. *Ibid.*, p. 27.

13. Available in Bradley's *Oxford Lectures on Poetry* (New York: The Macmillan Co., 1909), pp. 70–92.

14. A. C. Bradley, *Shakespearean Tragedy*, p. 38. My other quotations are from pp. 18–19, 26–28.

15. *Ibid.*, pp. 107 and 116–123.

16. *Ibid.*, pp. 344–349 and 483 (on Macbeth); 54, 194–195 (on Othello).

17. Though Bradley insists on moral "responsibility," it appears in a contradictory form. Of *Macbeth* he writes: "Speaking strictly we must affirm that he was tempted only by himself. He speaks indeed of [the witches'] 'supernatural soliciting'; but in fact they did not solicit. They merely announced events." The temptation "was already within him," yet leaving him "free to accept or resist the temptation." How free if already possessed, we might ask, but Bradley offers no explanation. His system allows him no real temptation, for that would involve solicitations, not an overpowering of one natural force by another. Bradley regards the witches as not "anything but women," but argues that for atmosphere's sake Shakespeare has used them to present the "popular superstition" (available to him in Reginald Scot's book) that they have received supernatural powers from certain evil spirits. *Vide* Bradley, pp. 341–344.

18. A. C. Bradley, *Shakespearean Tragedy*, pp. 11–16.
19. *Ibid.*, pp. 2 and 7.
20. *Ibid.*, p. 25 and, earlier, p. 6.
21. *Oxford Lectures* (1909), pp. 311–357.
22. Notable recent instances of an essentially Bradleyan humanism are H. B. Charlton's *Shakesperian Tragedy* (Cambridge, Eng.: The University Press, 1948), esp. pp. 1–17 and 230–243; and D. G. James, *The Dream of Learning* (Oxford: The Clarendon Press, 1951), esp. pp. 26, 91–97, and 116–123.
23. T. S. Eliot, "Shakespeare and the Stoicism of Seneca" (1927), reprinted in *Selected Essays* (London: Faber and Faber, 1932).
24. *Vide* Eliot's "Tradition and the Individual Talent," in *Selected Essays.*
25. L. L. Schücking, *The Meaning of Hamlet* (New York: Oxford University Press, 1937), pp. 1–30.
26. Lily B. Campbell, "Bradley Revisited: Forty Years After," *Studies in Philology*, 44 (1947), p. 180. The article rebukes Bradley for his squeamishness in naming God, and for reducing to virtually nothing the three elements of the supernatural, the abnormal, and the accidental.
27. *Summa Theologica*, I–II. 73.2; 74.4; 77.4.
28. W. C. Curry, *Shakespeare's Philosophical Patterns* (Baton Rouge: Louisiana State University Press, 1937), pp. 97–137.
29. Thus E. M. W. Tillyard, in his *Shakespeare's Problem Plays* (London: Chatto and Windus, 1951) does not treat Hamlet as a tragedy, or *All's Well* as a comedy, but writes, p. 6: "It is these two interests—in speculative thought and in the working of the human mind—pursued largely for their own sake that partly characterize the Problem Plays." Virgil Whitaker, in *Shakespeare's Use of Learning* (San Marino, Calif.: The Huntington Library, 1953), p. 196, thinks that "Shakespeare was more interested in the ideas themselves than in the movement of his plot" in *Troilus and Cressida* when Ulysses discourses on "degree" or when Hector expounds "the moral laws of nature." Tillyard and Whitaker seem to imply that thought takes precedence over plot.
30. L. C. Knights, "On Historical Scholarship," *The Sewanee Review*, LXIII (1955), p. 227.
31. H. C. Goddard, *The Meaning of Shakespeare*, pp. 398–400.
32. On this point, *vide* John Lawler, "On Historical Scholarship," *The Sewanee Review*, LXIV (1956), esp. p. 204.
33. *Vide* Augustine, *City of God*, esp. XIX. 24; XIV. 28; XV. 22; and Book I. For a full discussion of Shakespeare's play in the light of St. Augustine's categories, *vide* David Kaula, *The Moral Vision of*

Troilus and Cressida (Indiana University Ph.D. dissertation, 1955, published on microfilm).

34. Compare the seventeen images of tragedy from Satan to "Rich Croesus," rehearsed by Chaucer's Monk under the motto, "Let no one trust a blind prosperity." D. W. Robertson has an excellent essay on "Chaucerian Tragedy" in *ELH, A Journal of English Literary History*, XIX (1952), pp. 1–37.

35. Francis Fergusson, *Dante's Drama of the Mind* (Princeton: Princeton University Press, 1953), pp. 53–55.

36. M. D. H. Parker, *The Slave of Life* (London: Chatto and Windus, 1955).

37. Nevill Coghill, "The Basis of Shakespearian Comedy," *Essays and Studies: 1950*, Vol. III of the New Series of Essays and Studies Collected for the English Association, G. Rostrevor Hamilton, ed. (London: John Murray, 1950), pp. 1–28.

38. For example: R. W. Battenhouse, "*Measure for Measure* and Christian Doctrine of the Atonement," *PMLA*, LXI (1946), pp. 1029–1059; and J. A. Bryant, "Shakespeare's Allegory: The Winter's Tale," *The Sewanee Review*, LXIII (1955), pp. 202–240.

39. For example: S. L. Bethell, *Shakespeare and the Popular Dramatic Tradition* (London: King and Staples, 1944), esp. pp. 53–61 and 80–83; Francis Fergusson, "*Macbeth* as the Imitation of an Action," *English Institute Essays: 1951* (New York: Columbia University Press, 1952), pp. 31–43; Paul N. Siegel, "The Damnation of Othello," *PMLA*, LXVIII (1953), pp. 1068–1078; and R. W. Battenhouse, "Hamlet's Apostrophe on Man," *PMLA*, LXVI (1951), pp. 1073–1113; "Shakespeare and the Tragedy of Our Time," *Theology Today*, VIII (1952), pp. 518–534; "Shakespeare and the Concept of Original Sin," *The Drew Gateway*, XXIV (1954), pp. 78–90.

40. J. V. Cunningham, " 'Essence' and the *Phoenix and Turtle*," *ELH*, XIX (1952), pp. 265–276.

41. S. L. Bethell, *Shakespeare and the Popular Dramatic Tradition*, p. 82.

42. G. Wilson Knight, *Principles of Shakesperian Production* (Baltimore: Penguin Books, 1949), pp. 166–167.

43. J. A. Bryant, "Shakespeare's Allegory," p. 211.

44. According to Matthew 26 and John 12, Judas makes his final decision to betray when he covets to have given to his keeping alone the "alabaster cruse" of ointment which Mary of Bethany poured out on Jesus. There may be an analogue in Othello's coveting to have as his alone the "monumental alabaster" of Desdemona's body (V.ii.).

45. G. I. Duthie, Introduction to *Romeo and Juliet* (Cambridge, Eng.: The University Press, 1955), pp. xix–xxi.

46. Ulrici has remarked of the lovers: "they mar their excellence by making idols of each other, and fanatically sacrificing all things to this idolatry." Quoted in the Variorum *Romeo and Juliet*, H. H. Furness, ed., p. 452.

47. And with awareness of the play's humor too. When Mercutio jests at Romeo's love as "like a great natural that runs lolling up and down to hide his bauble in a hole," there may well be beyond the sexual innuendo another truth: Shakespeare may be suggesting that Romeo's love is that of the "natural man," which attains its greatness in a dedication to the grave. By Act V, Romeo is ready to "set up my everlasting rest" at the grave.

48. The religiousness of the love here is typical of the ritual of Courtly Love, which Denis de Rougemont in his *Love in the Western World* (New York: Harcourt, Brace & Co., 1940) has traced to gnostic heresy. Note, however, that Juliet attempts to resist Romeo's making a shrine of her, as if she sensed heresy in it. But as the Friar elsewhere says, "Women may fall when there's no strength in men." She follows Romeo into idolatry and suicide.

49. Richmond Noble, *Shakespeare's Biblical Knowledge and Use of the Book of Common Prayer* (London: SPCK, 1935), p. 20.

Miltonic Tragedy and Christian Vision

FEW CRITICS, or indeed theologians, would be rash enough to deny that Milton treated biblical subjects in a fair facsimile of classical form. *Samson Agonistes* has a cast of characters from the Book of Judges and even a Greek tragic chorus. *Paradise Lost* is a long epic concerning Adam and Eve and Satan, in which Milton has to turn from indulgent "familiar talk" of God with man and "change these notes to tragic." In *Paradise Regained*, a short epic, the Son of God avoids the tragic pitfalls of sin and Satan.

Yet it has been reasonably enough maintained, as by Dr. Johnson, that Milton is lacking in both tragic vision and biblical faith. *Samson Agonistes* has a beginning and an end, but does it have a middle? "The intermediate parts have neither cause nor consequence, neither hasten nor retard the catastrophe." If it has no middle, there is no tragic vision of life as a whole. And what is *Paradise Regained* but a "dialogue without action"? Similarly it may be stressed that Milton "unhappily perplexed his poetry with his philosophy"; that he was unduly suspicious of the Catholic doctrine of the Trinity, his God the Father being poetically as well as logically *Summus Deus;* that he slighted the Evangelical doctrine of the Atonement by writing no great work on the Cross and Passion; and that even his theism is suspect, since he has the world created out of God rather than out of nothing, and denies the natural immortality of the soul. Does Milton, then, really lack both tragic vision and biblical faith?

I shall maintain, on the contrary, that Milton is centrally a Christian poet; among English poets second (in this respect) only to Shakespeare (who has also been called an unbeliever, though never, so far as I know, denied the gift of tragic vision). In the many plays of Shakespeare and in the one play and two epics of Milton, I should say that we have almost ideal examples of tragic vision illuminated by biblical faith, and of biblical faith transforming the tragic vision of life. Even more explicitly than of Shakespeare we can say of Milton: here is Christian *vision*. Doubtless a Catholic theologian such as Maritain, or a Protestant theologian like Brunner, might find a formal heresy here or there; but, as careful theologians, they might be willing to admit the difficulty of avoiding heresy in the service of One who was a schismatic to the Jews and a traitor to the Romans; and they might acknowledge the still greater difficulty of any Christian poet having more than Edwin Muir's "One Foot in Eden." Perhaps it is enough, from the standpoint of Christian faith, that Christian poets do not, like Robert Graves, label themselves as ex-Christians and promote the worship of the White Goddess. For, as Dr. Johnson properly maintained: "The good and evil of eternity are too ponderous for the wings of wit," even of the poet and theologian; and at the last we must rest content "with calm belief and humble adoration."

COMUS, or the Mask of Humanism

Many of my colleagues in this symposium are stating or implying their view of what is central to the tragic vision and to Christian faith, and I do not want to enlarge on that general topic. But perhaps I had better mention that, in my own view, the most necessary (though never sufficient) approach to poetry and to revelation is through anthropology. Neither Milton nor the Bible can be apprehended, still less enjoyed or endured, without some appreciation of the fact that pagan tragedy, comedy, and epic on the one hand, and biblical liturgy, saga, and prophecy on the other, derive from and are reactions to a common primitive core of myth, ritual, and sexuality. Eve is Pandora and Pandora is Eve, as in their different ways the Panofskys and Robert Graves have brought to our attention.[1] But the former do not make clear the reason why Pandora and Eve are one, and the latter too closely confines his explanation to the warfare of the sexes and the rivalry of matriarch and patriarch in human society.

I at least would hold, more in the tradition of Frazer and Harrison, that tragedy and comedy, in other words drama, emerge out of the fertility cults, that the goat-songs of Dionysus and the revels of "*Komos*" or the spirit of fertility are in origin two aspects of the same thing—what was said and done both "tragically" and "comically."

In this religion of primal and savage man, the "myth" is the thing mouthed or said when the appropriate act (in culmination, the sexual act) is ceremonially or ritually performed. Both myth and rite are based on the implicit belief that there are analogies between speech and sex as forms of expression, and between human copulation and the progress from seed-time to harvest. And more important still, the secret of primitive knowledge is how and when to mouth the myth and do the deed so as to manipulate and control the annual fertility of the crops, to make "*Komos*" or the spirit of fertility work. Copulation might then as now be prescribed when the seed is deposited in the earth; men might copulate with trees if the harvest was threatened; mass-mating and sexual promiscuity might be encouraged in general, or certain members of the group might be designated to serve on behalf of the rest. In all its forms this is the fall into magic—the exploitation of the potency of man and nature, in the fatal but pardonable delusion of human omnipotence. And the prophetic denunciation in the Bible of idolatrous magic, and its liturgy of redemption, from the Passover to the Lord's Supper, are the Hebraic-Christian answer to the basic error of man. Moreover, the primitive does not die: it merely goes underground; medieval romance and seventeenth-century witchcraft are but outcroppings of "the old religion." Magic, idolatry, and a contorted sexuality which assigns omnipotence to human potency remained a continually recurrent phenomenon in the Christian era and still, in fact, dominate this post-Christian world of ours: indeed, their domination is a main reason for calling our age post-Christian. The story of Prometheus and of Dionysus, or the story of Adam and Eve, of Satan and Dagon and Christ, is, from the beginning, our story.

In the hands of the Greek tragedians (rather than the comic writers) the facts are faced, seen steadily and as a dramatic whole, from beginning to end; this is the tragic vision, the aesthetic transformation of life and death which makes both bearable. What transforms the story of the magical fall into either the message of Christian faith or the vision of Christian poetry is the direct or indirect appreciation and expression of the new and different ending to the tale—some sense that, in the long run, man is not merely reconciling himself to God, but that God is in Christ reconciling the world unto himself, according to that Gospel which we have heard with our ears. Or, as the Prometheus of Edwin Muir puts it:

> At the world's end to whom shall I tell the story?
> A god came down, they say, from another heaven
> Not in rebellion but in pity and love,
> Was born a son of woman, lived and died,
> And rose again with all the spoils of time

Back to his home, where now they are transmuted . . . .
And time itself is there a world of marvels.
If I could find that god, he would hear and answer.

The practice of magic and its connection with the manipulation of love and potency is so pervasive in human conduct and human history that it has become a bulwark of human imagination, and a staple of the works of imaginative writers. As Eric Bentley recently said of drama, and particularly of Shakespearean plays: "If the comedies were written in celebration of fertility, the tragedies were written out of a sense of the horror of infertility." And in Shakespeare's final play, *The Tempest*, by his treatment of the black magic of Sycorax and the white magic of Prospero and their dubious connection with the forms of love, Shakespeare awoke in Milton that "wonder and astonishment" which gave rise to his first stage effort, *Comus*. But the early Milton either did not fully understand Shakespeare—which would not be surprising—or, in writing a masque rather than a play, was confined by the nature of his form. At least the effect is different. Shakespeare appears to conclude that Prospero must return to Milan, abjuring the direct use of even white magic; the young Milton, however, was still content with the illusion that chastity can be magically preserved from "*Komos*" or the uncouth spirit of fertility:

> Love vertue, she alone is free,
> She can teach ye how to clime
> Higher than the spheary chime;
> Or if vertue feeble were,
> Heav'n it self would stoop to her.

Such humanistic illusion is but a refined form of the fall it seeks to avoid.

All is very different, though, when we come to Milton's

Christian tragedy, *Samson Agonistes*, written (I would hold) just a few years later and planned from the start as a Dagonalia —beginning with the story of Samson and Dalila; having, as the middle, the story of Samson and Harapha; and ending as the story of Samson and Dagon.

SAMSON AGONISTES as a Catholic Tragedy

The composition of *Samson Agonistes* is usually dated between 1640 and 1670, but it would be aesthetically and religiously right, and therefore chronologically proper, to put the date as close to 1640 as possible. By that time Milton had outgrown the rich but academically cloistered frame of mind and style of writing which makes his early poetry pleasant and gifted but humanistic rather than Christian—whether it is *L'Allegro* and *Il Penseroso*, or *Comus* or *Lycidas*. He had not yet been caught up in the apocalyptic mood of revolution in which he wrote the prophetic prose works of his political period, nor had he come to the composition of Protestant epic as in *Paradise Lost*, nor Puritan allegory as in *Paradise Regained*. But he had experienced tragedy and had broken through the mask of humanism.

What had made him grow up was the traumatic experience that he had on his grand tour of Europe in 1638, when he arrived in Geneva to find that his bosom friend, Charles Diodati, had, unknown to him, been dead for months. John Diodati, the uncle of Charles, to comfort the young Milton, opened to him the life-giving message of the Bible. It was as if Augustine had been converted—instead of simply departing for Carthage—on the death of that fellow student whose friendship had been "*Suavis mihi super omnes suavitates illius meae*" (Sweeter to me above all the sweetnesses of that my life). And it was in all likelihood when Milton returned to London and took in private pupils for a couple of years and had to revise textbooks for them that he expanded (from the ampler treatment by Polanus) what the pithy theologian Wolleb had to say on Fortitude and Patience. That Fortitude and that Patience (of which Samson and Christ are type and fulfillment) were also burned on his soul by what John Diodati said of Samson and Christ in the spirit of his Annotations to the Holy Scripture.

The result was neither Humanist nor Protestant but Catholic, the liturgical and holistic drama of *Samson Agonistes*. The Jews know the meaning of "Moses," of individual and general history, in the Passover; the Christian knows "Christ" in the Lord's Supper (or some poetic surrogate celebration of the victorious and redeeming death of Christ), with its transformation of human destiny. Hence *Samson* is the key to Milton, and for myself the peak also: before it he is a Humanist, after it a Protestant and Puritan, but here is Catholic Christianity.

Since *Samson Agonistes* is, in Milton's own phrase, a Dagonalia, the influence of Dagon is pervasive. We are introduced to Samson in Philistian Gaza on the very day on which

> a solemn Feast the people hold
> To Dagon their Sea-Idol (11–12)

whose companions are Baal-zebub and Astaroth (1231–1241), the lord of flies and the mother of vegetation. Milton thus preserves the twofold aspect of Dagon—his name being alternatively derived (as Milton well knew) from the words for fish or for corn. Either basis is proper enough, since fish-gods had corn-goddesses for their consorts, and both are fertility symbols.

On this scene enters Dalila, "that specious Monster, my accomplisht snare" (230), appearing to the chorus like a stately ship of Tarsus "with all her bravery on, and tackle trim" (716), but in her own words:

> With doubtful feet and wavering resolution. (731)

In her enters contorted sexuality, or love in the service of Dagon, that love for which Samson had fallen, blind in the eyes—and for which he has been blinded.

In the view of the Bible (as indeed of the Greeks) there are three major forms of love: erotic passion, domestic affection, and friendliness. All of them have their appropriate causes: the attraction of the sexes, family relationships, the mutuality of men and nations. But the Bible knows a fourth kind of love, which is essentially divine and divinely essential, an uncaused holy love for the unlovely and unworthy and nonexistent. It is a love on which all nature and human nature depends. No wonder then that the ultimate idolatry and fall is any magical abuse of love, above all the attempt to invert the levels of love, or to transpose the dimensions of love, as in the effort to manipulate the course of nature (which depends on the highest, holiest love) by studied prostitution of erotic passion. And this is what Dalila is, and this is what Samson had fallen for.

But, however cunningly the sorceress continues to display her own transgressions (cf. 819), Samson has learned from his chastisement; he will no longer transgress "the law of nature, law of nations" (890), nor fall into "wedlock-treachery endangering life" (1009). He is no longer a sinner but a saint, no longer under chastisement for succumbing to the world, the flesh, and the devil. He is now one whose virtue, whose patience, and whose fortitude are to come under trial.

This is the middle of the play, and with it appears Harapha, the giant, to accuse Samson of practicing

> black enchantments, some Magician's Art. (1133)

With great skill Milton's Samson turns the taunts of the adversary and inveigles the giant into rejecting the trial of mortal fight:

> By combat to decide whose god is god,
> Thine or whom I with Israel's Sons adore.
>   (1176–1177)

And the chorus declaims:

> Oh how comely it is and how reviving. (1267)

The saint is refreshed by his divinely sent trial, and we are prepared for the summons to the pomp and games of Dagon which the Officer now brings. Under this impact Samson will be seen in a still grander, indeed in a uniquely symbolic position, at once the climax of the tragedy and the fulfillment of its Christianization.

Tension mounts as Samson refuses to join the

> Jugglers and Dancers, Antics, Mummers, Mimics,

in the idolatrous service of Dagon. He begins to feel "rouzing motions" in himself which indicate that (in the dispensation of God) he may have to be

> Present in Temples at Idolatrous Rites
> For some important cause. (1378–1379)

So he becomes "content to go" (1403) and is intent on "some great act" (1389).

No one dares to appear as his antagonist; but soon we hear from afar the noise of ruin and destruction. Perhaps Samson is being slain; but the chorus suspects that by some miracle Samson is "dealing dole among his foes" (1529). Soon a messenger arrives from "the place of horrour" (1550); and their fears and hopes are at once confirmed. The "spacious Theatre" of Dagon

> Half round on two main Pillars vaulted high

has been pulled down

> with burst of thunder
> Upon the heads of all who sate beneath,
> Lords, Ladies, Captains, Councellors, or Priests
> (1651–1654)

and

> Samson with these immixt, inevitably
> Pulled down the same destruction on himself.
> (1657–1658)

The chorus asserts:

> O dearly-bought revenge, yet glorius (1660)

and, Manoa adds, one which

> to Israel
> Honour hath left, and freedom. (1715)

Even in the midst of the final holocaust Samson, like the Phoenix, "revives, reflourishes" with "ages of lives" (1707). For he is a "type" of Christ (as practically everyone from Jerome to John Donne and John Diodati agreed), victorious over the enemies of God, triumphantly ransoming his people at the cost of his own life.

There can, to my mind, be little or no doubt that Milton possessed and articulated the tragic vision, that *Samson Agonistes* is a real and great tragic play, in its beginning, in its middle, and in its end. I have similarly no doubt that Milton paid adequate tribute in literary form to the Atonement, and was possessed of biblical faith. The final Samson is a figure of the death of Christ. But Milton is neither merely a poet as such nor a Christian theologian as such: he is a Christian poet: his *Samson* is not pagan vision nor Christian preaching but Christian vision. The Christian poet makes us *see* it all; in this seeing we perceive more clearly than anywhere else that the miraculous redemption cannot be magically and automatically applied. What we hear is of faith, what we are made to see is wisdom:

> His servants he with new acquist
> Of true experience from this great event
> With peace and consolation hath desmist,
> (1755–1757)

devoid of that passionate perturbation of mind which comes from Philistian idolatry, from the attempt to raise human potency above divine omnipotence. But, like Prospero back in Milan, we must

Find courage to lay hold on this occasion. (1716)

PARADISE LOST as a Protestant Epic

The tragic theme of Milton is the ramifications of love, magic, and idolatry; and his method is symbolical; he gives us in his drama an intertwining sample. His basic meaning and method are much the same in *Paradise Lost*, the story of man's primal disobedience, the story of Eve and Adam, the tale of the "apple." But the epic is more complicated, for the fall of man is instigated by the fallen angels and turns on the logically prior fall of the angels. What, then, are we to make of Satan?

Let me put it in this way. We can look at things from the inside out and from the bottom up; or we can look at things from the outside in and from the top down. The former is the symbolic method, the method of Shakespeare above all, and of much of Milton. The latter is the allegoric method, of Bunyan and of much of Milton, including Milton's presentation of

Satan. Samson and Eve and Adam figure something forth; Satan, like Bunyan's Pilgrim, concretizes an abstraction. Symbols give insight, allegory illustrates.[2]

It would therefore be easier in learning the language of Milton to start with his symbolic narrative of Eve and Adam and see why allegory becomes necessary. And let us begin with Book IX, at the moment when Satan "having compasst the Earth, with meditated guile returns as a mist by Night into Paradise" (Argument).

Satan arrives in a mist; the Noxious Influence peers through a miasma, that atmosphere traditional to the Prince of the Air. He arrives in Paradise, a carefully tended oasis, the divinely given Garden which biblically oriented minds contrast with both the unfruitful desert and the cunningly exploited territories of Egypt, Canaan, and Mesopotamia. He enters into the serpent sleeping, just as, in the preview of Book IV, he had entered Eve's dream like a toad. And all Hell began to break loose in the garden.

Adam was a gardener, not a farmer. Farming, even vegetable farming, was the crime of Cain. Adam had a fruit-garden, not an orchard; and though the fruit became an apple of discord and tasted like the apples of Sodom, it was not (even in Milton, really) any apple that caused the pother. It was a fruit

> of fairest colours mixt
> Ruddie and Gold. (IX, 578)

It was the fruit of that tree from which the symbolic aprons of the protoplasts also came—the fig. It was a tree, moreover, fit for the serpent from a "circular base of rising foulds that tour'd" with "head crested aloft" and a "burnisht Neck of verdant Gold erect" (498-501).

The sexual dimension of the symbolism here must, again, be recognized, for the serpent erect is, at the most literal level, the male organ of sexuality. As T. S. Eliot said of his "The Waste Land," anyone acquainted either with Frazer's *Golden Bough* or with Jessie Weston's *From Ritual to Romance* "will immediately recognize in the poem certain references to vegetation ceremonies." And, at the most literal level, once more, the reference of the Eve story is to copulation for better crops, to imitating in particular the fertilization of the fig in order to ensure it—an extension of human potency which is, of course, not possible in the very nature of things, but is a fitting symbol of man's attempt to outdo divine omnipotence. Primordial indeed is the sign of the fig.

I do not believe it to be extremely important that Milton's Satan, reporting to the other devils on his successful assault on mankind, happens to refer to the fruit as an apple. Much more significant is the total imaginative picture in Book IX; not to mention the fact that Milton in his *Pro Se Defensio* naturally associated the foolishness of illicit love with the fig tree and the loss of Paradise. It would not indeed be of major consequence that the fatal fruit of the Bible or of Milton's poem could be shown to be of some other fruit tree, or even of the vine. The point is rather the continuing imaginative tradition concerning the fatal character of fertility rituals and idolatrous love.

In Eve the cultivation of the soil becomes a cult in itself; the magic of the misuse of love becomes idolatry. Despite, or just because of her

> dilated Spirits, ampler Heart
> And growing up to Godhead, (876–877)

Eve genuflects to false deity:

> From the Tree her step she turn'd
> But first low Reverence don, as to the power
> That dwelt within.   (834–836)

Eve was deceived; but, when Adam falls, he is "not deceav'd,
But fondly overcome with Femal charm" (999). The accent is
on charm, on magic, on the idolatry of love. In historical terms
the literal reference is not to the survival of vegetation ceremonies but to that tradition of eroticism (deriving from the
fertility cults) which has re-emerged in the Troubadours and
Cavaliers, Courtly or "platonic" love: the cult of romantic
adultery and romantic fornication.

If we may (as I think we must) interpret *Paradise Lost* in
terms of *Samson Agonistes*, Dagon-Dalila and fallen Samson
become Satan-Serpent and Eve-Adam; only in the drama we
are introduced to Samson as a sinner who becomes a saint,
while in the epic we are introduced to Eve as a saint who
welcomes the Trial of her Vertue (only to become a sinner),
and to Adam as a saint of God who degenerates into "love's"
saint. When Adam has inverted the career of

> The Danite strong
> Herculean Samson from the Harlot lap
> Of Philistean Dalilah, (1059–1061)

he is hailed by Eve in her "agonie of love" (858) as one for
whom the trumpets are sounding on the other side:

> O glorious trial of exceeding love
> Illustrious evidence, example high.

But exceeding means excessive.

We have been engaged with Milton's symbolic narrative,
with what Eve and Adam are all about; and we have seen that
neither of the protoplasts is wholly to blame. Eve especially
is deceived by a fair appearing good; her rebellion has cause.
So far the *symbolic* narrative.

But why should evil appear good? It is the work of Satan.
Caused rebellion depends on the ultimate enigma of causeless

rebellion, on a supra-human but infra-divine surd. (And though, from the causeless perversion of love, man can be rescued by the uncaused love of God, even God cannot save the Devil.) These are high and deep matters that may not perhaps be ultimately penetrable by even the bravest attempts to look at evil from the outside and from above. These are ideas that can hardly be symbolized, that can at best only be illustrated. Hence the *allegory* rather than the symbol of Satan, the personification of Evil—and the allegorical story of Sin and Death, in Books II and X.

In the very first book of the epic, the evil angels had been, in allegorical fashion, formally identified with the gods of the old religion, including Dagon and Ashtoreth (462, 438), and formally likened to the dubious heroes of romance (579 ff.). In the second book, Satan, on his journey from Hell to Earth, encounters a serpentine woman who had, in origin, sprung from the head of Satan, like Athena from the head of Zeus, a portress of Hell's fate. From dalliance with her, Satan incestuously begets a son "fierce as ten Furies" (671). And from the moment of birth the outrageous goblin brandishes his "fatal Dart" (568), begetting on his mother a brood of "yelling Monsters" who

> when they list into the womb
> That bred them they return, and howle and gnaw.
> (798–799)

Such is Sin-and-Death. Satan, however, promises to improve the lot of his "Fair Daughter" and his "Son and Grandchild both" (X, 384); so Daughter Sin, though "forbidden to unlock" the adamantine gates of Hell, undoes the doors she cannot close. Satan, Sin, and Death are then loosed on *Chaos* (690 ff.), which, as we might expect, turns out to be the world of primitive religion, of Hesiod's *Theogony*, of sable vested Night, of Orcus and Ades and Demogorgon, of Tumult, Confusion, and Discord. And through it all Satan moves like the heroes of pagan myth and epic, like the Argonauts or like Ulysses (1017 ff.).

It is only after such an allegoric approach to Satan that we are introduced to the story of his original revolt in Heaven, his rebellion against the favor of the Father to the Son, and the consequent War in Heaven which drove Satan to Hell. These are the least successful, but of course the most difficult, portions of the epic. Of them Alexander Pope not unjustly averred that Milton made God the Father lecture like a school divine or professor of theology. The symbolic contact with earth is, in other words, it is true, almost lost.

Yet there is something to be said in defense of Milton's allegory, and of this we can be put in mind by recognizing that *Paradise Lost* is a play within a play, an epic within an epic— the story of man within a story of angels. And as such the theme of "man's first disobedience" is surrounded by that of satanic disobedience. Pride goeth *twice* before a Fall; and the two tales, of caused rebellion and causeless rebellion, reinforce and illuminate each other. In each case the point is the supreme folly of our refusal to accept the limits of creaturely existence. The case of Satan, like that of the Philistines, is hopeless. There is a surd of irredeemable evil in the nature of things; even the uncaused love of God can do nothing permanently effective for totally causeless rebellion. And for this, for something we all hope is forever beyond our own experience, allegory rather than symbolism is perhaps the more suitable vehicle of expression.

Further, the ingenuity with which Satan constructs the case against the Omnipotent in Heaven prepares us for the way in which he can twist rhetoric to cause the Fall of Eve in Book IX. In Satan, cultivation of the mind becomes a cult in itself; and, appropriately, Satan is a more abstract and allegorical figure than Eve.

Thus Milton's Satan fastens on the Etymological Ambiguity in the Genesis story; "And hath God said, from all the fruit of this garden ye shall not eat?"

> Indeed? hath God then said that of the Fruit
> Of all these Garden Trees ye shall not eate
> Yet Lords declar'd of all in Earth or Aire?

> To whom thus Eve, yet sinless. Of the Fruit
> Of such Trees in the Garden we may eate,
> But of the Fruit of this fair Tree, amidst
> The Garden, God hath said, 'Ye shall not eate. . .
> (656 ff.)

Satan has failed in the first round; but he has learned from the failure, and becomes more like

> Some Orator renouned
> In Athens or free *Rome*. . . .
> to some great cause addresst.
> (670–671)

He "stood in himself collected" and then proceeded to Testimonial Sophistry: God knows that on the day ye eat of it, your eyes will be opened and ye shall be as Gods.

> O Sacred, Wise, and Wisdom-giving Plant,
> Mother of Science, Now I feel thy Power
> Within me cleere, not onely to discerne
> Things in thir Causes, but to trace the wayes
> Of highest Agents, . . .
> ye shall not Die:
> How should ye? by the Fruit? it gives you Life
> To Knowledge? By the Threatener, look on mee,
> Mee who have touch'd and tasted, yet both live,
> And life more perfet have attaind then Fate
> Meant mee, by ventring higher then my Lot.

> Shall that be shut to Man, which to the Beast
> Is open? Or will God. . . .
> > not praise
> Rather your dauntless vertue . . .?
> Goddess humane, reach then, and freely taste.
> > (679 ff.)

And who of us would not say as Eve said or do as she did?
Are we not persuaded by propaganda to snatch at omniscience
and omnipotence?

> What hinders . . . .
> To reach, and feed at once both Bodie and Mind?
>
> So saying her rash hand in evil hour,
> Forth reaching to the Fruit, she pluck'd, she eat.
> > (781)

Milton is not casting a baleful look at love, or sexual inter-
course, or the family. Genesis is not "agin" generation or the
generations. This is an instance and symbol of humanity de-
humanizing itself, of reason not erect but prone; by "some
faire appeering good surpris'd" and falsely dictating (360);
through some "specious object by the Foe subornd" (361),
falling into deception unaware (and therefore forgivably, but
at what cost to Divine Omnipotence).

Nor is it correct to regard Milton as somehow on the side
of Satan. In Milton, as in the Bible, we hear throughout our
story: "In the beginning, God" and "Providence thir guide"
(XII, 647). Some angels may not want to keep their place;
men may reach for forbidden fruit and want to try out evil—
even after the appearance of Him who brought back "Through
the world's wilderness long wander'd man" (XII, 312). All too
often

> > Truth shall retire
> Bestuck with slandrous darts, and works of Faith
> Rarely be found. . . . (XII, 535–536)

But for man as such in God's time, the End is sure:

> New Heav'ns new Earth, Ages of Endless date
> Founded in righteousness and peace and love.
> (XII, 550–551)

The Christian tradition is both incurably Catholic and incurably Protestant—or, if you prefer, incurably symbolic and almost incurably allegorical. Within the Bible itself one finds the symbolic parables of Christ transformed by the disciples into allegories (as in the case, for example, of their allegorization of the parable of the Sower). Augustine, founder of the Catholic Middle Ages, is also the favorite theologian of the Reformation and of contemporary Neo-Orthodoxy—and did not Augustine allegorize even the parable of the Good Samaritan and see the course of human history in terms of an allegoric conflict between the City of God and the City of Satan? In the late Middle Ages, the Mass and the drama both became more and more allegorized; and, though Luther and the *Book of Common Prayer* are richly symbolical, Calvin and the Huguenots became increasingly allegorical as the Counter-Reformation adopted an ever greater literalism. (Only in our day, in the liturgical movement, has symbolism within Rome regained its rightful place.) So, though I rejoice that the major myth of *Paradise Lost*, the myth of Eve and Adam, is symbolic, I recognize the necessity of the satanic allegory. And just as *Samson Agonistes* is a fully Catholic tragedy, *Paradise Lost* tends equally to become a fully Protestant epic.

PARADISE REGAINED as a Puritan Allegory

With Paradise tragically lost, what does it mean to envisage Paradise regained through the Temptation of Christ in the Wilderness? Quite apart from the interpretation of *Samson Agonistes* as dealing centrally with the Redemption and so making a "redemptive" interpretation of *Paradise Regained* unnecessary, we have Milton's own affirmation, at the end of his epic on the re-establishing of Eden in the wilderness, that only now is the Redeemer about to begin his dramatic labors:

> on thy glorious work
> Now enter, and begin to save mankind.

Even at the level of being the story of Christ's consecration to his prophetic office, *Paradise Regained* is singularly undramatic. Here is no tragedy or epic in the usual sense; here is neither Catholic nor Protestant vision. This is Puritan allegory; and whether the poem is allegorical because it is Puritan, or vice versa, it might be unwise to affirm with too nice a distinction.

Milton had behind him the Protestant allegorical tradition that the biblical Temptations of Christ were meant to give the Church proof of assured victory against all endeavors and subtleties of the evil spirit—a guide to new dangers of idolatry, of the desertion of God's truth by Christians in the conduct of their prophetical office. Such had been its significance for Diodati, for instance. But Milton is developing from a Protestant into a Puritan; a Bunyan was eventually born in him. And his Puritan allegory of Christian history in terms of Christ and Satan sits rather lightly on the Bible.

Two of the biblical Temptations—the turning of stones into bread and the casting of oneself down from the pinnacle of the temple—are given but the briefest and most cursory treatment. Almost the whole epic is a series of variations on the temptation to the kingdoms of this world, a revised and more puritanical vision of how Paradise may be lost.

The Eve theme has come to appear in Milton's imagination as that of a "crude apple"; or, as he explains (when Belial wants to "set women in his eye" [II, 153]), the story of the fatal fruit was really hocus-pocus—the devils were just pretending to be pagan gods (II, 173 ff.). So Satan tries a dose of Renaissance culture—a pleasant grove, a table richly spread in regal mode, with cakes and wine, Ganymedes and Nymphs, and harmonious airs of chiming strings, no fruit forbidden but "sweet restorative delight" (373). Not unexpectedly, the Son of God can say

> Thy pompous Delicacies I contemn. (390)

Luxuries cost cash, as Satan proceeds to mention:

> Great acts require great means of enterprise. (412)

But the Son of God is aware that mercantile Renaissance civilization is impotent in itself. Without Virtue, Valor, Wisdom, who can attempt either to "gain dominion or to keep it gain'd" (434)?

This gives Satan his clue, and he proceeds to parade the Virtue, Valor, and Wisdom of the World. Why not imitate the erected Spirit of Alexander or of Julius Caesar? Swift comes the answer: such imperial virtue degenerates into Machiavellian virtue; such leaders receive not glory from God but wish themselves to be titl'd Gods. Well, why not imitate the valor of the Maccabees, and free the country by arms from heathen servitude? And the reply comes that one must not force the Father's hand; Christ's humble origins indicate no such career. Nor is the politic wisdom of the world in much better shape. The regal arts and crafty league, the fox as well as the lion, lead to Dagonism, notoriously in the case of the Kingdom of Israel itself which

> fell off
> From God to worship Calves, the Deities
> Of Egypt, Baal next and Ashtaroth. (III, 415)

The climax comes when Satan displays the real Wisdom of the kingdoms of this world, the grandeur of Rome and the glory of Greece. He calls up both the imperial

> Civility of Manners, Arts, and Arms (IV, 83)

of the first century A.D. and its artistic and philosophic base in the fifth century B.C. in

> Athens the eye of Greece, Mother of Arts.

But these arts arrogate all glory to themselves and their creators—and will do so again in any Renaissance revival of them.

The Devil gives the Greeks their due—especially the dramatists, lofty and grave, in whom the tragic vision is focused, while they treat

> Of fate, and chance, and change in human life;
> High actions and high passions best describing.
> (IV, 265–266)

But, as the Son of God answers, concerning the tragic vision as systematized by the philosophers:

> Alas what can they teach and not mislead;
> Ignorant of themselves, of God much more?
> (IV, 310)

> Much of the Soul they talk, but all awrie,
> And in themselves seek vertue, and to themselves
> All glory arrogate, to God give none
> Rather accuse him under usual names,
> Fortune and Fate. . . . (IV, 312–316)

And is not this in fact so? Is not the tragic vision, man's aesthetic atonement for his failure at omnipotence, itself too self-sufficient?

At least so it must appear to the Christian allegorist, the Puritan, looking at good and evil from the outside and topside.

And by the time Milton completed *Paradise Regained* the whole movement for which he stood was politically on the outside too: he who had been Foreign Secretary under the Cromwellian regime was just a suspicious character—which hardened his Puritanism. But it never quite froze, even in his late vision of Christian history. He preserved a wit which Bunyan and indeed Spenser never had, as is well borne out by the conclusion of *Paradise Regained*.

Just as Eve's fall was presaged by a dream, so Christ's victory over the world ends with a dream—in the midst of a storm. Satan very cleverly admits "this Tempest as this desert" (IV, 466) can be no portent of disaster in Heaven, but it may foretell woe to man. Perhaps superstition and magic are still allowable at the human level. Such signs come not from God; however, only the Son of God recognizes that such matters are "harmless, if not wholesom, as a sneeze" (IV, 458).

Christian art has always the tendency to become more Christian than artistic, to swallow up the tragic vision in the victory of faith. Even in *Samson Agonistes*, we are almost propelled from the moving and amusing arts to the ministrations of the redemptive order; indeed, the tragedy is, as it were, a liturgy for the almost unchurched Milton. In *Paradise Lost*, the tragic narrative is immersed in and partially subordinated to the devout allegory. No wonder then that in *Paradise Regained* the tragic vision is almost submerged in the allegorized presentation of faith. But in the first two-thirds of *Samson Agonistes*, the Ninth Book of *Paradise Lost*, and the Fourth Book of *Paradise Regained*, we can experience all that is best in the tragic vision of the Greeks and hear all that is holiest in the voice of biblical faith. In these literary forms of Christian vision we have an answer that is both artistic and Christian to the problems perennially posed by human idolatry and the magical fall.

NOTES: Chapter 3

1. For the Christian comparison of "the story of the forbidden pithos with that of the forbidden fruit" *vide Pandora's Box* by Dora and Erwin Panofsky (New York: Pantheon Books, 1956), especially chap. I; and for the pagan interpretation of the similarities *vide* Robert Graves, *The Greek Myths*, 2 Vols. (Baltimore: Penguin Books, 1955), especially Vol. I, pp. 22, 35, 148, and also his review of the Panofsky volume in *The New Republic*, 135:16 (August 13, 1956). As B. Reicke comments in his article on "The Knowledge Hidden in the Tree of Paradise" in *The Journal of Semitic Studies*, Vol. I, No. 3, July, 1956, "There is no question of deriving the Hebrew tradition from the Greek myth, but its meaning can be illuminated by this well-known legend," including, of course, the Adamic action of Prometheus in stealing the forbidden fire. The Adam-Eve topic is the Prometheus-Pandora topic; and, as Mr. Reicke continues, "An important presupposition is that human procreation is a principle of civilisation. Such a synecdoche is often found in ancient vegetation mysteries where man's procreative faculty was obviously considered an indispensable factor of the growth and exuberance of the fields. Thus man's transition from innocent naturalism to a conscious technique, by means of which he can successfully exploit and rule the life of nature, is here very instructively represented as a dangerous transgression finally leading to suffering and death."

2. In a subsequent essay on "Milton, Vico and Mythopoeic Method," I hope to develop the view that poetic and religious truth, if viewed from this standpoint, are not opposed but allied to scientific truth.

The Anguish of Pascal

WE HAVE BECOME so obsessed in our time with the new sciences of genetics and psychoanalysis that we easily disregard what is in front of us. Learned presuppositions may lead us to postulate premises which are simply not supported by the facts. This is more likely to be the case when the life of genius comes under consideration, genius being too often associated with abnormality. Yet the fact that Blaise Pascal was in bad health and that he died at the age of thirty-nine does not allow us to reduce his philosophy to that of an invalid, as Aldous Huxley invites us to do. Granted that unbearable pains are likely to darken one's outlook on life, Pascal's anguish is not to be explained away in terms of neurosis, as Cabanes believes, or of ophthalmic headaches, as Onfray suggests. In the words of Henri Peyre of Yale University, the vision of a Pascal continues to be more revealing than that of a healthy optimist who has never suffered from dyspepsia.

Hereditary factors seem to have been essentially healthy on both sides. Pascal's forebears on his mother's side, whom we may trace back as far as the thirteenth century, were mostly tillers of the soil; one was a priest, one a notary public. Well received in local gatherings, they were loved and respected for their charitable gifts and habits of piety. Pascal's maternal grandfather, Victor Bégon, established himself in Clermont (Auvergne) as a merchant toward the end of the sixteenth century. There was a tinge of mysticism, balanced by plebeian realistic common sense, in Antoinette Bégon, his mother. She was remembered as a level-headed, "very pious and very charitable" lady, and may be truly said to have recapitulated, as it were, a family tradition of dedicated souls. On the father's side we find honest, hard-working men of solid good sense, tradesmen—dealers in carts, perhaps—who made their way up into the middle class by unremitting toil. Recognition had come to them in this capacity as far back as the fifteenth century when they were raised to the aristocracy of the petty *noblesse de robe*. They also finally settled in Clermont. And one of them, Pascal's great-grandfather, was so successful a merchant that he was able to purchase the position of Inspector of Deeds. His son, Martin Pascal, became Tax Collector for the city of Clermont, and later Treasurer of the Bureau of Finance. An independent thinker, he became known for his Protestant leanings and his keen interest in the Renaissance. He sent his eldest son Etienne, Pascal's father, to Paris to study law. After pursuing his studies, young Etienne became the King's Counselor in the local electorate, and as Deputy President of the Court of Aids (which was sovereign in matters of taxation) Pascal's father became one of the most prominent men in the country. Endowed with a high sense of duty, he was essentially a Christian gentleman. The premature death of his wife Antoinette left him with three children to educate, two daughters and a son, Blaise. So Blaise grew up as the genial end product of a long tradition of disciplined hard work under God. And whatever sense of anguish may later have appeared in his make-up can hardly be traced to a hereditary line thus culminating in the most fully rounded, the best balanced and most trustworthy soul that French tradition has ever produced.

Should we now turn our attention to the moment in history when Blaise Pascal appeared on the scene, this same impression would find further confirmation. When the Pascal family left Clermont and settled down in Paris, the seven-year-old Blaise was entering his most formative years, educationally speaking.

This was the age of Richelieu, the dawn of France's Golden Age, a time of discipline and stability. Politically, this was true both in France itself and also with regard to her position in the life of Europe. In Paris at that time an ancient courtly tradition was revived, preparing the way for the reign of the *honnête homme* in a polite society where any manifestation of self-centeredness was shunned. The French language of Malherbe and Guez de Balzac was further refined and carefully catalogued, to become worthy of the new moral and social ideal. Four years after the Pascal family arrived in the capital, Richelieu gave the French Academy its credentials. The standard French dictionary and grammar were initiated. Two years later Descartes wrote that great intellectual autobiography of the *honnête homme* called the *Discourse on Method*. The disciplined inner man he pictured drew the personal attention of such a portraitist as Philippe de Champaigne, who captured a meditative mood concentrated in the eyes of his subject. The serene maturity of outlook of the painters of that day marks them as men aware of their moral and spiritual responsibility. These were the days when new forms of Stoicism were revived in a Christian context, and a high ideal of humanity was developed which was incarnated in the heroes of Corneille's drama as well as in the utter dedication of such founders of religious orders as St. Vincent de Paul. What a solemn moment for Pascal to be initiated into the meaning of Christian manhood! Surely, then, there was not the least incentive to the anguish of uncertainty. Like his great contemporaries, the adolescent Pascal knew where he was going, and why. All about him he could see men readying themselves with an inner armor to do battle for causes they held sacred. There is deep significance in the fact that this was the moment when the pitiless disciplinarian Richelieu himself singled out the elder Pascal to work on the rehabilitation of the province of Normandy.

And yet it is perhaps still more significant to find Corneille, a short time later in Rouen, giving a first reading of his great Christian play *Polyeucte* in the Pascal home.

Think now of Pascal's environment and surroundings during these formative years. We need not recount the feats of the boy prodigy, who at the age of eleven started writing a treatise on sound after having noticed at the dinner table that a porcelain plate vibrated when a knife struck it and that the noise stopped as soon as someone's hand touched the plate; who, at the age of twelve, rediscovered himself the thirty-second proposition of the First Book of Euclid, in spite of the fact that his father had thus far kept him away from mathematical treatises. What is of particular interest, however, is that henceforth the young Pascal attended the learned meetings of the Free Academy, which in due time became the French Academy of Sciences. There he took an active part in the discussions, and his opinions were greeted with respect by some of the most learned men of Europe. Then, when barely sixteen years old, he produced the famous *Essay on Conic Sections*, which made Descartes jealous, gave inspiration to Leibniz, and laid down the foundations of projective geometry. As a result, the adolescent lived mostly in the company of learned, older men. His attention was practically monopolized by scientific curiosity, leading to the invention and construction of the calculating machine. On another occasion, inspired by a conversation with an intendant of fortifications, he began his research on the problem of the vacuum. Imagine this youth establishing the *fact* of the vacuum by infinite variations upon Torricelli's experiment, altering the size, length, and shape of the receptacles used, and varying also the several liquids employed. Having laid down the foundations of his work with such care, he was now well on his way to the invention of the barometer and its applications, to the opening up of the science of hydrostatics with such applications as the hydraulic press. . . . No, indeed: this young man was not a divided soul. There was not in him a shadow of anxiety: he was too sure of himself for that.

Let us say, then, that up to 1646—that is, up to his twenty-third year—there was in him no evidence of uneasiness, still less of anguish.

II

We are now aware, however, of a change of climate.

In January, 1646, Pascal's father suffered a fall on hard frozen ground and dislocated his hip. He was attended by two capable and most dedicated gentlemen who happened to be recent converts to Jansenism. This religious teaching, claiming to be derived from St. Augustine, had Calvinistic overtones which increasingly aroused the suspicion of Roman Catholic authorities. Jansen, the initiator of this theology, had died in 1638, and his tenets had been published in 1640 under the title *Augustinus*. His fellow worker St. Cyran, who had become Confessor at Port-Royal and made of this religious community the center of Jansenism, had been imprisoned in the year of Jansen's death for disruption of ecclesiastical peace. Theirs was a movement that seemed to be sponsoring a rather dangerous type of extremism in religion: yet Blaise Pascal's ardent soul was quickened by this very extremism of the new teaching, with its emphasis on man's impotence, God's sovereignty, and unconditional election.

One of the most immediate results of this Jansenist quickening was that this passionate convert who never did anything by halves became a most zealous reader. He read the new Jansenist literature and, in the manner of the neophytes of Beroa, turned to the Scriptures to see if what he was now being told was true. A Roman Catholic by birth, he was led in this manner to rediscover the Bible, and henceforth it played such a vital part in his life and thought that one may be tempted to detect in this fact an all-important clue to the understanding of Pascal.

Looking at the record, it would seem, however, that the most important result of his encounter with Jansenism was that it lent new impetus and, as it were, a new motivation to Pascal's self-assurance. Passionate by nature, he had already become an imperious young man. Educated by his father, he had never gone to school or mixed with boys of his own age. I, for one, have always felt that he certainly missed having been asked in earlier years by fellows of his own age the question we have all heard, "Who do you think you are?" Growing up as he did at home between his two sisters, also aware of his father's predilection for the precocious genius he so evidently was, he had developed a tendency to lord it over the household. And now he had become further aware of his own election, of God's purpose for his life. The fact is that God had used him to convert his father and sisters, and even his new brother-in-law. Again, shortly after his own "conversion," we find him investigating the case of an elderly Capuchin friar, candidate for an ecclesiastical appointment in Normandy, a certain Jacques Forton, who had taken on the name of Saint-Ange. The newly converted Blaise knit his brow as he scrutinized the beliefs of the candidate. Without going to the extreme of Sainte-Beuve, who called Pascal on that occasion a "denouncer and quasi-inquisitor," or that of Jovy, who described the incident as "a theological ambuscade," one must admit that the self-appointed judge, who surpassed the Archbishop's grand vicar *in pontificalibus* during the whole procedure, was sure of himself, to say the least. For it had seemed right to the Holy Spirit and to him that this burden should fall upon an obviously misguided friar. Again, read the retort of the young scientist when the Jesuit Father Noël, proceeding upon the authority of Aristotle, challenged his admittedly masterful views on the reality of the vacuum: "One cannot deny you the fame of having upheld a peripatetic physics as well as that can be done. . . . And certainly the skill with which you have defended the impossibility of a vacuum on the slender grounds which remain to support it, makes it easy to judge that with similar effort you would have incontrovertibly established the contrary opinion in view of the vantage-ground which experiments provide." The merits of the case are not in question here. The plain truth is that Pascal's fame was spreading all over the scientific world of Europe. This may partly account for the self-assured, and even arrogant, tone of his pronouncements, however revealing of his genius they may be. We leave it to the reader to judge for himself, as he considers at length the letter to Father Noël (October–November, 1647) from which the above quotation was made.

And yet a deeper note becomes increasingly audible, a theme of pathetic quality in a solemn, aching, minor key. The very fact that his own fame was spreading all over Europe and that he was conscious, nay, proud of it, constituted for Pascal an incontrovertible danger signal. Probing Scripture on this subject, he discovered in Exodus 20:4–5 what vengeance the living God may take upon idolaters. One of Pascal's fragments which is preserved in the second Guerrier Collection acknowledges that it is impossible for God to be the End, if he is not also the Principle. Either God, or self. Self-centeredness is the essence of all sin. This same fragment proceeds from this basic implication to this terrible warning: "We lift our eyes on high, but lean upon the sand; and the earth will dissolve, and we shall fall whilst looking at the heavens." The deeper note in a minor key that now broke out at the very core of Pascal's being initiated the leading theme of his anguish, the fear of becoming a castaway. You will find it echoed in the concluding lines of the *Memorial* of November 23, 1654, as the Fire of the heavenly vision fades away: "Let me never be separated from Him." And the supremely moving evidence is that of Pascal's very last words, his cry of anguished hope at the end: "May God never abandon me!"

This, then, becomes clear—our second conclusion: the reason Pascal's anguish appeared only after his twenty-third year, that is, after 1646, is that during that year he began to view his human situation in the light of Scripture. Then it was that the Bible came to him in a most personal way. Yet it came to him, a Roman Catholic, at the hands of the Jansenists. So the question that arose was the question as to whether or not he, as a Jansenist, would be able to exercise his mental activity upon it without destroying in the process the security implied in his Roman Catholic faith.

III

It should be made clear at this point that Pascal remained at all times faithful to Roman Catholic practice. As a child he had learned from his father that a clear line of demarcation should be drawn between objects of reason and objects of faith. This basic distinction which Etienne taught his son became the principle of Pascal's contention with Father Noël. As he saw it, the very persons (here, obviously, the Jesuits) who appealed to authority (here, Aristotle's authority) in physical science were the same persons who launched a naturalistic, rationalistic method in theology. It was, therefore, necessary, after restoring to experimental science the naturalistic and rationalistic methods which properly belonged to it, to restore to theology the authority which was its proper due—ultimately the authority of the Roman Catholic Church. Such submissiveness was to the individual a matter of useful relationship in the context of a sacramental life which assimilates the members to the head—the visible head being the Vicar of Christ on earth. He alone disposes of the nurture of the sacraments which a faithful Roman Catholic needs in order to live and continue to live. This life he thus lives on earth is the *inchoatio vitae aeternae*, the inception of eternal life. When Pascal, therefore, was anguished at the possibility of becoming a castaway, when his prayer culminated with the cry of dereliction, "Let me never be separated from Thee!" his immediate context was that of "communion with the head of the Church who is the Pope," as one of his private letters later stated it. And the most elementary intellectual honesty constrains the student to admit that he never wavered from that basic position.

As an adept of Jansenism, he never thought of himself as departing from Roman Catholic doctrine. Quite the contrary. He saw in Jansenism a restoration of the Church to her pristine purity. An ever closer study of Scripture confirmed him in that view. Interpreted in this context, the Saint-Ange controversy, to which reference has already been made, clearly indicates that one of the important consequences of Pascal's Jansenist quickening had been a renewed interest in the Church. One of the major conclusions at which he had arrived was that the best way to be a zealous and genuine Roman Catholic was the Jansenist way.

Thus far, however—that is, up to 1648—he had known Jansenism only through Jansenist writings, except of course for an edifying contact with the two Jansenist gentlemen who had nursed his father with such utter devotion. But by this time Pascal had moved to Paris for reasons of health, with his younger sister Jacqueline, and he immediately made contact with the Jansenist community there. While the experience proved a happy one for Jacqueline, it ended in near catastrophe for Blaise. A letter to his elder sister, dated January 26,

1648, tells of his first visit to Monsieur Rebours, one of the confessors at Port-Royal. Pascal had immediately told him that, having read the books of the Jansenists, he had been won over to their sentiments. Anxious to serve the good cause they now had in common, he suggested the possibility and advisability of demonstrating many of the views involved, admitting that one ought, though, to believe them without the aid of reasoning. But it was now the Jansenist's turn to knit his brow in suspicion. The fact that Pascal was a geometrician only made things worse, for it argued the excessiveness of his confidence in human reasoning. In vain, Pascal tried to clarify his good intentions. His self-justification heightened Rebours' suspicion, and his excuses were interpreted as obstinacy. The entire interview took place in equivocation and ended in embarrassment. And yet what Pascal had in mind was in essence that science of the defense and explanation of the Christian religion which the Roman Church has always encouraged under the name of apologetics. The Jansenist's exclusive dependence upon the downreach of divine knowledge, on the other hand, meant that the sovereignty of divine grace left no room for human intellectual striving. Any suggestion to the contrary merely exposed sinful pride. An age-old issue, this, one which has been raised afresh in our own day by Karl Barth.

Here, then, was Pascal, a man who, during the past two years, had learned the hard way that he must live a God-centered life, that henceforth his sole aim should be the glory of God. And now that he could at long last personally bring the good-will offering of his knowledge and capabilities to the religious masters he admired most, he was rejected. We should know by now what such rejection would mean to him! Those of our contemporaries who in minor ways and in a different context have met with similar misunderstandings and enforced isolation may further appreciate what the resulting anguish in Pascal's soul must have been. When he confessed to his elder sister in the same letter that his weakness was great, the context makes it clear that there was infinitely more at stake than his poor health. Was he, in effect, a blind leader of the blind? This was the question which troubled him. "I have felt my incapacity incomparably more since the visits in question, and very far from having won from them enough light for others, I have carried away from them but confusion and disturbance for myself which God alone can calm." Let us heed this "God alone" on the part of a man thrown upon his own by ecclesiastical authorities—and let us heed it for at least two reasons: (1) Pascal interpreted perseverance as nothing but the continuation of the infusion of grace, and not as the effect of one single grace which lives forever, as he expressed it in a letter again to his elder sister, dated November 5, 1648. To him this meant that perseverance amounts to a revelation of our own true status with God. Not to persevere is to be cast away. (2) Increasingly thrust back on his own by Jansenist disapproval—such disapproval in itself being a bad omen—Pascal was losing ground. More and more he practiced self-mortification as if to be purged of all carnal impressions. He requested his relatives to refrain even from expressions of gratitude.

Yet more trials were at hand. On September 24, 1651, his father and most trusted friend died, he who "would still have been a necessity to me for ten years, and helpful to me all his life." Whereupon his younger sister, for whom he had always had a special predilection, left him to enter Port-Royal as a nun. He then fell back upon the friendship of the Duke of Rouannez, only to realize that he had hardly enough money to keep up his new social relationships. Hence his reluctance to give to Port-Royal the amount a nun's dowry required. As the

Jansenists saw it then, the measure was full. The man was simply a backslider who had surrendered to Mammon. No one was surprised at his leaving Paris with his new friends, bent upon what has been called his worldly period. The fact that this period proved most fruitful in the development of Pascal's genius need hardly detain us here. It was then that he was initiated into the discovery of the *esprit de finesse*, the knowledge of the "heart," imperfectly translated "intuition" ("The heart has its reasons which reason does not know" [Fr. 277]). I suspect his friends of having tried to teach him how to dance, yet with little success ("Dancing: we must consider rightly where to place our feet" [Fr. 139]). They must have taken him to gambling houses, an experience which later inspired in him the argument of the Wager. The clear result of his observation of card players was to put Pascal on the track of the calculus of probabilities which he formulated with the eminent Fermat. What concerns our subject most, however, is that Pascal soon realized the emptiness of the world. He plumbed to their very depths the words of the *Imitation of Christ*, "As oft as I have been among men, I returned less a man than I was before." Pascal put it this way: "I have discovered that all the unhappiness of men arises from one single fact, that they cannot stay quietly in their own chamber" (Fr. 139). His was truly a "sickness unto death."

It was then that he experienced what he himself called, and I translate literally, "a great abandonment on the side of God." He became conscious of a great void, nay, of an abyss of nothingness at the very core of his being now "unrelated." Read in this context, Fragment 483 of the *Pensées* in the Brunschvicg edition constitutes the most probing diagnosis of his own plight first of all: "The separate member, seeing no longer the body to which it belongs, has only a perishing and dying existence. Yet it believes it a whole, and seeing not the body on which it depends, it believes it depends only on self, and desires to make itself both center and body. But not having in itself a principle of life, it only goes astray, and is astonished in the uncertainty of its being." Further reading from this same fragment, as it reveals a Christian coming again into his own, provides an essential clue to the *Pensées* as a whole. These collected fragments, developed in later life, were destined to become a Vindication of Christianity. There is no doubt, however, that this great unfinished symphony originated in personal notations, in diaries which recorded moods, events, experiences, notes on reading, entries which were subsequently developed and progressively reshaped with the great apologetical design in view. This suggests that the best way to approach the *Pensées* is to try and set fragments, as far as feasible, into the warp and woof of Pascal's life experience, thereby coming to a better awareness of the use that was henceforth made of original notations to exalt the Christian religion.

The immediate context of Pascal's thoughts relating to the "misery of man without God" is that of the period that followed the worldly period and immediately preceded the illumination of the night of November 23, 1654. As already stated in the preceding paragraph, Pascal had then become aware of an abyss of nothingness at the very core of his being now "unrelated." The total impact of this experience was one of "fear and trembling," as dramatically expressed in the anguished outcry, "The eternal silence of these infinite spaces frightens me," perhaps the greatest free verse in world poetry in the original French (Fr. 206). "Unrelated" man, that is, can only view the universe with quiet desperation. "For, I ask, what is man in nature? A nothing compared with the infinite, an all compared with nothing, a mean between nothing and all. Infinitely unable to grasp the extremes, the end of things and their principle are for him hopelessly hidden from him in an impenetrable secret, for he is equally incapable to see the nothing whence he springs, and the infinite in which he is swallowed up" (Fr. 72). Such a dreadful feeling of insecurity may easily turn into panic as the frustrated mind utters the admission, "Impossible!" For just as we are hemmed in between everything and nothing, our infirmity condemns us to perceive but "the appearance of the middle of things, in an eternal despair of ever knowing either their principle or their end" (Fr. 72). Indeed, it is at this point that the misery of our pitiable state is laid bare. Our state is one of inconsistency, feebleness, corruption, malignity. We are at the mercy of the most deceptive powers, be they imagination, vanity, ennui, pride, self-love, sickness or any form of blindness. A sense of futility attends our vain efforts at reading the script of our own life. And yet the paradox is that we are actually aware of our own misery. We think: We desire the good. We love truth, and we love glory. The fact is that we cannot bear to be despised. Just as there is in us an agonizing anguish at the feeling of being hopelessly thrown out in the midst of those dumb, and dark, and frightfully infinite spaces, there is an aching anguish of revolt against the unbearable implications of such a lot. A lump chokes our throat and causes us to set our face against the baleful decree. All this notwithstanding, the measure of human anguish is not yet full. For in the very moment in which we are trying somehow to regain our bearings, even in the midst of such despondency, we become time-conscious: "We set sail over a vast expanse ever uncertain, ever adrift, carried to and fro! Whatever point we think to fix and fasten ourselves to, shifts and leaves us; and if we pursue it, it escapes our grasp, slips away, fleeing in eternal flight. Nothing stays for us. That is our condition, natural, yet most contrary to our inclination; we have a burning desire to find a sure resting place and a final basis whereon to build a tower rising to the infinite; but our whole foundation cracks, and the earth yawns to the abyss" (Fr. 72). One can readily see how such a dreadful picture of the human situation could later be used in a Vindication of Christianity to suggest the urgent need of recovery on the part of a creature now become a chaos of incompatible and contradictory elements.

The point I am making is that the original context of it all is Pascal's own anguish in the days he was left alone, "in a great abandonment on the side of God." He came to the point of loathing the sight of men for the plain reason that it is only when men are truly related to God that they may be truly related to one another. The anguish of Pascal can only be rightly understood and evaluated in the context of a drama where lengthening shadows portend an "eclipse of God" in the midst of which a man becomes unable to read the script of his own life situation. Yet already it must have become clear that there was a deeper context to the drama itself.

IV

Pascal returned to mathematics from mere habit. His heart was no longer in an exercise of the mind which he increasingly considered to be a beautiful "trade"—perhaps, after all, *only* a "trade." He turned to the philosophers, and, as we know only that which we are, he was torn between the skepticism of Montaigne and the stoicism of Epictetus. This experience also would be later transposed into a solid piece of apology, the substance of which may be found in the admirable "Conversation with Monsieur de Saci." For the time being, however, Pascal left Montaigne only more crippled in spirit, just as he left Epictetus astonished at his own weakness. Descartes he found uncertain to the point of uselessness. Then, reason having failed him, he turned to the life of faithful liturgical practice, hoping that in this way his soul might be opened to the inspiration of God. This is the deeper significance of his greatly misunderstood formula, "Take holy water and allow your reason to be dulled." But let no one conclude from this that we have here anything like autosuggestion, or a wishful will to believe. For Pascal's anguish at this juncture was so excruciating precisely because he clearly distinguished all such human efforts as he attempted from the genuine motion of divine grace. He believed that the gift of sanctifying grace comes to the whole man and is itself a wholly divine gift; and he was certain that apart from it there can be no supernatural life in us. What he failed to understand was that the very striving he was undergoing implied the supernatural impulsion in him of actual grace. As a Jansenist, he could only interpret his present plight as a sign of perdition. And henceforth there could only be mortification and self-abasement.

So it was that on the night of November 23, 1654, Pascal opened his Bible at the seventh chapter of the Gospel According to Saint John, in which Jesus is shown preparing himself for his sacrifice on the cross. It was then that for two full hours Pascal lived in the illumination of that mysterious "Fire" and received with "joy, joy, joy, tears of joy" the assurances recorded in his *Memorial*. There is no doubt that he received them essentially as a message of election. To what degree and to what extent was that message conditioned by the presuppositions of the one who received it? The God who revealed himself in that encounter was "God of Abraham, God of Isaac, God of Jacob, not of the philosophers and scholars." Could it be that the phrase "not of the philosophers and scholars" appears at this point as a Jansenist mode of apprehension? Everyone will admit that it is an addition wherein Pascal appropriates a biblical passage—as he does throughout the document with reference to the other eight biblical quotations. That the *Memorial* at all points combines revelation and personal interpretation is an undeniable fact. Thus "I have separated myself from Him" is coupled with the quotation *"Derelinquerunt me fontem aquae vivae,"* this very concern with separation being, as we have seen repeatedly, Pascal's main concern. The theme in fact is soon repeated with greater emphasis still: "I have separated myself from Him: I have fled from Him, denied Him, crucified Him. Let me never be separated from Him." And, without overlooking here the problem of authenticity raised by the addition "total submission to Jesus Christ and to my director," it must be admitted that the passage fits in perfectly with the general tone of the document.

Pascal's *Memorial* is the profoundly moving record of a divine message as apprehended by a penitent Jansenist. The phrase, "Renunciation, total and sweet," naturally issued in total submission to Jansenist doctrine. Never again would a Monsieur Rebours have to knit his brow. Not only did Pascal die to all that might have been objectionable in the old self, but he gave up his name and thereafter used a succession of pseudonyms. Not only did he sell his coach and his horses, his fine furniture and silverware, but he sold also his library, keeping only, with a few devotional books, his edition of Augustine and his Bible. And only an unbearable toothache, coupled with horrible headaches, could later cause him to indulge in the solution of the insoluble problem of the cycloid. Yet he would take no credit for it. No wonder the Age of the Enlightenment indignantly exposed the "deviation" that deprived the world of the great mathematical and scientific achievements of which Pascal was still capable. No wonder those eighteenth-century men recast the edition of his works to emphasize his "real" contribution, as contrasted with speculations ascribed to Christian "obscurantism" and "superstition."

There are those who feel, however, that, in so doing, men like Voltaire and Condorcet did not properly allocate responsibilities and that they pronounced too summary a judgment.

V

"Certitude. Certitude. Feeling. Joy. Peace," said the *Memorial*. And so it would seem that this chapter concerned with Pascal's anguish might now come to an end. Yet there is a true peace, and there is a false peace, as Pascal himself was soon to express it, although in a different context of events.

Pascal had gone to Port-Royal for a retreat that he might have wished could extend to the end of his days. What came to him, however, was not peace but a sword. For by January, 1656, Port-Royal had become a storm center. From the Sorbonne, from the Court, and from Rome the accusation of heresy against Jansenism was taking on an ever more threatening shape. The Jesuits had just obtained a condemnation against Arnauld, the head of the Jansenists, and a final judgment was pending, in which the whole movement ran the risk of breaking up under the blow of a verdict of heresy—and such a verdict in the seventeenth century was a black prospect indeed. It was then that Arnauld called upon Pascal to lend his genius to the defense of the party. Admittedly Pascal was not a theologian, but Arnauld himself would provide the documentation as the need arose. Overnight, the former mathematician and physicist not only turned into a great writer but became the most resourceful creator of modern French prose, truly preparing the way for the comedy of Molière and the eloquence of Bossuet. Whatever one may think of the merits of the cause for which he entered the lists, the *Provincial Letters*, as they came out one by one under the *nom de plume* of Louis de Montalte, are acknowledged today as one of the literary masterpieces of all time.

Since the *Letters* singled out the Jesuits in a direct indictment, they soon led to a war of words and sarcasms, accusations and counteraccusations. Indeed, the polemical situation became so hot after the publication of the fourth "Letter" that Pascal once again began to be overcome with doubts and perplexities. Could this, he wondered, be the rightful role of a Christian? Yet, at that very moment, his ten-year-old niece, a boarding pupil at Port-Royal, was miraculously healed from a lacrimal fistula thought to be incurable. And this event was immediately seized upon by Pascal and his Jansenist colleagues as a sign from heaven in the midst of battle. So, after adopting a new seal commemorating the event and after adopting as his motto the text from St. Paul, *scio cui credidi* (I know in whom I have believed), Pascal resumed his campaign with a vengeance. His fifth "Letter" was a terrible analysis of Jesuit ethics, which proceeded with implacable and vengeful irony. The following "Letters" went into a pitiless indictment of casuistry and of the "subversive" innovations made in theology in order to gratify the ways and means of casuistry. The Jesuits reacted all the more violently as the identity of their accuser remained a mystery to them. In the long run, however, they detected in him a marked sensitivity to the insinuation of heresy. Accordingly, they sharpened their insinuation into a direct accusation which touched Pascal to the quick and brought forth on his part a most laborious justification, together with emphatic professions of orthodox faith, which are also echoed in private letters of the period. Pascal made his sixteenth "Letter" too long and rewrote the eighteenth thirteen times. A nineteenth "Letter" remained unfinished, and there the *Provincial Letters* came to a close. At the end of the year they were condemned in Rome. "If my letters are condemned at Rome," he wrote in agony, "what I condemn there is condemned in Heaven: *Ad tuum Domine Jesus, tribunal appello*"

(To thy tribunal, Lord Jesus, I appeal). At no time had his mental torture attained to this. And yet there is ample evidence that, true to his utter persuasion that the cause he had defended was the right cause, he subsequently resumed his attacks on the Jesuits under cover of the intervention of churchmen, for certain sections of the clergy were now on the move.

Such was his dedication to the cause of the Christian religion, as he had come to view it, that he now devoted all available time to his projected Vindication of Christianity. That is, although a very sick man, he insisted upon carrying on the activities related to the great cause to which he was committed, for the sake of true religion and for the sake of his own soul. In the midst of physical, mental, and spiritual suffering, Blaise Pascal attained holiness.

And yet anguish would be his lot to the very end. While his Jansenist fellow workers, apart from a very few, weakened under pressure, Pascal felt constrained to expose what appeared to him as sheer expediency on their part. During an emergency meeting at Port-Royal, he actually fainted at the sight of such failure of soul, and, when he came to himself, he explained to his elder sister that, in the face of such faltering half-heartedness in a holy cause, he could not help it. His own precious younger sister, having been forced to sign a Formulary of recantation required by the Church from monastic orders as well as from the clergy, died of a broken heart. Pascal received the news with the comment only, "Blessed are those who can die like that!" The end of his pilgrimage was drawing near, and he was aware of it. His main concern in this respect was to die well. Standing on crutches on a street corner in Paris one day, he could not help observing the silliness of so many vehicles carrying single travelers to a similar destination. The result was his invention of the omnibus and the organization of the first bus company. Yet he would not take advantage of this new manifestation of his genius, but rather asked for an advance payment on his share, which he sent to the poor of Blois who had suffered from a bitter winter. The poor he loved because Jesus had loved them. He wanted to die in their midst. His wish having proved impossible, he took a poor family into his own house. And when one of the boys was taken sick with smallpox and he was pressed by his sister to send the family away for the sake of her children, he decided that he should be the one to leave. Whereupon he turned his own home over to the impoverished family and went to spend his last days in the home of his brother-in-law.

Those last days were truly agonizing. The priest who attended Pascal not only did not know him well, but seemed to have been pressed by Church authorities to obtain from the dying man some kind of recantation from Jansenism. As for Blaise, he would no longer be drawn into the thicket of controversy. Time was short. He knew himself to be at the gate of eternity. All that mattered was not to die as a "detached" member. Yet it was not until the very end that he was allowed to receive Holy Communion, the Body of his Lord that would communicate itself entirely, truly, really, substantially to his soul, to nourish it with life divine. To the preliminary questions on the great mysteries of faith, he answered in the affirmative with holy impatience. In tears he received the sacrament of extreme unction, then fell back with the outcry of hopeful anguish, "May God never abandon me!"

VI

Now the reason that our approach to the understanding of Pascal's anguish has emphasized the biographical dimension is that Pascal was essentially an existentialist thinker, and any exploration of his work must, therefore, seek to interpret it in the context of his life. This is doubtless the way he meant to be read, as he stated his ideal of the genuine writer in Fragment 29 of the *Pensées:* "When we see a natural style, we are astonished and delighted; for we expected to see an author, and we find a man." It is, indeed, because he was so profoundly human that he spoke so relevantly to our human situation as such. So in this concluding section we would attempt to bring out the ways in which Pascal is to be regarded as an anatomist not only of his own personal predicament but of the more general human quandary.

Our opening section has made it clear that Pascal's anguish was an *acquired* feature. Granting that the child is the father of the man, we found in Pascal's early manhood no evidence of neuroses or psychoses such as might have been produced by singular events in childhood; no sign of unhealthy influences to be ascribed to emotionally traumatic experiences associated with childhood fears or anxieties. Here, then, is the paradox that dominates our conclusion as a whole: the very man who is most currently designated as an incarnation of human anguish started out in life with amazingly well-integrated mental functions—emotion, imagination, intellect, and will. The first most encouraging lesson he teaches us is that there is such a thing as a healthy mental organism, even in the most richly endowed human nature. Genius and normality belong together. And thus, beginning with a carefree, mentally healthy individual, we must, in order to reach his paroxysm of anxiety, explore in its successive stages the whole gamut of the rise of anguish in a great soul.

A first stage appears when Pascal who had been thus far a conventional Christian was confronted afresh with the claims of Bible Christianity. With this new revelation of his true status in the sight of God there came into his life a new sense of disquietude. He became, to use the words of Péguy in our day, "a monster of uneasiness." A pagan admittedly would not have known that anguish. Should the reader answer this assertion by calling to mind the depth of Sophocles and the sacred horror of Oedipus in the face of an obscure destiny, then allow me in turn to point to the inner conflicts of Hamlet or of Lady Macbeth in a Christian climate. What new depths have not been fathomed with Shakespeare! Likewise, picture side by side the Athena Parthenos of Phidias dedicated to the goddess Minerva, and one of our own medieval cathedrals whose restless, unfinished lines rise up to heaven in a tormented search for the living God! A new sense of mystery pervades the paintings of da Vinci and of Rembrandt; the same uneasiness is felt in the sculpture of our churches, in the sonatas of Beethoven, and in the longings of Bach and César Franck that seem to echo a prayer of St. Theresa—or Pascal's *Mystery of Jesus.*

Should the reader again object, wondering what kind of advantage this profound disturbance may represent for the ordinary man who thus makes a deeper plunge into the Gospel, an enlightened Pascal would provide the Christian answer. There is a true peace, he would say; and there is a false peace. There is the true peace that the Savior alone can give, and there is the false peace which the world can indeed give but which is horrible to the Savior of the world. Again and again the point at issue for Pascal was the opposition of "the children of light" and "the children of this world" of which the Bible speaks, according to St. Luke 16:8. To the very end we find him proceeding on the basis of this fundamental biblical distinction.

There is, therefore, according to him, a blessed form of anguish. Such anguish comes to the fore as the Word of Truth exposes the false optimism of natural man, and brings to light the disruption of this man's communion with God: I mean the disruption of a contact which in the divine order involved the genuine identity of a creature meant to show forth the image of the Creator. The peace of mind of natural man is the false peace of man in revolt. The normal result of the action of the Word of God on such a man is that it meets at first outward defeat. This tragic truth runs through the whole of the Old and New Testaments. Only "at-one-ment" as offered in and through Jesus Christ can relieve the plight of a man who has realized his situation. Until this happens, however, a soul made aware of its true condition remains a divided soul. The Greek word for "worry" in the New Testament, in fact, suggests a being divided against itself. Unless assent to divine truth, under the inspiration and with the aid of God's grace, moves the will aright, a frustrated, anguished personality is likely to disintegrate. And here, once more, we should heed the now familiar line of cleavage, and speak with Pascal in terms of true remedy and false remedy. There is no doubt as to what he would have to say today to those who "scramble for serenity" in a vain quest for a false peace of mind.

The phases observed in the development of anguish with reference to the inner man have their natural counterpart in his apprehension of the world of nature. Paganism denied anguish and attained perfection. The serenity of its mental activity could no longer satisfy the soul of modern man, however. And whenever one of our scientists recovers his humanity and speaks as an individual person of flesh and blood, he realizes that his usually detached speculation may well have little if anything to do with the deeper reality of the things that are. Such became the state of mind of Pascal during the last years of his short life. Writing to his friend, the illustrious mathematician Fermat, in this vein, he said: "For to speak to you frankly about geometry, I consider it to be the highest exercise of the mind, but at the same time I know it to be so unprofitable that I make little distinction between a man who is merely a geometrician and a skilful artisan. . . . Yet at present there is this further consideration: I am engaged in studies so remote from such preoccupations that I can scarcely remember that they actually exist." These studies were concerned with his intended Vindication of Christianity. Without going to such extremes of discrimination, a scholar worth his salt is bound to wonder sooner or later whether his own intellectual discipline is not merely a "trade," in view of the deeper reality of the things that are—and this, essentially, because he lives in a Christian climate.

The virulence of the deeper undertones in the Pascalian view of the world of nature and of man owes its aching effects to that same Christian context. The modern freethinker whom Pascal had in mind when he wrote his *Pensées* would be induced to labor under the awareness of what he disbelieved. The feeling of an absence is not the same thing as an absence of feeling. Either the living God of Scripture exists or he does not. In a domain beyond the limitations of human infirmity there is a "game" going on, the meaning of which differs according to whether this is God's universe or nothing but a meaningless assemblage of elements. The significance or insignificance of our own life is here at stake, and we have no choice but to take sides on the issue forced upon us. For we are already involved. How involved and whither headed? That is the question, a question likely to bring about increasing mental agony to one who becomes aware of its implications. Before one comes to see that his very destiny is at stake in the inescapable alternative, he will at least realize that the relevance of his own apprehension of the landscape of reality is involved. For surely "the silence of these infinite spaces" is not the same to him who stands without hope in the world as it is to him who stands in awe before the majesty of the heavenly Father. Again Pascal would say in this connection that there is a false apprehension of the landscape of reality as there is a true apprehension of that same landscape. And if the cosmos *is* the Creation of the great Doer of redeeming acts, then the plain fact is that the man who rejects the very thought of this fact does not see what is actually there, however learned he may otherwise be. And this is contrary to sanity, which is health of intellect. There is accordingly a blessed form of anguish in the intellectual realm also. It is good for one to awaken to a genuine cosmic anguish, that he may stretch out his arms to the Redeemer. For God *is,* and this world in which we live is his creation ruled by his providence.

There are sacred halting places where a man wishes he could make an abiding tabernacle. Such is the high place where Pascal brings us within full view of the Christian solution to a predicament basically ascribed to a double-mindedness born either of the pride of stoicism or of the sloth of skepticism, those "two sources of all vice." I refer especially to the glorious passage in Fragment 435 of the *Pensées:* "The Christian religion alone has been able to cure these two vices, not by expelling the one through means of the other according to the wisdom of the world, but by expelling both according to the simplicity of the Gospel." The trouble, however, is that somehow we have lost the sense of that divine simplicity. Ever since the days of the Reformation the seamless robe of Christ has been rent asunder.

As the aftermath of that dichotomy begins to be felt, a new element of anguish appears in individual souls torn between two extreme ways of apprehending the same basic Gospel. Allowing for a certain degree of oversimplification—such as is inevitable within the confines of a single essay—it may be said that these two extremes are represented by Roman Catholicism on the one hand, and by Calvinism on the other. Pascal admittedly would have shunned the very mention of Calvinism. His "Short Exposition of the Problem of Grace" (1656?), for example, presents the most severe indictment of the Calvinistic doctrine of predestination. According to this doctrine, as Pascal summed it up, God, in creating men, "created some to be damned and some to be saved by His absolute will and without foreknowledge of merit [whatever on their part]." It is a fact, nevertheless, that the Jansenist doctrine which Pascal embraced had real affinities with Calvinism on this question of grace and election. Unimpressed by 7,595 references to the writings of Augustine (mostly to his works on grace) found in the monumental work of Jansen, the Church of Rome has condemned under the name of Jansenism features which strangely approximate the famous five points of Calvinism, and this to such a degree that an authoritative Roman Catholic treatise in our day (Cayré's *Manual of Patrology*) brands together as "false Augustinians" the "founders of the Protestant and Jansenist movements."

Thus we come to the consideration of an extreme form of anguish ascribable to unresolved tensions within a religious profession—a perennial aspect which has been once more strikingly illustrated in our age by John Henry Newman. Having thus far shunned the practice of quoting myself, I may perhaps be pardoned for reproducing here the concluding paragraph of *The Clue to Pascal*, published almost fourteen years ago. This I do, not only because this short paragraph characterizes the form of anguish now under consideration, but to show how early in his Pascalian research this characterization forced itself upon a Protestant interpreter:

Let the most strictly evangelical Protestants measure with a glance the abyss which separates them from the most holy, most intelligent, the least scholastic, and the most audacious Catholic student of the Bible, and the most reverent before the Sacred Word who ever lived under God's great sky. Never was a Roman Catholic nearer evangelical Protestantism, nor farther away. In this supreme antinomy is summed up for us the secret of Pascal, and of his anguish.

It is noteworthy that a similar interpretation of anguish has found its way into one of the most widely read works of our day. I refer to Professor C. G. Jung's book *Modern Man in Search of a Soul*. In this book the eminent psychoanalyst forcefully states that among his many hundreds of patients a constant prerequisite to a restoration to mental health has proved to be the finding or recovery of a *consistent* religious outlook. This simple truth, rediscovered in the light of recent research, is the truth we ultimately learn from the Pascalian experience of anguish: a man cannot safely go through life, still less face death, without consistency in his religious profession. There were moments when Pascal's conversation had unmistakably Protestant overtones. The *heart*, in the Pauline sense of the word, held a considerable place in his thought. And so, while heeding the directive power of tradition, he was satisfied to probe his Bible very much in the manner of a Protestant listening to the Holy Spirit speaking in the Scripture. He thus lived in the obedience of faith under a strong sense of divine guidance. So much so that when confronted by an agonizing situation he would appeal directly to the Tribunal of the Lord Jesus. On the other hand, he believed, as a Roman Catholic, that he could be in a *useful* relationship with the Lord, as far as his salvation was concerned, only through the Lord's terrestrial Vicar. To him, then, "all the virtues, martyrdom, austerities, and all good works" were "*useless* outside of the Church, and the communion *with the head of the Church who is the Pope*." Hence unbearable tensions when the voice of the Pope seemed to contradict the voice of the Holy Spirit speaking through Scripture; when, for instance, during the controvery of the *Provincial Letters,* the Pope seemed to be misled by the pressure of the Jesuits' influence in Rome.

Pascal never missed an opportunity to profess the most orthodox Roman Catholic faith; yet he lived, and moved, and had his being in the company of men who insisted upon testing the Church by such private views as they had developed on their own. Priests like Saint Ange, bishops, and even the Pope fell under their self-appointed jurisdiction. But the fact that the Jansenist critique of Rome or of the Jesuit order may have been pertinent on a particular count or occasion is emphatically not the point at issue. The point at issue is that a Roman Catholic is never led to assent to ecclesiastical authority, still less to papal acts, by any *intrinsic* criterion of the evidence accessible to him. Whether in terms of doctrine or of ecclesiastical discipline, he is bound to assent because of the *extrinsic* criterion of an evidence grounded in the credibility of the Church. This is the ultimate implication of what came to full expression in the dogma of the infallibility of the Pope. There is, in other words, no place in Roman Catholicism for Protestant attitudes, nay, not even for such a minimal approximation of them as was involved in the doctrines of the Jansenist movement.

The individual person who feels constrained to say, "God help me, I cannot otherwise," and insists upon acting accordingly, merely emulates the precedent established by Martin Luther, whose words he has just echoed. This is the ultimate implication of the Reformation.

Should a man attempt a *both/and* solution in this matter of supreme allegiance, he is bound to go through life as a divided soul, that is, as an anguished soul. A divided allegiance, however well-intentioned, will ultimately cause him to lose his grip upon Reality. Having lost contact with the living God, he will inevitably become unable to read the script of his own life or to keep proper relationships with his fellow men and with this created world in its divine wholeness. It stands to reason, moreover, that only such a clear-sighted and firm allegiance originating in a free act may allow a man to be truly tolerant and even appreciative of the position taken by those of his fellow men with whom he disagrees cordially.

Pascal's motto, "I know in whom I have believed," remains one of the most pertinent of all mottoes, provided *I* live up to all its implications. Apart from such consistency, there can only be a succession of semantic nightmares in anguish and endless misery.

Goethe's Faust:
The Tragedy of Titanism

THE SPECIAL CONTEXT established by this symposium leads us, at the outset, to raise two basic questions about Goethe's drama—first, is *Faust* a tragedy; and, then, can the general perspective from which the drama is written and from which the character and destiny of the hero are seen be regarded as Christian? Is the drama, in other words, a Christian tragedy? Neither question can be answered bluntly and categorically, as we shall see, for *Faust* is, in many respects, a drama so unique that the usual categories are not readily serviceable. Goethe himself, to be sure, called it a tragedy, perhaps because the tradition connected with the hero made him a tragic figure; he wanted to preserve this tradition, particularly that aspect of it which pictured Faust as the victim of a compact between himself and the Devil. But the question as to how, in general, the drama shall be characterized is by no means a question that is easily answered, chiefly because there is such extreme disparateness between its two main parts. The first part, in its outlook and arrangement, differs so greatly from the second part that hardly any connection seems to exist between the two, with the exception of the Prologue in Heaven, which is common to both, and the last scene which directly resumes and consummates the Prologue. And it is this extreme internal complexity of the drama that raises for us, initially, the question as to whether it can be adequately described by the phrase "Christian tragedy" or, indeed, by any such univocal term.

The first part is often called "*Gretchentragoedie*," because it deals with the tragedy of Margaret, who is, indeed, the central figure in Part I, which focuses upon her love of Faust, her surrender to him, her transgressions, and her punishment which culminates in her imprisonment and execution. This whole chain of action is, undoubtedly, a tragedy and may even be conceived as a Christian tragedy, since Margaret is sincerely devout and since her Christian faith, her Christian contrition, and her Christian trust in the grace of God are the governing motives of the drama. The dramatic form which Goethe employs here represents, however, a certain eccentricity, for there are no acts and scenes: instead, we have twenty-five pictures showing the various adventures Faust undergoes, as he travels through the world to seek pleasure and distraction, under the guidance of Mephistopheles (whom Goethe offers as type and example of the Devil). The main event in this series of adventures is his encounter with Margaret and the ensuing passion which unites and finally separates them.

The second part of the drama has a more conventional form, since it is composed of five separate acts; but these acts are very unequal in length as well as in significance, and their inner connection is very loose. There is no obvious progress of action or plot—indeed, there is no plot at all that unifies these five acts and makes them parts of one dramatic whole. There is no conflict dominating the development, no crisis, no catastrophe of the sort that is central to Shakespearean tragedy. There is no unity of time and space, not even in the moderate sense of a modern tragedy. And it is even more difficult to decide whether the second part, or the two parts taken together, are Christian, if we regard Faust as the hero of the whole drama. Goethe uses biblical figures, to be sure: the Prologue, for example, obviously imitates the conversation between the Lord and Satan which precedes the narrative in the Book of Job. And in the last scene we meet "holy anchorites," fratres and penitents taken from biblical imagery. Even the Virgin Mother makes her appearance. In the fourth act Goethe quotes biblical writings like the Epistle to the Ephesians, where it is said that "we wrestle not against flesh and blood, but against principalities," and so on. And, of course, the figure of the Devil is biblical altogether. But in the vast scheme of historical allegories and legendary personages not only biblical but also, and even more abundantly, ancient mythological allusions are to be found. So the question as to whether or not *Faust* is a Christian tragedy cannot be settled merely by reference to the imagery. One has to penetrate deeper into the core of the poem: one has to consider Goethe's ultimate intentions and convictions, as they are expressed in the character and destiny of Faust. One has, in other words, to look at the drama as a whole.

But is there any ultimate intention at all? Is the drama a whole? Can we distinguish its essence from its paraphernalia, its accessories, its bypaths and digressions, its enormous display of scientific and philosophical ideas and symbols? This has frequently been doubted or denied. Scholars and critics have argued that there is no inner unity whatsoever, no consistent development, no central topic—in fact, that it is really no drama at all in the traditional sense. And it is true that if a drama is to be regarded as a script for actors and as something performable in the theater, one may seriously question whether this is what we have in *Faust*. For without interventions, accommodations, and curtailments by shrewd directors and stage managers, it is hardly adaptable to the theater. The superabundance of visions, the lack of continuity, the embarrassing variety of personages, places, and settings, the apparent disorder of events and their consequences—all this seems to point to the inability of the poet to discipline his imagination and to master his subject, particularly in the second part.

Some students of Goethe would insist that *Faust* was composed over so long a period of time—about fifty years—that he lost the initial vision and was, therefore, unable to hold fast to the original plan that had been conceived in his youth. And this would, indeed, seem to be a not unreasonable view of the matter, for, in almost all fields of experience, Goethe did undergo tremendous transformations in the course of his long life—especially in his aesthetic ideals, in his style, and in his religious and philosophic opinions. But just this consideration may lead to another conclusion. It is true that, throughout the long years, from the early days when he wrote the *Werther* and the *Goetz von Berlichingen* until he composed the last scene of *Faust*, Goethe's outlook did undergo great change. Still he always remained essentially the same man—this unique "entelechy," this individual "monad," as he liked to call the organic being that, in growing and unfolding, only enriches its inborn nature. "You cannot escape yourself," is one of his sentences. And another one says: "To be a personality implies the highest happiness on earth. Every destiny can be endured, if you do not miss yourself; one may lose everything, if one only remains what he is."

Now it is possible to argue—and it is, indeed, my conviction —that this inner unity and continuity of his own personality was conferred upon the hero of the drama that accompanied him throughout his whole life and in which he enshrined his most fundamental ideas and his most deeply held convictions. Indeed, Faust *is* Goethe, and Goethe *is* Faust. Seldom was a poet so identical with his creation. In this respect one has perhaps to compare Goethe's relation to Faust with Dante's relation to the hero of the *Commedia* or with Shakespeare's relation to Hamlet. What we must see, in other words, is that the central intention of *Faust* is the imaginative account of Goethe's own innermost struggles, his disappointments, and his victories, his hopes and his aspirations, these being gathered together in one great vision of a man favored by God but also tempted by the Devil. If we look at the drama in this way, the manifoldness of its content can be unified and integrated: viewed from the angle of this perspective, Parts I and II can be seen as truly members of the same body. The "*Gretchentragoedie*" depicts Faust and Goethe in the period of their utter confusion, when the selfish wish to enjoy life is still unhampered and undisciplined; and, in the second part, we see Faust slowly and gradually gaining clarity about himself and his true aims.

The Prologue in Heaven is the key to the whole drama. As God permits Satan to hurt Job severely, in order to probe the purity of his devotion and the integrity of his character, so the Lord in the Prologue delivers Faust up to Mephistopheles:

> Enough! What thou hast asked is granted,
> Turn off this spirit from his fountain-head;
> To trap him, let thy snares be planted,
> And him, with thee, be downward led;
> Then stand abashed, when thou art forced to say:
> A good man, through obscurest aspiration,
> Has still an instinct of the one true way.[1]

Mephistopheles is content with this permission, but he, of course, does not believe that the Lord's confidence in Faust is justified. He answers:

> Agreed! But 't is a short probation.
> About my bet I feel no trepidation.
> If I fulfil my expectation,
> You'll let me triumph with a swelling breast:
> Dust shall he eat, and with zest,
> As did a certain snake, my near relation.

Of course, as the drama unfolds, both the Lord and Mephistopheles are, in a way, to be vindicated. Faust is actually led astray; he does eat "dust" for quite a while. But, in the end, "the instinct of the one true way" is stronger than all temptations. Faust defeats the hope of Mephistopheles: he returns to his better self; he overcomes the devil within himself and clings to the ideal that was shining in his heart before he succumbed to Mephisto. And, as Job eventually recognizes the folly of attempting to contend with the Almighty and surrenders to God, so Faust too stands the test ordained for him by the Lord.

Now there are two wagers in the play which must be carefully distinguished from each other, since a proper assessment of their respective outcomes is essential to an understanding of the entire drama. In the first wager Mephistopheles bets that events will prove the Lord to have been mistaken in his trust of Faust, and it is evident that this is a wager that he loses. It is not so evident, however, that he also loses the second wager (which is with Faust), though one would assume that the loss of the first wager would necessitate the loss of the second as well. As Faust undertakes his pilgrimage through the world, he purchases the services of Mephistopheles as guide by agreeing that, in the moment in which his relish of life is so reawakened that he desires a given moment to linger, in that moment Mephistopheles may claim him as his own: then, in the nether world, the master-servant relation will be reversed, and he will jump to the tune that Mephistopheles will call. Faust does not believe that Mephisto can ever succeed in bringing him, by the blandishments of sensualism, to the point at which he will want to prolong the passing moment, but Mephisto is convinced that he can. This, then, is the second wager, and, toward the end, it does indeed seem that Faust is the loser, for he utters the words which were supposed to be the cue marking the victory of Mephistopheles and handing him over to the magician. He cries out to the Moment:

> Ah, still delay—thou art so fair!

But these words, when they are finally uttered, no longer have the meaning which the earlier pact with Mephistopheles would seem to have given them. For, at that earlier time, Faust had in mind the moment which would satisfy his sensuality and lust and make him wish that it might last forever, the moment in which he would abandon his high aspirations and infinite strivings. But now, at the end, he is actually looking toward an infinite future in which his loftiest ideals would become a reality, and in this anticipation he feels that this is his greatest and happiest moment, a moment which should never pass away. Mephistopheles does not, however, understand this momentous difference. He believes that he has defeated both the Lord and Faust. And, in fact, Faust dies, after having spoken these fateful words. But, to Mephisto's amazement, he beholds the angels bearing Faust's soul away, and he is forced to recognize that he is himself less powerful than the Lord, that he has, indeed, lost his cause:

> A great investment has been thrown away:
> By lowest lust seduced, and senseless passion,
> The old, case-hardened Devil went astray.

This, of course, implies a subtle irony, for Mephistopheles had himself intended to seduce Faust by senseless passions, and now he must admit that he has himself been the victim of blind impulses.

At the end of the drama Faust is a man of very advanced years: so his death is, therefore, the natural and necessary end of a life rich in experience and deeds. Seen from this angle the drama is not a tragedy. Although the hero does commit guilty acts and does incur misfortune and disappointment, he also succeeds in many ways. He enjoys his energy and creativity to the full, and his death is the natural culmination of a long and fruitful life. The transfiguration which crowns his life clearly indicates, in other words, that the drama concludes not in tragic frustration but rather in a beatific vision not altogether unlike that which marks the end of Dante's pilgrimage.

Yet there is tragedy in the life of this man, precisely because his aspirations do so far exceed his grasp. He is a magnificent example of human titanism, of man's inordinate capacity for striving and of his infinite creativity. In him all the distinctively human gifts are greatly intensified, just as they were in Goethe himself. He reaches out for the excessive and the extreme, for unlimited knowledge and unlimited action, for an all-embracing vision of the universe and for an all-penetrating unification with the core of reality. But in all these aims and longings he feels disappointed. Everywhere he encounters barriers too high to be surmounted, and in his despair he laments:

> What am I, then, if 't is denied my part
> The crown of all humanity to win me
> Whereto yearns every sense within me?

He does not want forever to be told: "Thou shalt abstain," "thou shalt renounce." It is the oft-quoted *"Faustische Drang,"* the Faustian Impulse, which urges and plagues him:

> In each soul is born the pleasure
> Of yearning onward, upward and away . . . .

This ever inciting, pressing, stirring, agitating impetus, this dynamic force in his heart, is the source of all his activity, but also of all his sorrow and grief. It enables him to experience life on deeper levels than it is commonly the lot of man to do, but it also makes him vulnerable to deeper shocks and hurts, to more crushing disappointments, than it is generally the fate of man to endure.

Man is too small to be a god, but he is too great to be a beast. Thus he is tossed about on the troubled sea of life and never finds complete rest. He is forever tortured by an inner "anxiety," to use the word of Kierkegaard. He is lacking that state of balance which is natural to the beast, because he wants to transcend his natural limits. This, again, according to Kierkegaard, is the deepest root of his sinfulness, and it is the root of Faust's wish to use "magic" and to bargain with the Devil. Mephistopheles knows that there is this weakness in his victim: indeed, Faust becomes his prey precisely because he aspires too high, or, to speak in the language of the Book of Genesis, because he wants to be "like God." But Mephistopheles does not understand and appreciate the noble source of this languishing for ultimate consummation. He only sees the lower desires, the passions and lusts, the craving for sensual pleasures or, at the most, the ambition to obtain power and glory. He believes that Faust will be perfectly happy once his lowest instincts are gratified and that then he may claim him as his own. And Faust himself shares this view when he enters into the compact, for he is at the point of complete despair. After having studied all the sciences, he has come to see that man can never know the truth. So he now decides to give up all his learning and throw himself into the world, to feel its woe and its bliss. Yet even before he and Mephistopheles set out on their journey together, he begins to doubt the ability of this questionable friend to understand his deepest yearnings. It is the good instinct in his soul that raises the question:

> Canst thou, poor Devil, give me whatsoever?
> When was a human soul in its supreme endeavour
> E'er understood by such as thou?

But he suppresses his doubt and risks the dangers which lie ahead. He no longer has any choice. He is prepared even to lose his soul, to encounter "shipwreck," to be smitten by the storm of his passions.

It is, then, the duplicity of human longing that is at the bottom of Faust's transgression and of his final doom. Both lust and aspiration, sensuality and ambition, are strangely mixed up in the human soul, and man is unable to distinguish them clearly. So he is "confused," as the Lord remarks of Faust in the Prologue. Or, as Faust himself says, there are "two souls" within his breast—

> And each withdraws from, and repels, its brother.
> One with tenacious organs holds in love
> And clinging lust the world in its embraces;
> The other strongly sweeps, this dust above,
> Into the high ancestral spaces.

Which will prove superior in the long run? Will he ever arrive at the state of clarity when he can separate the two streams of his craving? Will he ever overcome his confusion? It is this question which the drama in its two parts answers. World and God, Tempter and Savior, fight within Faust's breast, as they fight within every man. But they fought with greatest intensity, and in all spheres of human creativity, within the poet of the drama himself. And he came finally to the insight that God alone can separate the two souls, that from him alone is redemption to be expected.

The tension in Faust has, though, still another aspect. For his confusion is not only the result of the duality within him of a lower and a higher part: it is also the result of the duality between two opposite ways of finding ultimate satisfaction, the duality of contemplation and action. Faust has an insatiable thirst for knowledge; he wishes to comprehend the whole universe, to penetrate into the very core of all truth. This was why he had studied all the sciences and had read all the literature of Antiquity and of the Middle Ages. But nothing could ever quench this infinite thirst. Symbolically, this disappointment marks the transition from medieval book-wisdom to the modern empirical approach to nature. Faust is not content to contemplate the sign of the "Macrocosm," as he sees it in a medieval manuscript; instead, he wants to know the earth and is delighted to see the sign of the Spirit of the Earth. "New strength and heart to meet the world incite me," he jubilantly exclaims. But it is not only the contrast between book-knowledge and direct experience which characterizes his inner tension: it is, more specifically, the opposition between contemplation or intuition and practical activity. This it is which moves him to flee the narrow world of his study and to seek the great wide world outside.

The "All" which medieval philosophy describes is magnificent, but it is merely a picture:

> How grand a show! but, ah! a show alone
> Thee, boundless nature, how make thee my own?

To make nature his own it is not enough to observe it, to investigate it, to find out its laws and modes of operation; for what he really longs for is action. It is his dream "To pierce the ether's high, unknown dominions,/To reach new spheres of Pure activity!" Contemplation, theory, speculation—this is too passive a way of penetrating the universe. Faust wants to perform deeds. "Restless activity," he says, "proves the man." To work, to create, to embrace, to change the world—this is what he really wants to do. And when Mephistopheles promises him pleasure, he retorts:

> But thou hast heard, 't is not of joy we're talking,
> I take the wildering whirl, enjoyment's keenest pain . . . .

And all of life for all mankind created
Shall be within mine inmost being tested . . . .
And thus, my own sole self to all their selves expanded
I too, at last, shall with them all be stranded!

It is not pleasure that he is seeking: it is activity, life, destiny, even if it should all end tragically.

It is with such high hopes as these, then, that he begins his journeying through the world. Mephisto does not understand the mind and heart of his companion—or, rather, he understands only one side of Faust, that side which would "eat dust." And so he tries first to distract him with debauchery. But Faust cannot be seduced by gluttony and drunkenness for long. And, indeed, the painful lesson that he purchases at such a great cost, as a result of his affair with Margaret, is of how vacuous and sterile the life of sensuality really is. For Margaret is destroyed by his exploitation of her innocent affection and devotion to him, and she ends in prison, awaiting the death penalty. "O had I never been born," Faust complains in despair. But still he clings to Mephistopheles and commands him to rescue the girl. "Thou shalt live," he tells her. But Margaret now turns away from Faust. "I shudder to think of thee," she says, and she surrenders herself to the mercy of God: "Judgment of God! myself to thee I give." The "*Gretchentragoedie*" thus ends in a religious mood. But it is only Margaret who is in this mood: Faust himself feels merely his loss and her distress.

In the second part of the drama the horizon of Faust's experience considerably widens. His private affairs are no longer the focal issue but rather the world of public interests and concerns, the world of state finance and welfare. Lust of power now inspires his ambitions and incites his activities. It is a less selfish, less sensual, goal that he now pursues. It is the "ancestral spaces" which now begin to pique his appetite. And he will later soar even higher to the realm of the Beautiful, to the realm of Art—and, finally, he will aim at the true ideal of a free society of working people who own their land. While Faust climbs up this ladder of aspiration and effort, Mephistopheles descends from his superior place step by step. He loses sight, as it were, of Faust's impulses and is degraded to the function of a slave who carries out what his master requires. But to the very end he has his hand in the play, since Faust is sometimes tempted to employ dubious means in order to realize his ends.

In the first act we see Faust at the court of the German Emperor, where he undertakes to improve the economic situation by distributing bank notes of Mephisto's manufacture. The Chancellor is naturally enchanted. "In my old days I'm blest and most content," he exults. But the Emperor has some misgivings:

> A most enormous cheat—a crime, I fear!
> Who forged the Emperor's sign-manual here?

Mephistopheles, however, succeeds again, as he earlier succeeded in bringing Margaret round: he persuades the Emperor to accept these financial transactions, and the Emperor most solemnly thanks them for their ruinous "help":

> You've given our empire this prosperity;
> The pay, then, equal to the service be!

By this device, then, Faust ascends to power and authority in the state, and he is even appointed custodian of the state treasury. But he remains unsatisfied and soon wants to move from the world of politics to the world of Beauty, as Goethe himself often enough had occasion to move from the court of Weimar to the sphere of art and poetry. Faust's way of announcing this new desire is for him to say to Mephistopheles that he wants now to see Helena and Paris, "the model forms of Man and Woman." That is to say, he wants to be given a vision of Greek antiquity, that remote and vanished world in which all of life was organized in accordance with the demands of Art. But Mephistopheles is embarrassed and regards such an idea as "absurd." Antiquity is a "strange sphere" to him. He begins to feel uncomfortable in his association with Faust. It is not as easy to command Helena, the beautiful Greek woman, as it was to seduce Margaret or to produce "paper-ghosts of gold":

> I've no concern with the old heathen race;
> They house within their special Hades.

The Devil is, after all, a biblical figure, and in the artistic world of Greek imagination and creation he is not at home. It is the world of high "ancestral spaces" of which Faust has spoken, the world for which the nobler of his two souls is longing, and the more resolutely he turns in this direction, the less secure Mephisto's hold upon him becomes.

Faust's intention now, in other words, is to leave the material world, the Visible and Tangible, the realm in which Mephisto is so consummately competent. He purposes to enter the realm of the aesthetic imagination. What is Nothing to Mephistopheles he hopes will be the All to him. He even welcomes the dread and the danger that he may have to face:

> My breast expands, let the great work begin!

Mephistopheles is anxious and unsure whether Faust will ever return from the "Mothers" who symbolize the "ancestral" element. He implores them to release Faust again: "O Mothers! Mothers! let but Faust go free." Faust has to work hard and "with a fervor tragic" in order to win that "heavenly gain" which is hidden in the Beautiful:

> Who would that treasure lift, the Beautiful,
> Requires the highest Art, the sage's Magic.

But he is delighted beyond measure to discover what was always at the bottom of all his dreams and longings:

> Have I still eyes? Deep in my being springs
> The fount of Beauty, in a torrent pouring!

Goethe-Faust has now, then, arrived at the center of his entire existence. This is the turning point of the drama, the point when Faust returns to himself and Mephisto becomes a dupe. Here Faust is in his own element, at the source of his creativity and his greatest joy. Even the lovely image of Margaret which he beheld in Part I grows pale when he compares it with the image of pure Beauty itself:

> The form that long erewhile my fancy captured,
> That from the magic mirror so enraptured
> Was but a frothy phantom of such beauty.

Margaret was, after all, only an earthly woman, while Helena is the pattern of Beauty itself, the essence of all that an artist might ever hope to attain. So he confesses that love and imagination, inspiration and adoration, find their ultimate object in her. But the image cannot suffice: he needs Helena herself. And, after having seen her image, he is resolved to seize and to hold her:

> Ye Mothers! Mothers! crown this wild endeavour!
> Who knows her once must hold her, and forever!

But, while he tries to grasp her, he is prostrated by a sudden explosion. Mephisto takes his body upon his shoulders and complains:

> You have it now! One's self with fools to hamper,
> At last even on the Devil puts a damper.

This occurrence foreshadows the events of the second and third acts, for, though Beauty is the highest goal, there is still a magic in its attainment, and a magic which might destroy him who longs for it.

The world of classical beauty, of mythological and poetical imagination, of philosophic speculation and scientific observation which now unfolds before our eyes, in all the riches and splendor at the disposal of the poet, the world of Greek antiquity with its fabulous and magnificent figures—this is all something that is foreign to Mephistopheles. He is "from the north, and in the age of mist brought forth." Though he was the guide and the lord amongst the German ghosts and phantoms, he is now utterly incompetent amongst the Greek sphinxes and sirens and nymphs. Whatever he touches loses its beauty and turns to ugliness. He finds himself in a labyrinth where there is no door:

> Where am I then? and whither sped?
> There was a path; 't is now a dread.

Only amongst the Phorkyads, symbols of ugliness and disgrace, does he feel at home, for they, like himself, are the creations of Chaos.

Then at last, in the third act, we meet Helena, on her own ground, "before the palace of Menelaus in Sparta." As Goethe himself fled from the little town of Weimar, when the air was no longer bearable in the narrow circle of his administrative duties, so Faust too has left the German court; and as Goethe went to Italy, where, for the first time, he saw the masterpieces of classical antiquity, so Faust is brought to Greece where he joins the model and pattern of ancient perfection. We see Helena first in the marvelous surroundings of her royal home and of the chorus of her maidens. But this splendor is darkened through the appearance of one of the Phorkyads. It is the

Devil who emerges in the midst of Beauty. It is Ugliness it-self. And the lesson is that pure beauty cannot exist on earth. "Earth's residue," as it is later said, is never pure and fair, "though 't were asbestus." There is a thorn in the flesh that cannot be eradicated even by the craftsmanship of the most highly gifted artist.

But for a while Faust is happy in possessing the most beauti-ful wife that ever was on earth. The marriage between him and Helena reflects symbolically the union of German and Greek poetry which was for a time the ideal of Goethe's mind, and one which he believed to have been realized in works of his own like *Iphigenia* and *Tasso*. Both were the fruit of his jour-ney to Italy and his intimate acquaintance with the classical culture he enjoyed there. But, after a time, this ideal began to fade, and Goethe turned romantic, as the *Faust*-drama, and especially its second part, clearly indicates. And in our drama the fragility of this marriage between the Hellenic and the Germanic is symbolized by the violent death of the son of Faust and Helena. Euphorion's overflowing imagination and unbounded vitality make him a fine representative of his father's titanism, and his ultimate fate is, expectably, the fate of the titan. He is not content to live on earth: he wants to emulate Icarus and will not heed his parents' warning that unrestricted flight is unlawful and forbidden:

> I must clamber ever higher,
> Ever further must I see . . . .

So, refusing to heed the counsels of reason and prudence, his parents' darkest fears are borne out, and he crashes to his doom.

In the last two acts the scene of Faust's activity shifts again. He returns to German soil and to the world of politics, but, this time, with greater wisdom and with nobler ends in view. He now aspires to found an ideal community in which all men might be free and happy. And, in order to carry out this great program, he determines to reclaim vast areas of land from the sea. But, first, in order to gain the Emperor's assistance in his project, he assists him in quelling a civil war that has broken out. After this disturbance has been put down, he claims his reward, and, in the final act of the drama, we behold his completed work—a great kingdom which has been brought into being out of vast watery wastes.

Despite Faust's protestations to Mephistopheles of the disinterestedness of his motives in this whole project, his actions are by no means without moral ambiguity. There is, for example, an old couple, Philemon and Baucis, who own a little garden on a piece of territory which Faust wishes to include within his realm:

> Accurséd chime! As in derision
> It wounds me, like a spiteful shot:
> My realm is boundless to my vision,
> Yet at my back this vexing blot!

So his soldiers invade the garden and demolish the little hut and garden, and the old people perish in the tumult. Mephisto drily remarks:

> The pair had then an easy lot:
> They fell, and died upon the spot.

Faust, however, attempts to shift the guilt from himself to Mephistopheles and berates him, saying:

> Deaf unto my command were ye!
> Exchange I meant, not robbery.
> The inconsiderate, savage blow
> I curse! Bear ye the guilt, and go!

At this juncture, Guilt, Want, and Care appear in person to threaten Faust himself, but he defies them. Although he admits that he has "stormed through his life," seizing "each appetite by the hair," he still insists that man should not turn to heaven: rather, it is the Earth alone which should be the field of his aspirations:

> A fool, who there his blinking eyes directeth,
> And o'er his clouds of peers a place expecteth!
> Firm let him stand, and look around him well!
> This World means something to the Capable.
> Why needs he through Eternity to wend?
> He here acquires what he can apprehend.
> Thus let him wander down his earthly day;
> When spirits haunt, go quietly his way;
> In marching onwards, bliss and torment find,
> Though, every moment, with unsated mind!

This is exactly the same mood in which we met Faust at the beginning of the drama; the essential view of life and the world is unchanged. And it is not only the essential view of Faust but also of Goethe as well. This is his creed: it is the Renaissance love of the earth, the Renaissance faith in man's mission here on this planet where he is born and has to live, and where he should labor and work without looking beyond to an eternity which he can never know and never reach. When Care objects to this creed and insists that man can really achieve nothing, Faust responds:

> Desist! So shalt thou not get hold of me!

And, when Care then hurls back at him to retort:

> Throughout their whole existence men are blind;
> So, Faust, be thou like them at last!

Faust, now actually blind, replies:

> The Night seems deeper now to press around me,
> But in my inmost spirit all is light . . . .

He remains convinced that his work will go on and will be crowned with success in the end:

> Quick diligence, severest ordering
> The most superb reward shall bring;
> And, that the mighty work completed stands,
> One mind suffices for a thousand hands.

And at last, in a moment of exuberance, when he anticipates the fructification of his labors, he utters the fateful words:

> And such a throng I fain would see,—
> Stand on free soil among a people free!
> Then dared I hail the Moment fleeing:
> "Ah, still delay—thou art so fair!"
> The traces cannot perish,—they are there!
> In proud fore-feeling of such lofty bliss,
> I now enjoy the Highest Moment,—this!

The time has now come for Faust's death, and he passes from the scene, to the bewilderment of Mephistopheles. And Mephisto is bewildered just because Faust wished to hold the "poorest, emptiest moment" fast forever. What is Nothing to him is, as we have seen, the All to Faust. For Faust it was activity alone that mattered, not pleasure, not glory, not power, but the mind that "unweariedly" aspires and plans, toils and labors.

And at the very end Goethe gives us his versions of Dante's *Purgatorio* and *Paradiso*. It is to these realms that Faust's soul is borne away by the angels, and there we find many penitents on the various levels of purgation, amongst whom once again we meet Margaret. She welcomes her former lover to the blessed place, and, as his spirit soars into the loftiest heights, she assures us that he is now a "new-born Being." In this the Mater Gloriosa encourages her, saying:

> Rise, thou, to higher spheres! Conduct him,
> Who feeling thee, shall follow there!

And the Angels sing:

> Whoe'er aspires unweariedly
> Is not beyond redeeming.
> And if he feels the grace of Love
> That from On High is given,
> The Blessed Hosts, that wait above,
> Shall welcome him to Heaven!

Unmistakably Christian motifs figure in the culmination of the drama. Yet there is one essential thing that is missing—namely, the evidence of any genuine contrition in Faust. Here is a man who has committed crime after crime in the course of his long career, from the defamation of Margaret, the poisoning of Margaret's mother and the murder of her brother, up to the destruction of the innocent old couple in the garden. Time and again he has exhibited moral defects of the grossest sort: yet he remains till the very end unshattered by any profound act of repentance, and the best lesson that Goethe has to offer us is that it is enough to "aspire unweariedly" in order to be redeemed. How infinitely humbler are the great voyagers and pilgrims of spiritual history! How much more capable of contrition is Job! How much more aroused is the conscience of the hero of the *Commedia!* How much more conscious of his guilt is Hamlet! And, when we think of figures like Orestes or Oedipus, must we not conclude that even in Antiquity the human spirit was capable of being far more deeply smitten by a sense of its moral inadequacy than it seems possible for Germany's greatest poet to have been?

NOTE: CHAPTER 5

1. All quotations are taken from the Modern Library edition of the Bayard Taylor translation. The beauty of the German text cannot, however, be rendered by any translation; and even the precise meaning is, I am afraid, sometimes lost.

Soren Kierkegaard:
Faith in a Tragic World

THIS ESSAY IS NOT intended to be still another introduction to Kierkegaard. But, for some readers, this may be the first encounter with this engaging Dane, and they ought, therefore, to know that he wrote over thirty books, a sprawling journal of twenty volumes, and, besides, did most of this within an eight-year period. Born in 1813, matriculating at the University of Copenhagen in 1830, writing and publishing a remarkable thesis in 1840–1841, he was, by his thirtieth year, 1843, launched on a literary career for which there are no analogues in European history. By 1850, a few years and many books later, he was almost ready for retirement. A brief and spirited attack upon the Church gave his writing new focus during 1854 and 1855, and then he died.

The delightful irony, humor, and enthusiasm which pervade his numerous pages were present in the last hours too. After falling to the floor at a party, partially paralyzed with the immediate effects of his mortal illness, he stutteringly said, as those who were present gathered anxiously around, peering intently at him, "Oh, let it lay—the maid will sweep it up in the morning."[1] When hospitalized, Kierkegaard was asked by his best friend, a cleric, whether he believed in God, and he laughed and said, "Of course, what else?"[2]

Sören's brother, Peter, a somewhat stuffy and prosaic guardian of Denmark's cultivated Lutheranism, preached the funeral oration and skillfully emasculated his brother's polemical literature of its urgency, all the while contending that it was important to understand and yet somewhat exaggerated. How this would have made Sören laugh! And Henrik Lund, Kierkegaard's cousin, so angry at the Church's generous enfoldment of his relative at the last moment, helped stage a gentle riot at the graveside. Before the Dean of the Cathedral could get his words said, some students read the indictment of the Laodicean church from the Revelation of Saint John and matched this with Kierkegaard's last stinging diatribes against the Lutheran church. But this attempt to tip the balances in his favor took place as Kierkegaard ironically suggested it would—after he was dead!

It was altogether fitting. Kierkegaard often noted that the universals of discourse sometimes unjustly portray the particularity of existence, but it is also true that sometimes the writings of a great poet-dialectician, and even that poet-dialectician himself, get thrown into the web of human history with no apparent congruence between them. If no one else laughed, Kierkegaard did himself. He learned to see the humor of himself, a reflective master and a creative artist, in Copenhagen, a market town if there ever was and is one. At this distance, his discerning readers have little trouble in noting with irony the juxtaposition—Kierkegaard and little Denmark, Kierkegaard and a mediocre church, Kierkegaard and those piddling professors at the University of Copenhagen, Kierkegaard the genius and all those literary and historical critics who, as an author in *Either/Or* says, resemble the poets to the hair, the only differences being that the critics have neither the songs in their hearts nor the words on their lips.

Some of Kierkegaard's readers have seen this contrariety and wept. Georg Brandes, a distinguished critic and man of letters, himself a Jew in an erstwhile Christian land, early concluded after reading Kierkegaard's prose that he, Brandes, was not a genius like his compatriot and that he would have to content himself with much less. In addition, he argued that the tragedy of Kierkegaard's life was the confinement of such genius to the niggardly Scandinavian "milieu."[3] But, interestingly enough, Kierkegaard too knew about the contrariety, the opposition, even the contradictoriness of it all, and he laughed. Instead of attempting to change his environment or looking for more encompassing intellectual syntheses, he decided to wed his particularities—Denmark, its fishwife language, its church, its limitations, intellectual and otherwise—to his own person and authorship. And, what is more, he did it with religious enthusiasm. The result is a singular and penetrating literature which is both the author's education and the reader's. What seemed tragic to others became for Kierkegaard a Christian vocation.

II

Kierkegaard said repeatedly that his authorship was dialectical. By this he implied several things, one of which surely (though it is often overlooked) is that his books are not exemptible from the rules of logic. Despite the numerous loose criticisms of Kierkegaard on this point, it is perhaps time to be boldly assertive. So let us say, then, quite bluntly, that he was, after all, a logical realist. That is to say, he believed that logicality—the minimal rules of inference, of definition, of order—had to rule absolutely all meaningful discourse. His point is surely not that religious language is logically contradictory or that speech must be illogical in order to be properly religious. He is not a champion of ruleless speech or of the view that language can only be immediate and expressive in its significance. There is no tragic and irresolvable ambiguity within discourse itself. On the contrary, he took it for granted that language is the locus of logicality, and few authors have so assiduously cultivated the virtues of clarity, of exactness, and consistency. Indeed, Kierkegaard's diatribes are never directed against logicality but are rather directed against those who believe that logical canons somehow control and dispose actuality. In this connection, it should be observed that Hegel, his *bête noire*, evokes such devastating criticism from him, precisely because his is a philosophy which purports to be a penetration into the logic of existence, into the very rhyme and reason of actual being.

But, again, Kierkegaard is not concerned to say that existence is senseless, that it has no order or no governing principles at all. He is not *against* science, nor is he an irrationalist in a metaphysical sense, who asserts that actuality is a chaos. He never says that nature and history are without rules or that they are unintelligible. He simply insists that he does not know them, and he is modest enough to suggest that the empirical sciences have it as their task to ascertain what the orders and congruencies, if there are such, actually are. Kierkegaard believes that God must know the order in which both natural and historical events fall, but he resists the philosopher's temptation to characterize, on God's behalf, all time and all existence. In fact, he refuses to anticipate the researches of the scientist or to pretend that he is God: on this issue he abdicates, with a grace and a modesty that are rare in one so reflective and otherwise gifted.

That thought, that the intellectual life, has its own kind of order, Kierkegaard does not deny. He speaks often of self-reflexive knowledge, the kind of knowledge one has when one thinks about thinking. But, unlike some philosophers, he does not suppose that he can see through his thoughts into the very ground of being itself. He discovers by thinking only the conceptual being of thoughts—that is, how ideas exist as the objects of thought and what the necessary relations are that obtain amongst them.

But there is another kind of order in reality that is different from that which characterizes the realm of thought: it is the order of actual existence, and it is evinced in the sequences of historical and natural events. As far as I can understand Kierkegaard, he does not stand opposed to metaphysics, if by it one means the science of the general traits of existence. But then metaphysics is a very tentative and hypothetical science of what is: it is not an inventive or conjuring science; it does not produce reality but describes it, and this in a very ordinary sense. Its accomplishments are high-level generalizations. On these points, Kierkegaard often praised Aristotle, Hegel, and other philosophers for the skill with which they managed to make a vast amount of detail subject to a few categories.

The point at which Kierkegaard tended to be severely critical, however, of the great philosophies (and, particularly, of Idealism) was the point at which he believed them to obscure the profound differences between these two domains. Sometimes they describe the realm of essence, of conceivability, in categories that are really appropriate only to the realm of existence—or it may be the other way round. The urge to unite essence and existence, the actual world and the order of conceivability, occasions their identification in some *tertium quid*. The philosophers of daring invent a more inclusive reality, an ontological realm, the really real, where the unities obtain, where the logos is also natural and historical and the fundamental breaches are overcome. All of this Kierkegaard believed to be unwarranted philosophic legerdemain. He insisted, instead, upon the opposition and irreducibility of these orders. And to their duality he regarded the proper response as being passionate and subjective, for surely, he insisted, there is no objective and logical assimilation of this bifurcation.

But, if Kierkegaard is novel as a philosopher, he is not novel for saying this much, for his real distinctiveness lies elsewhere: it is, in fact, the evocation of a third kind of order that most fundamentally distinguishes his authorship.

III

Kierkegaard contended that the life of passion was also orderly—not quite in the same way, to be sure, as the life of thought, but orderly nonetheless. Almost alone among philosophers and students of human nature, he suggested that the life of subjectivity has its types, its rules, its principled movements. And he proposes a typology under the rubric of "stages."[4] Here it is that we may discover how much his endeavors as a reflective man involve a recasting of certain fundamental problems in relation to which traditional theology and philosophy have signally failed. Possessing a consummate mastery of several of the Greek tragedians and of a large body of the mythological and imaginative literature of Europe, he was quick to note the disparity between theological and philosophical theories of human existence, on the one side, and the literary descriptions on the other. His aim was to provide exact categorization, in philosophical and theological terms, for all those multifarious features of actual existence which have been so much more profoundly expressed in imaginative literature than in systematic thought.

Furthermore, not only was he convinced that the features of lived actuality are scanted by the theoretical systems of existence, but he also felt that in them Christianity is excluded too. For, if logical order is so defined as to include empirical existence in its grasp, or vice versa, if causality is so inclusive as to subsume logical rules, then existence, even the lived existence of a person, loses its dramatic qualities, and a mere progression from one theoretical category to another becomes the mode of anticipating any human life. God, in such a systematic view, becomes only the way of unification, the point of coherence, the Reality in whom the order is realized. Against all of this Kierkegaard urged another view. He argued that man was the point of unification, the synthetic agent, whose dramatic urgency was defined by the necessity of putting together these diverse orders and thereby making sense of his own existence. And even if God does hold all things in his hand, he is still not himself an object of knowledge, and Kierkegaard thought it ridiculous, therefore, to pretend a synthesis on his behalf.

In this situation he saw fit to draw attention to something he believed had been omitted. He eschewed invention at this juncture and sought, instead, to look harder at the actual facts, to analyze what he could, and to write as acutely as possible about what he had discovered. His conclusion was that living a human life meant a confrontation with exciting oppositions, for both actual and conceived existences compete for human loyalties and provide the goals of endeavor.

The miscellany that lived existence presents is not, however, incapable of precise description, for, as Kierkegaard suggests, it too involves relations which, though not of a logical sort, are yet clearly specifiable. This is, indeed, a separate order— the third, in fact—and its operative principle confronts us with an *existential* dialectic which evokes in the human agent a *passionate, interested* response.[5] These adventures in inwardness are not quite the same as logical or temporal events. Kierkegaard's purpose is to show by his description that the subjective life is legitimate, that it is ridiculous to abjure it altogether, and altogether naïve to assume that it is merely a byproduct of culture, an internal effect of external historical or natural causes, or even a kind of "bad innocence" requiring extirpation in order that logical awareness might blossom.

Contrary to many philosophers, Kierkegaard tries to show that the inner cosmos of subjectivity is not a mere reflection of the passing objective scene, and that it is not governed by logical rules and causal laws. It is not a mirror, not an imperfection to be castigated as either primitive or derivative. Yet the task of being human does involve the effort to bring these three orders of actual existence, of thought, and of passion into some kind of integral unity. The actual world is already with us, and so too are our passions and our thoughts. Knowledge presupposes the synthesis of the real and the ideal—if, that is, it is truly knowledge of actual existence; and ethical existence presupposes that possibilities of an ideal sort can be effected in action. We can think about thinking, and even our thought is subject, sometimes, to our interests and concerns. We behave teleologically toward others and toward the world; and we live our lives by directing deeds and thoughts to the things which concern us most. No human life, in other words, is either pure thought or pure passion, and the harmonization of these two dimensions of the life of selfhood is, as both Spinoza and Pascal understood, the problem of character.

Kierkegaard was, fundamentally, a student of human subjectivity, and he early learned that we cannot think to good purpose about either the world or our thoughts unless we control our dispositions, our hopes, and our wishes. We cannot, in other words, allow internal chaos to govern our thinking about the objective and patterned features of existence. And, indeed, in his view, the perfection of character demanded of every man is to be defined in terms of the achievement of the kind of temper, the kind of disinterestedness and detachment, that will enable the intellectual life to proceed without being unduly hampered by the distractions of subjectivity.

Already then we can see the extent of the involvement of the three orders. The disciplining of subjectivity is the neces-

sary condition for a proper apprehension of both the order of
reflection (logicality) and the order of actual existence. A
temperamental and subjective requisite must be met. Kierkegaard nowhere disparages this temper of objectivity but always insists that it is a perfection essential to knowledge.

Every person has, of course, his subjectivity, his enthusiasms
and interests, constituted initially and in large part by others.
The identifiable interests for most of us are easily traced to
church, to nation, ethnic loyalties, egoism, biological urges,
and so on. But Kierkegaard believed that any subjectivity constituted by others was immature. A moral man is one whose
subjectivity is not a mere by-product of the engines of society
but is, instead, an intentionally constituted and controlled inwardness which is a consequence of clearly perceiving the
available alternatives and options for life. Again we are brought
to a point at which the orders overlap. For reflection alone
orders the possibilities, and, without it, we are conditioned
creatures who can have no notion of the plurality of modes of
personal existence or of the tensions between them.

The aesthetic, ethical, and religious ways of life which are
described in the writings of Kierkegaard are the three ways
in which subjectivity can, in fact, be constituted. Each of these
is, intellectually at least, co-possible with actuality and, therefore, in skeptical fashion, Kierkegaard indicates that nothing
knowledge has to offer concerning either the logic of discourse or the character of history and nature is incompatible
with any kind of subjectivity. We can be aesthetes, ethicists,
mildly religious, ardently Christian, with or without knowledge of what history teaches and nature is, with or without
an awareness of the rules of valid inference. There is, thus, a
certain kind of order in subjectivity, but it is not subject to
the same determinations as the other orders, even though these
orders are relevant in the ways that have been indicated.

Thinking thus leads us to an opposition and a choice which cannot be resolved simply by more thinking.

IV

Now we have established the context in terms of which it becomes possible to understand Kierkegaard's definition of the tragic and the comic. In the *Concluding Unscientific Postscript*, we read that both are "based on contradiction," but that "the tragic is the suffering contradiction, the comical, the painless contradiction."[6] And by "contradiction" here he means the kind of opposition between the fundamental orders of reality that we have described.

Kierkegaard insists that things are not simply tragic or comic as such. Indeed, neither term presents us with an ordinary category under which illustrative instances and events are to be subsumed. The tragic and the comic are not names for metaphysical or ontological attributes. Neither is existence by itself either tragic or comic. Instead we must remember that these words are relational words. They bespeak the way men relate themselves to the oppositions, to the contrarieties, between thought and things, or between one passion and another; and so, therefore, it is not events, apart from men, which are tragic or comic, but, rather, it is the relations in which men place themselves which become tragic or comic.

Kierkegaard's thesis against Hegel is that the totality of existence is not a single and homogeneous order. If it were, all opposition would be obliterated, all tension gone. But it is precisely the oppositions, the diversity of orders, that make living so dramatic and that make literary tragedies and comedies so illuminating of existence. Kierkegaard's writings are an attempt to document the fact of the diversity of orders, so that the nature of the tragic and the comic may be more fully understood.

The characteristic of the humorist is, first, to discover the contradiction and, then, to discover a way out, the incommensurateness becoming an occasion for humor only if there is a way out. Kierkegaard's writings are rich in descriptions of incongruities which are funny. The Hegelian lunatic who threatens to blow up the whole world with a syllogism is funny because he takes the asserted relationship between being and thought so literally. The man who buys beer at six cents a bottle and sells it for five is ridiculously funny when he explains his action in virtue of the principle that "it's the quantity that does it." The man who excuses his illegitimate child by saying, "But, it is so little . . ." is confusing moral accountability with the absurdest kind of quantitative consideration. The German-Danish clergyman, misled by similarities in linguistic form within the Danish and German languages, reads his biblical text as, "The Word became pork" instead of "The Word became flesh." And the man who is refused his license to open a brothel because he cannot produce a baptismal certificate is probably as funny as the woman who seeks official permission to become a public prostitute.

The humorist is always a disinterested spectator of the oppositions and the contrarieties. Hence he is not subjectively hurt, his interests are not involved, and, as long as his interests are not involved, he is not pained by the contradiction. Indeed, anything contradictory can be funny if one succeeds in establishing a detached and disinterested relation to the opposition. The flexibility by which one can pass from concern to dispassionate neutrality provides the measure by which the impasse can appear comic. One can laugh at the incongruity of the British pilot who, coming in after a bombing mission with two bombs a-hanging which are certain to explode when he lands, keeps radioing the control tower for advice. The tower is silent. After numerous entreaties the nasal voice of the pilot is heard, "I say, old boy, only twenty gallons of petrol, what shall I do . . . ?" Finally comes the answer: "Say after me, Our Father which art in Heaven . . ." To hear it now is to laugh, but just suppose one were the pilot, the pilot's wife, even the man in the tower: then the "Our Father" might not seem the most desirable way out. When the opposition of wish and fact is such that the wish must be given up, then the subject will surely be in despair. When this occurs, and the interests are so ordered that what is occurring or what will and must occur is reprehensible, then one no longer laughs. And this is the making of tragedy.

As soon as interest re-enters the context, then what reflection does is to articulate the alternative ways in which interest may be expended, and this is precisely the condition in which there seems to be no way out at all. Thought perfects the indecision rather than resolving it, and subjectivity is thus plunged into despair by the very logicality which seems initially so provident.

Kierkegaard suggests that men of reflection can even despair finally of thought itself. For sometimes diverse and incompatible resolutions to intellectual questions seem to be equally plausible, and skepticism may thus become a kind of tragic view of reflection itself. But even this is not so severe a matter as despairing of the validity of one's own existence, for when one doubts the validity of one's personality, then despair becomes intimate and pervasive and infinitely more telling in effect than the doubts one might have in the purely cognitive dimension.

Now Kierkegaard's thesis about human life is that, though existence does not lack systematic features, it is not itself a system. For we live in the kind of world in which the Lord of creation is crucified; in which we must do all things while knowing that without God we can do nothing; in which we must believe in God's providence while enduring the direst of circumstances. Yet the greatness of Christianity, he contends, is precisely revealed in its adequacy to just this kind of world; and herewith he distinguishes the faith in Jesus Christ from all other ways of resolving the contrarieties of actual existence. Christianity does not remove the contradictions, nor does it suggest that from another vantage point they do not really exist. No, instead, it translates the oppositions into their subjective and personal components and asks that we encounter them there. Men must die to the world, must crucify the flesh, must live eternal life in time, must rejoice in all things.

The contrarieties are real; but there is a way out, and the point is that the despair to which they give rise can be removed. Humor is, of course, one way out. But it is the disinterested way out, and its effectiveness presupposes an emasculation of all earnestness: certainly it is not the Christian way, for Christianity proposes faith as the answer. Faith is not a dispassionate form of personal existence: it is, rather, the maximally passionate form: it is simply a particular determination of subjectivity. Indeed, it is a fundamental proposal of Christianity that God is in business to transform the subjectivity of men, and, through that subjectivity, the entire world. The Christian's faith is not a resolution of the contrarieties but is the refashioning of the self, so that the contrarieties do not overwhelm him but actually become the context in which his redemption takes place. The consequence of his encounter with the Christ is, in other words, the discovery that his fate is not dependent upon the incongruities of existence but rather upon the way in which he goes forward to meet them: he discovers, that is, the possibility of rebirth and inward transformation—the possibility that, being ordered to and by the relation to Jesus Christ, he may overcome the world.

V

In a somewhat quixotic sense, then, Kierkegaard might be said to have fashioned a tragic view of human life. But surely only in a quixotic sense is this the case. His great gifts were enlisted in the effort to demonstrate that the average man's way of construing the world in terms of frustration, contingency, and chance is far closer to the truth of things than the esoteric philosophical and religious views which insist that reality is one and that the plurality of things and principles is a mirage. Kierkegaard's writings are, in a way, no more tragic than the world of experience itself in which gross immorality can be causally efficacious, in which logical fallacies are often historically important, and in which the evil that good men do is often counterbalanced by the good that evil men do. To suppose, therefore, that everything will be discovered to work for good and that all strands will be discovered to weave one garment, if only we sufficiently distance ourselves from the human scene—this is surely the quixotic view. But Kierkegaard is a realist whose aim is to philosophize about the world, not to philosophize us out of it.

Few authors have phrased so exactingly as did Kirkegaard the pragmatic significance of Christian faith for such a world as ours. For him faith is a way out, not of the world, but of despair. It is his thesis that Christians can rejoice, that, indeed, they can even laugh, for theirs is the way, the truth, and the life. The opposition that one discovers between Christ and oneself may, of course, itself be a source of tragic despair. And one way to resolve this despair is to refuse to entertain Christ as an ideal requirement, in which case Philistinism is the consequence. But the other way is to let the requirement be an occasion for repentance, which is a leave-taking from one's present selfhood, into a new one.

The latter is Sören Kierkegaard's delineation of the Christian's triumph over an otherwise tragic world.

NOTES: CHAPTER 6

1. Quoted in P. A. Heiberg, *Sören Kierkegaard i Barndom og Ungdom* (Copenhagen: Wroblewski, 1895), p. 46.
2. The conversations with Emil Boesen are printed at the end of the last volume of *Efterlade Papirer*. Other details of this relation can be read in Carl Koch's *Sören Kierkegaard og Emil Boesen* (Copenhagen: Schönberg's Publishing Co., 1901).
3. *Vide* Georg Brandes, *Recollections of My Childhood and Youth* (London: William Heinemann, 1906).
4. *Vide* most particularly *Stages on Life's Way*, trans. by Walter Lowrie (Princeton: Princeton University Press, 1940); also *Either/Or: A Fragment of Life*, Vol. I, trans. by David F. and Lillian Marvin Swenson, and Vol. II, trans. by Walter Lowrie (Princeton: Princeton University Press, 1944); and the *Concluding Unscientific Postscript*, trans. by David F. Swenson and Walter Lowrie (Princeton: Princeton University Press, 1941).
5. *Vide* David F. Swenson's essay, "The Existential Dialectic of Sören Kierkegaard," in *Something About Kierkegaard* (Minneapolis: Augsburg Publishing House, 1944).
6. *Concluding Unscientific Postscript*, trans. by David F. Swenson, p. 459.

Dostoevski—Tragedian of the Modern Excursion into Unbelief

IT IS AN INTERESTING FACT of the modern literary life that, whereas, since the middle years of the nineteenth century, we have had many distinguished minor figures in poetry and only a few really great practitioners of the art, in the novel we have had, relatively speaking, few important examples of the authentically minor talent but very many examples of great genius. In the English-speaking world we have had George Eliot, Nathaniel Hawthorne, Herman Melville, Henry James, Joseph Conrad, James Joyce, D. H. Lawrence, and William Faulkner; out of western Europe have come Flaubert, Zola, Proust, Mann, Kafka, and Mauriac; and Russia has given us Turgenev, Dostoevski, and Tolstoy. This is the great and the central legacy in the novel that we inherit from, roughly, the last hundred years: it is surely this remarkable constellation of genius that sufficiently explains the ascendancy in our period of the novel over the older genres, and amongst its masters there is none whose accents are for us today more compelling than those of the Russian Dostoevski. He, we feel now, is one of the great directors of the modern conscience, who really understood the ache that is within us; and in his books our most secret nightmares and the deepest issues of our bewilder-ment are given a kind of terrible lucidity that shows us how narrowly in its progress the modern mind has skirted the brink of absolute perplexity and despair.

Our conviction of the exact pertinence of Dostoevski's vision to the crises and distempers of our age is, I suspect, a consequence of the clarity that we find in him about what continues to be a major predicament of modern man—which is the brutalization of his nature that is threatened by his captivity to ideas and to the intellect. We live, of course, in a time in which, as W. H. Auden has said, the individual must "do deliberately for himself what in previous ages had been done for him by family, custom, Church, and State—namely, the choice of the principles and presuppositions in terms of which he can make sense of his experience."[1] And not only is he thus bent back upon himself by the absence of coherent traditions that furnish guidance with respect to the ultimate issues of existence: he must also engage in the common adventure of life in a period of history in which it is widely supposed that there has been such an erosion of the religious terrain as makes it necessary for a man himself to create the absolute values that the mind requires for its peace and sanity. So to *exist* has, in a way, been to *think*, and the Cartesian formula—*Cogito ergo sum*—has, to a considerable degree, summed up the lone and final certitude of the modern voyager. He has not been able to live out of any deep center or equilibrium of being, beneath the level of the mental or the ideational, for the circumstances of his culture, with all the spiritual disorder that they have involved, have condemned him to the terrible despotism of the mind. "We are the people of the idea," says Lionel Trilling, "and we rightly fear that the intellect will dry up the blood in our veins and wholly check the emotional and creative part of the mind."[2]

It is, indeed, a profound horror of the absolute sovereignty of the intellect in modern culture that forms, from Blake and

Wordsworth to Melville and to D. H. Lawrence, a major theme in our literature. But in no writer of the past hundred years does this response to the modern predicament gain so trenchant an expression as it does in Dostoevski. For he, above all others, was occupied with the modern "tragedy of mind" and perceived that the autonomization of the mind must be, in our time, the necessary consequence of the belief that God is dead. Fishing in the deepest waters, he took hold, in other words, of our distress at its real root, and we can, therefore, in his books, find out more of what it actually entails than we can in any other source.

And yet to make this claim for Dostoevski may seem only to obfuscate matters. For, if he describes the problem of modern man as one arising out of his atheism, it would not at first appear that this is really *our* problem. Where, we would ask, are the people whose sense of the tears in things is motivated by the regretful conviction that ours is today a world without radiance? Do our friends go about proclaiming, with Nietzschean passion, the death of God? No, we will say: however much the basic fact of their lives may no longer involve the fact of God, our conversations with them, when they are not punctuated by the confidences of intimacy, are likely to be focused upon the disorders in our collective life, and what we are constantly attempting to do is to take some measure of the contingencies which harass our togetherness in the modern world. For, again as Trilling says, we feel that our present "fate, for better or worse, is political,"[3] and this is the character of our present preoccupations. So, if it was some divine abdication that focalized the concern of this nineteenth-century Russian, how, it may be asked, can he be considered to speak to our present condition?

Well, to this query, should it be put, it must be granted that, yes, our immediate and most conscious concern today is not with the death of God but with the death of the City, of what the Greeks called the *Polis:* it is with the death of the human community. What we yearn for are the cultural and political instruments by which we might create a stable international order that would make a technical civilization sufferable: what we seek is "a city which hath foundations"; but the author of the Epistle to the Hebrews tells us that the builder and the maker of that city is God.[4] And, indeed, we do perceive, intermittently and anxiously, that our severances from one another may be a reflection of our severance from a transcendent *Other* and that perhaps the former will not be healed until the latter has been repaired. "We must love one another or die," Auden told us some years ago; and he might well have added that we can, however, encounter one another as "presences" (which is the *event* of love) only if for us the world is itself grounded in "Presence."[5] Here it is that we are at the real point of juncture between God and the moral order, and it is at this point that we may see that, when Dostoevski attributes the disorientation of modern man to his denial of an order of "presence" transcending the empirical dimension, he is really speaking far more directly to our actual condition than might at first be supposed. At any rate, this is the unifying witness of all his writings, and Ralph Harper gives us a true summation of his mind, when he tells us that

> For him [Dostoevski] the crisis of civilization was a crisis of presence and absence, encounters and alienations. His great heroes were always alienated men who longed for a presence they had lost touch with or never had long enough to remember clearly. They all understood that the problem of God and the problem of love or friendship or law were inseparable because they both were the problem of presence, seen in different dimensions.[6]

We might say that what Dostoevski exhibits in the concrete, dramatic structures of his novels is the ontology of modern secularism, its version, that is, of the reality that man is up against in this world. And the main tenet of that bill of particulars is that ours is a universe without governance or guiding principle and that, therefore, in so far as it is truly a *universe*, or a field of reality constituting a unified and meaningful realm, it becomes so as a consequence of a heroic act of the human mind which "furnishes the world and determines the way of life."[7] The limiting condition of man's existence is, in other words, his complete autonomy—which is, of course, a condition involving no limits at all. He must, therefore, himself invent the purposes of life and the modes of action, creating Good and Evil and creating the categorical imperatives of morality. "Every moral action on the part of the autonomous man is a creative act, for, in it, he recreates himself and his own freedom."[8] Indeed, living in such a void as the universe becomes when all limits have been banished from it, the autonomous man must recreate himself anew each day, in order to retain any sense of his identity. And carrying the whole meaning of his existence by himself, he is constantly in the ironical position of having to struggle desperately to retain some sense of his identity, because, since he beholds nothing in the world except his own image, the world seems to afford nothing against which he might really test himself and whereby he might, therefore, be given a deeper sense of himself. So, amidst this essentially empty world, he gives himself to first one and then another gratuitous action, by means of which he hopes to gain the assurance that he craves of his own substantial reality. These actions almost always involve violence, either against himself or against others; and they end in futility and defeat, because the autonomous man, refusing to acknowledge the interpersonal character of human existence, with all the metaphysical implications that it involves, can never discover who he really is. He remains trapped within the solipsistic prison of his own ego, and what, as a result of his anguished experiments in self-realization, he finally apprehends is not his own self's integrity but rather the tragic thing that the mind itself is when, suspended in the void of unbelief, it can find no higher reality than itself and is thus doubled back upon itself in the stark desolateness of its vacancy and isolation.

It is, then, the world of this lonely soul that Dostoevski made his own, charting its hitherto unexplored recesses with the bravery and the depth of insight of the true tragic poet. And we should perhaps first of all turn to a little book that he published in 1864 called *Letters from the Underworld*, for it is here that we get one of his earliest and most revealing portraits of the autonomous man of modernity who is engaged in "the experiment . . . of replacing the true balance of living by the despotic activity of the independent mind."[9] Is it a *novela*, or is it a diary, or a confession? We are not sure, but, like Rilke's *Notebook of Malte Laurids Brigge* and Valéry's *Evening with M. Teste* which give rise to similar questions, its impact upon us is unforgettable and permanent.

There are two main divisions of the *Letters*, the second consisting of a long story which, in terms of action, illustrates the character of the hero whose "confessions" form the first part of the book. He is a man of forty years of age who has for a long period held a minor post in the Civil Service— from which, however, he has recently resigned, after receiving from a distant relative a small legacy of six thousand roubles. And, as his story begins, we find him in his retirement eking out a miserable existence in a shabby room on the outskirts of St. Petersburg. He has had an education of sorts and has read widely: indeed, he considers himself to be a consummately brilliant dialectician and observer of the foibles of men, and, in every way, a real figure. But he has somehow never had any gift for incontestably bringing his brilliance to bear upon the world, so that it might be known and properly appreciated. In his external aspect he has appeared so ineffectual and ordinary, so blundering and awkward and shy, that he has very nearly succeeded in being the man whom no one notices is there. And he never ceases to be pained by the pathetic contrast between his own sense of his powers and the public estimate of his worth. But he insists that his essential reality is to be found not in the public self but in the secret, "underworld" self, and this it is, therefore, that he sets out to reveal in the long monologue which forms the first half of the *Letters*.

This "underworld" self is a curious admixture of tendencies toward sadism and masochism, toward the most excessive forms of pride and of humility. He regards himself as infinitely superior to all the "superficial" people of his acquaintance, but he is constantly given to contemptuous dismissals of himself as a mere "insect." He wants to be liked and admired by everyone, and yet he recalls that, during his days in the Civil Service, "whenever people approached my office table to ask for information, or what not, I used to grind my teeth at them, and invariably to feel pleased when I had offended their dignity." His dominant emotions are contempt and envy —contempt of "them," of "everybody," and envy of the success with which they, in their gross normality, are able to get on with the business of living. And it is for the sake of commanding from "them" an act of recognition that this bilious and exacerbated little cypher goes into a tavern one evening to pick a quarrel not with anyone in particular but with whomever may first chance to cross his path. But the upshot of this rather nasty adventure is only that he is brusquely pushed aside by a husky young officer who then pursues his own way without taking any further notice of him. And it is this same man who forces himself upon some acquaintances one evening as they are holding a party for a friend who is about to depart for a new position in the Caucasus—but who, before the end of the evening, manages, by his churlishness and bad temper, completely to spoil the celebration. As the others leave in disgust, he is overcome with feelings of frustration and self-loathing.

In such moments it is his habit to escape into debauchery, and so he enters a brothel. There he consorts with Lisa, a pretty little girl from the provinces who has just recently joined the establishment. And after he has taken her body, he lectures her on the degradation of her life, painting such a direful picture of what lies at the end of her road that the girl is reduced to tears. He is simply carried away by the force of his own rhetoric and speaks so movingly that she is persuaded that she must, indeed, attempt a fresh start. So she calls on him at his lodgings a few days later, expecting to be taken in and given assistance. But, instead, he greets her with laughter and scorn, telling her that he had only been playing a game with her, "the game of forcing your tears, your humiliation, your hysterics." And, when, perceiving how inwardly broken and tormented he is, she embraces him, in a spontaneous gesture of pity and affection, he deliberately misconstrues her intent and offers her money, as though the embrace had been an act of solicitation. At this Lisa throws the money upon a table and leaves, realizing that in this man there is neither goodness nor decency.

Now we may ask who this man of the "underworld" is and what is the meaning of the strange ambivalences that form his enigmatic character. And when this question is pressed we must say, as he himself insists, that he is a "man of acute sensibility" and also a man of thought. Indeed, like Paul Valéry's Monsieur Teste, he *exists* in his *thought*—which is perhaps to say that he does not *exist* at all, but only thinks; and, as John Middleton Murry remarked forty years ago in his fine book on Dostoevski, this is a man whose "thought has paralysed his being, until he can only sit down and contemplate the world that is, which he abhors yet can by no means escape."[10] And though the hero of the *Letters* represents an extreme instance of this malaise, the condition itself is constantly reflected in most of the central characters in Dostoevskian fiction, for they are people in whom the mind can never know any surcease from its labors, since the only meaning in their world is that which the mind itself is constantly calling into existence. This it is that constitutes, in Dostoevski's view, their modernity, for he sees the unhappy fate of modern man as consisting in the emptiness which his secularism compels him to find in the universe—an emptiness, indeed, so chilling and so exasperating that the mind is stretched to the very end of its tether. The tragic principle, in other words, as he encounters it in the tonalities of nineteenth-century life, is, in his definition of it, the principle of unbelief. And though, in the hero of the *Letters,* the mode of its functioning is not theatricalized in the grandly operatic manner that characterizes the delineation of Raskolnikov and Svidrigailov of *Crime and Punishment* or Pyotr Verhovensky and Stavrogin of *The Possessed* or Ivan Karamazov, we yet find in him a clear kinship with these great personages of Dostoevski's later work, for he, like them, is a captive to the awful solitude that overtakes the human spirit when it finds itself inhabiting a world from which the gracious reality of "Presence" has been banished.

The chief difference perhaps between the hero of the *Letters* and the agonists of the great tragedies *(Crime and Punishment,*

The Idiot, The Possessed, and *The Brothers Karamazov*) is
that he, unlike Raskolnikov and Verhovensky and Stavrogin
and Kirillov and Ivan Karamazov, is almost wholly passive: he
only squirms and quavers in the dungeon of his isolation,
whereas they hurl themselves into life with an almost consuming energy and violence, in order that their freedom and
independence might be proven in the absoluteness of the concrete act. It is, indeed, these great Faustian characters of
Dostoevski who illustrate the bitter dialectic that is fundamental to his conception of the tragic predicament—that,
when, by an act of negation, man chooses to live in a metaphysical void in which nothing has any meaning and no
values can be affirmed, if he is not betrayed into utter inaction
(the hero of the *Letters*), he will be betrayed into some form
of moral dilettantism (in which case other men will be regarded as mere puppets to be experimented with) or into some
form of blatant self-deification whose premise will be that
everything is permissible. But whichever of these alternatives is embraced, it is clear that the apostate radical will be
prepared, ultimately, to commit either suicide or murder.
For when life is regarded as being essentially and ultimately
absurd—which is what it is for the nihilist—then "the dark
victory in which heaven and earth are annihilated"[11] is for
him the only kind of victory that is really possible. And it is,
in a way, such a Pyrrhic victory that the tragic hero in the
Dostoevskian drama seeks.

Crime and Punishment is the first of the great novels in
which these issues are fully dramatized. It deals, on the surface, with a morose and destitute student, Rodion Raskolnikov,
who murders an old pawnbrokeress in order to rob her of her
hoard and who then plays a cat-and-mouse game with the
police till, being overcome with exhaustion and panic, he is
finally taken by the clever police investigator Porfiry. But the

most cursory examination of the book immediately reveals that what we have here is not merely a "thriller" compounded of crime, detection, and punishment, and it is only on the most superficial level that Raskolnikov appears as a murderer who has killed for money. For he is a half-educated intellectual who has published an article in which he expounds the thesis that there are some men who, by reason of their natural superiority to the common herd, are above the law, above all moral standards—and, being convinced that he belongs to this élite, he has murdered the old moneylender Alyona Ivanovna with an axe, simply for the sake of asserting the transcendency of his will. She is, he has persuaded himself, a bloodsucking, tightfisted old usuress who does not deserve to live, a mere "louse." "I wanted to become a Napoleon: I wanted to have the daring . . . and I killed her."

Of course, Raskolnikov is finally persuaded by Sonia, who loves him, of how humanly impertinent are the presuppositions upon the basis of which he has acted, that none can judge another worthless and a "louse" and thus dispose of him. Indeed, he is brought at last to the point of acknowledging that "I am perhaps viler and more loathsome than the louse I killed . . ." Yet there is evidence that suggests that this is, though, a conclusion at which he arrives only because, in his very remorse and contrition, he discovers what is for him the tragic proof of his having been unable to summon the courage demanded by his principles. He realizes finally, in other words, that in himself there was not the necessary strength really to live in the power of the absurd. And we must therefore conclude that the kind of absolute autonomization of the mind and the will that is represented in the curiously sinister figure of Svidrigailov (who pursues Dounia, Raskolnikov's sister) is something that remains perhaps only potential in Raskolnikov. But however much Raskolnikov's commitment to his principles may ultimately be rendered uncertain by the incompleteness of his "emancipation," he stands as a major embodiment in Dostoevski's novels of that modern nihilist spirit which, in undertaking to reconstruct human life on the basis of some self-willed invention of reason, only succeeds in wrecking it with the destructiveness of its own demonry.

Of the books of Dostoevski, however, that deal with this issue there is perhaps none that is felt to speak more immediately to the condition of our age than *The Possessed*, in which the implications represented by a Raskolnikov or a Svidrigailov are extended into the concrete actualities of the political life. Though everyone will, of course, acknowledge *The Brothers Karamazov* as Dostoevski's masterpiece, it is *The Possessed* that is felt to be the great book *for us*. And we have not to cast about at any great length for the reason that explains this, for in this book Dostoevski is concerned to explore the moral complications internal to modern radical ideology, and this is, of course, a subject than which there is none that recent history has more fully prepared us to take an interest in. It has, indeed, been the astonishing metamorphosis that has taken place in Soviet Russia of modern socialism that has been one of the great decisive experiences of our generation, and into which we are thrust once again by the complex moral ambiguities represented by the revolutionaries in *The Possessed* who, for the sake of tactical expediency, permit themselves every conceivable duplicity and every performable crime. When today we read this book that was written almost fifty years before the Russian Revolution, we feel, as we are whirled through the vortex-like movement of its intrigues and betrayals and violence, that we already have, in a way, lived it all through, and Dostoevski's evident desire to sound a warning no longer seems the eccentricity that it once represented for a generation whose political radicalism was uninformed by the disenchantment about radical politics that the events of the past quarter-century have made accessible to us.

Irving Howe has reminded us that "*The Possessed* is a caricature of radicalism, a grotesque, a slander and a scandal; it would be absurd," he says, "to suppose that the Russia it presents is a reasonable copy of the Russia of Alexander II or that the radicals spawned in Dostoevsky's malice are the actual radicals of mid-nineteenth century Russia."[12] And this is doubtless true: surely the criminal Machiaevellianism of Pyotr Verhovensky, in whom Dostoevski gives us his most concentrated image of the revolutionary radical of his age, has nothing visibly in common with the humanistic libertarianism of such leaders of Russian radical thought as Herzen and Chernichevsky and Mikhailovsky or with such earlier continental theorists as Fourier and Saint-Simon and Proudhon. But Dostoevski never intended to be the kind of "secretary of society" that Balzac and Flaubert and Zola were holding up as the ideal for the novelist, and his sympathy for the kind of precise sociological documentation that the naturalistic movement generally in nineteenth-century letters tended to advocate was very limited. What he wanted to offer was a large mythic image of the modern secular meliorist whose activity in the collective life is guided by a socialistic bias, and whose dedication to some vision of social harmony is so fanatical as to destroy all the ethical scruples that he might otherwise have about the means that may be employed in the implementation of this vision. And though it is true that in an empirical sense Verhovensky does not truly represent the revolutionary movement of Dostoevski's period, is it yet not true, on the other hand, that he is a marvelously prescient symbol of the demagogues and careerists and cabalists who have been the heroes of those totalitarian movements in our own time in which we have seen the declension and the degeneracy of Western socialism. So to dismiss him, as some historical critics have done, as being merely a splenetic expression of the malice toward nineteenth-century radical ideology into which Dostoevski was betrayed by his political conservatism is hardly to draw a full enough circle of definition about his significance.

It is true, of course, that Dostoevski was profoundly and bitterly at odds with the Socialist movement of his time and with all that he could see as being portended by its promotion —but what we must recognize is that this was a theologically principled rejection, and deeply so. He tells us, for example, in *The Brothers* that if Alyosha had decided that

> God and immortality did not exist he would at once have become an atheist and a socialist. For socialism is not merely the labor question, it is before all things the atheistic question, the question of the form taken by atheism today, the question of the tower of Babel built without God, not to mount to Heaven from earth but to set up Heaven on earth.

And here it is that we are enabled to see that, despite the over-riding political concerns that control *The Possessed*, it has, nevertheless, its relation to the predominantly religious interests that determine the tragic dialectic of *Crime and Punishment* and *The Brothers Karamazov*. For Pyotr Verhovensky and his fellow conspirators Shigalov and Kirillov and the others are presented as type and example of what Dostoevski considered to be the central disorder of the modern spirit. And that disorder, in his definition of it, is, as we have seen, essentially a religious disorder: it is the condition in which man finds himself when, to his own satisfaction, having effectively sundered any linkage between himself and the Transcendent, he discovers that this disorientation actually brings no real satisfaction at all and, furthermore, imposes upon him the enormous burden of himself bringing into existence whatever meaning life is to have. And, modern man finding himself in this extremity, Dostoevski believed that the strategem that is ultimately to be expected of him is one that will involve some form of resort to the tactics of socialism: that is to say, what he will try to do is to achieve a definitive and an absolute settlement of human destiny in purely historical terms. Ivan Karamazov remarks on one occasion that "those who don't believe in God discuss socialism and anarchism and the reorganization of mankind on a new pattern, which are the same questions, only tackled from the other way up." And this is, in a way, the burden of one whole side of Dostoevski's testimony; for the fact that he perceived and so wonderfully dramatized in his fictions (most memorably perhaps in *The Possessed* and "The Legend of the Grand Inquisitor" in *The Brothers*) is that once life has been emptied of meaning by the death—or the banishment—of God, the only thing left for men to do is rigorously to *organize* it into some semblance of meaning. And, all things being permissible, there will, of course, be nothing to check the self-will of those self-appointed few who do the organizing—so that in the utopia of social harmony the equality of the multitude will be the equality of slaves. As Shigalov (the theorist of Verhovensky's "cell") confesses: "I am perplexed by my own data and my conclusion is a direct contradiction of the original idea with which I start. Starting from unlimited freedom, I arrive at unlimited despotism." But the rub is that the unlimited freedom is for only one-tenth of the human community, the other nine-tenths becoming a mere herd and, "through boundless submission," attaining "something like a primeval paradise."

So Pyotr Verhovensky and his colleagues in *The Possessed* are devotees of that same modern experiment in autonomy to which Raskolnikov and Svidrigailov are committed, the only difference being that they carry it into the fateful and expensive realm of *Realpolitik*. And though in the "Byronic" Stavrogin this audacious adventure achieves a kind of meretricious grandeur, the pathos of it is to be seen in Kirillov, who reasons that, if there is no God and no will greater than his own, then he must himself be a kind of God and his will must itself be omnipotent—a fact, however, which, on "the most vital point," he must express by killing himself, for he wants to assume the burden of a kind of inverted Messianism whose function will be to announce the dawn of a new age in which man, no longer fearing death, no longer seeks belief in God or the reassurance of belief in immortality.

Everything in Dostoevski moves, of course, toward the resounding climax of his entire career which was made by *The Brothers Karamazov*. For this is his masterpiece, and this is the book which alone would have entitled him to admission into that heaven for novelists wherein we believe are to be found the creators of *The Red and the Black* and *Moby Dick* and *War and Peace* and *The Magic Mountain* and *Remembrance of Things Past*. Yet, when it is set beside *Crime and Punishment* (1866) and *The Idiot* (1869) and *The Possessed* (1872), the greatness of *The Brothers* (1880) appears to be not a consequence of the new dimensions of Dostoevski's vision which it reveals but rather a consequence of the completeness with which it summarizes the themes already implicit in the great books that precede it. The history of the tragic family is, of course, superbly done, and the management of the old father's death is one of the great triumphs of the novelistic art. But, our compass having to be so brief, these and other felicities must be brushed aside, in order that the central line that has been established here might be hewn to without deviation—and my point is that this is a line that may be seen as being directly continued into *The Brothers* from the other great books. The strange psychological quirks and ambivalences of Grushenka and Katerina Ivanovna have already been explored in Nastasya Filipovna in *The Idiot* and in Lisa in *The Possessed*. The sensualism of Dmitri has its analogue in Rogozhin in *The Idiot*, as Kolya's representation of the precocity of the schoolboy already corrupted by modern intellectualism is also prefigured in *The Idiot* by Ippolit. Alyosha and Father Zossima also put us in mind of Prince Myshkin in *The Idiot* and Father Tihon in *The Possessed*, but, appealing as are these "saintly" figures in *The Brothers*, Dostoevski no more succeeds in making their virtue relevant to the world that is described in his fiction than he does in his handling of the earlier representatives of this category of his characters. And then, finally, at the incandescent center of *The Brothers* is Ivan Karamazov, in whom Dostoevski accomplishes a powerful recapitulation of that erring and tragic adventure in negation and rebellion, of which the previous protagonists have been such figures as the nameless hero of *Letters from the Underworld*, Raskolnikov, Svidrigailov, Verhovensky, Kirillov, and Stavrogin.

There is, however, one special thing in Ivan that sets him apart from many of his progenitors in the Dostoevskian drama, for he does not deny the existence of God: on the contrary, he passionately affirms it, and he purposes, like Goethe's Mephistopheles, to talk to him as an equal, to bring him into the dock, and to put him on trial. He does not choose to debate the question of his existence, for, as he says to Alyosha, "I have no faculty for settling such questions, I have a Euclidian earthly mind, and how could I solve problems that are not of this world?" No, on this ultimate issue he will not commit himself to any controversy: indeed, controversy on this question is forsworn by the deepest dispositions of his being, and what he finds it impossible to accept is not the fact of God but rather the miserable fact of the world which is held to be under his governance. As he says to Alyosha: "It's not that I don't accept God, you must understand, it's the world created by Him I don't and cannot accept."

Ivan's problem is the problem of theodicy: how, that is, are the sufferings and the tears of man to be reckoned with—or, rather, do they not demand to be reckoned with in terms of some principle higher than that presumably ordained by the necessities of a providentially structured natural law? Yes, to be sure, conventional religion teaches us that in that ultimate geometry of which God is the mathematician all contradictions will be reconciled and all dissonances will be harmonized. But, says Ivan, "if the sufferings of children go to swell the sum of sufferings which was necessary to pay for truth, then I protest that the truth is not worth such a price." Why should they "pay for the eternal harmony . . ."? No, he declares: "It's not worth the tears of that one tortured child who beat itself on the breast with its little fist and prayed in its stinking outhouse, with its unexpiated tears to 'dear, kind God'! It's not worth it, because those tears are unatoned for." And his point is that they *must* be atoned for, not "in some remote infinite time and space, but here on earth"—for, if we suffer (as, indeed, on the most generous construction of things, it appears to him that we do) only in order to "manure the soil of the future harmony for somebody else," then surely we have been thrown into a most outrageous world. "I must have justice"—this is the persistently recurrent note in the tirade which he hurls into the face of God. Indeed, it is the principle of justice to which he holds God accountable and against the measure of which he finds him wanting: for Ivan the kingdom of God is not worth the tears of a single child, and if this is its price, the price is too high. So he refuses it, because it is based upon injustice: "I renounce the higher harmony altogether." And when Alyosha murmurs, "That's rebellion," he replies:

"Rebellion? I am sorry you call it that. One can hardly live in rebellion, and I want to live."

But in the name of what does one live, when one has denied that life is ultimately meaningful? If the immediate chaos of existence is not to be understood in the context of an ultimate order, can one then act in the name of, or with the sanction of, anything other than chaos? In this extremity, has virtue any reward—or evil any retribution? These are the bitter issues with which Ivan must wrestle, and he does finally conclude that, yes, all things are, indeed, permitted: "Everything is lawful."

Here, then, we have the strange irony that Ivan Karamazov incarnates, of the man who, as Albert Camus says, "trembled at the suffering of a child" and who, "from the moment that he rejects divine coherence and tries to discover his own rule of life, recognizes the legitimacy of murder."[13] And, as Camus sees with such clarity, the ironic element here, surprising though at first it may seem, is yet an inescapable aspect of the dialectic within which Ivan is caught, for "the bitter end of metaphysical rebellion" is "metaphysical revolution":

> The master of the world, after his legitimacy has been contested, must be overthrown. Man must occupy his place. . . . But what does becoming God mean? It means, in fact, recognizing that everything is permitted and refusing to recognize any other law but one's own.[14]

This is the dreadful logic to which Ivan is committed: indeed, this is what he has chosen—to be logical: his determination to protest against the tears of humanity has committed him to the denial that goodness has any *effective* sanction in the universal scheme of things, so that his dilemma, as Camus reminds us, becomes that of being "virtuous and illogical, or logical and criminal."[15] The "visitor" who comes to him during the

delirium of his illness is right, in other words, when he tells
him: "You are forever angry, all you care about is intelligence. . . ." For this is, indeed, the primary focus of Ivan's
ultimate loyalty: like all Dostoevski's major representatives of
the modern disorder he would live out of the self-sufficiency
of his own intellect—to do which, of course, is to become
God: and when man has thus divinized himself, then "everything is lawful," even crime. And Ivan does, indeed, allow his
father to be killed. He goes mad afterwards, to be sure, for
he cannot retain his sanity betwixt the horns of the intolerable
dilemma (illogical virtue or logical crime) within which he is
caught. But, though he, for special reasons internal to himself,
remains within the private universe of his own anguish, "The
Legend of the Grand Inquisitor" in *The Brothers* does not
allow us to forget those demonic careerists of *The Possessed*
(Verhovensky, for example—or Shigalov), for, as it reminds
us, it is inevitable that metaphysical insurrection should extend
itself from the dialogue between man and God to the relations
between a man and his neighbors. Once achieved, in other
words, in the sphere of religion, it must also be achieved in
the human polity, for toward this conclusion its inner dialectic
presses inexorably.

This is, indeed, what Dostoevski means when he tells us that
socialism is, above all else, a question of atheism. For, in his
view, it is essentially the effort of the modern secularist to
bring the kingdom of Heaven down to earth, and he perceived
that, once this is done, the new administration must inevitably
involve for the human community the reign of a Caesarism
which can, in principle, admit of no bridling at all. It is of this
that the old Inquisitor is prophetic, and the logic of the experiment in autonomy is thus brought to its conclusion by this
"Legend" that Ivan relates to Alyosha, of Christ's return to
earth, of his appearance in Spain during the Inquisition, and of

his confrontation by the "Grand'" Inquisitor, who imprisons him and who then proceeds pedantically to "correct" him by pointing out to him that the happiness of man is really to be guaranteed only by offering him bread and relieving him of the burdens of freedom. The tragic lesson, in other words, that is here being dramatized and that is adumbrated at many other points in these great books might be formulated in this wise, that Hitler and Stalin dwell in all men who venture really to live upon the premise either that God is dead or that he is hopelessly impotent.

So Dostoevski is, then, our great modern tragedian of unbelief, and, in the imaginative literature of the last hundred years, his marvelous fictions continue to be the most important repository that we have of the data that the Christian consciousness would bring forward in its rejection, ultimately, of the legacy of the Enlightenment. He is reactionary, unsentimental, illiberal: he makes us ask questions about what is behind the masks that we conventionally wear, and he is never surprised about what is there to be found; before the moral faults and duplicities of men he is always sober and competent. "His gift," as Alfred Kazin says, "has been icy and merciless clarity; and awareness of man, as man, in his social loneliness, his emotional cheating, his fertile and agile hostility, his limited power to love. . . ."[16] "He knows," says Kazin,

> that men live as they do because they think as they do, and that their thoughts cannot be replaced by other thoughts until they have reached the bottom of their own. He asks: "Do you know who you are?"[17]

And, like Baudelaire and Kierkegaard in the nineteenth century and Eliot and Kafka in our own, he performs a fierce surgery upon the modern soul.

NOTES: Chapter 7

1. W. H. Auden, "Yeats as an Example," *The Permanence of Yeats,* D. Hall and M. Steinmann, eds. (New York: The Macmillan Co., 1950), p. 348.
2. Lionel Trilling, *The Liberal Imagination* (New York: The Viking Press, 1950), p. 286.
3. *Ibid.,* p. 100.
4. "By faith Abraham, when he was called to go out into a place which he should after receive for an inheritance, obeyed; and he went out, not knowing whither he went. By faith he sojourned in the land of promise, as in a strange country, dwelling in tabernacles with Isaac and Jacob, the heirs with him of the same promise: For he looked for a city which hath foundations, whose builder and maker is God." Hebrews 11:8–10.
5. The term "presence," in its usage here, originates in the writings of the contemporary French philosopher Gabriel Marcel.
6. Ralph Harper, *The Sleeping Beauty* (New York: Harper & Brothers, 1955), p. 57.
7. László Vatai, *Man and His Tragic Life* (New York: The Philosophical Library, 1954), p. 11.
8. *Ibid.,* p. 14.
9. D. A. Traversi, "Dostoievsky," *The Criterion,* Vol. XVI, No. LXV (July, 1937), p. 602.
10. John Middleton Murry, *Fyodor Dostoevsky: A Critical Study* (New York: Dodd, Mead & Co., 1916), p. 90.
11. Albert Camus, *The Rebel: An Essay on Man in Revolt* (New York: Vintage Books, 1956), p. 7.
12. Irving Howe, "The Political Novel," *Tomorrow,* Vol. X, No. 9 (May, 1951), p. 54.
13. Albert Camus, *op. cit.,* p. 58.
14. *Ibid.,* pp. 58–59.
15. *Ibid.,* p. 58.
16. Alfred Kazin, "Dostoevsky and the Age of Anxiety," *The Inmost Leaf* (New York: Harcourt, Brace & Co., 1955), pp. 253–254.
17. *Ibid.,* p. 256.

Nietzsche: The Conquest of the Tragic Through Art

For the fact that in life things actually take such a tragic course would hardly explain the original of a form of art; provided that art is not merely an imitation of the reality of nature, but in fact a metaphysical supplement to the reality of nature, placed beside it for the purpose of conquest.

—THE BIRTH OF TRAGEDY

WHEREAS MOST PHILOSOPHERS have been eager to communicate their visions and to proclaim the results of their thinking, Nietzsche was a philosopher who liked to hide. Not only was he capable of producing pages filled with a not inconsiderable obscurity but, like Kierkegaard and even Rousseau, he employed the device of a mask for purposes at once of communication and self-concealment. Moreover, Nietzsche's use of irony adds to the general difficulty of understanding his thought, which has very often been misconstrued in the past by a too literalistic interpretation of essentially ironical utterances. These difficulties are not lessened but rather increased when we approach *The Birth of Tragedy*, which is the book that will be at the center of our attention on this present occasion. This work introduces many subjects in its course, including a historical account of Greek tragedy, a theory of tragic pessimism, a metaphysic of tragedy and of art, and, not least of all, a criticism of late nineteenth-century German culture. And since these themes interpenetrate each other, the consequence is that *The Birth of Tragedy* is by no means an easy work to comprehend.

In order to achieve the greatest possible clarity, the discussion has been arranged in such a way as to move consecutively through a consideration of the following topics: the setting of *The Birth of Tragedy* in the pattern of Nietzsche's development; his special concern for Greek life of the late sixth century and the pessimism he attributed to it; his view of tragedy and the accompanying philosophy of Dionysus; his doctrine of art as metaphysics; the conquest of tragedy through art and the special sense in which pessimism is the truth about human existence; and, finally, the comparison with Christianity, the last topic representing the purpose of the entire study.

I

The Birth of Tragedy, the first published product of Nietzsche's peculiar and erratic genius, "was begun," as he tells us in *Ecce Homo*, "in the thunder of the battle of Wörth" during the Franco-Prussian War. And, he continues, "I thought out these problems on cold September nights beneath the walls of Metz, in the midst of my duties as nurse to the wounded."[1] Thus, while the main ideas expressed in the work grew out of his studies and lectures on ancient Greek civilization, Nietzsche's own personal experience of pain and suffering must also be kept in full view in any attempt to understand and estimate what he then called the philosophy of pessimism. It is possible to go further and show, as perhaps cannot be done to the same degree for any other significant philosopher, that Nietzsche's entire thought can be correlated with and interpreted by means of a minute account of the course of his life. The finding of the man behind the thought and in the thought has been attempted many times in the past, and not always with justifiable results, since the temptation to view his philosophical position from the perspective furnished by the tragic end of his life has always been great and few have been able to resist it. There is, however, no need to follow the biographical interpretation here; the presentation of Nietzsche's position with regard to the meaning and nature of tragedy can and must be accomplished in systematic fashion, for only if we can break through and grasp his doctrine in this way will it be possible to discover exactly how the tragic becomes an object of conquest by art and how this solution is finally to be estimated from a Christian perspective.

In 1869, Nietzsche accepted a call as Professor of Classical Philology at the University of Basel, and *The Birth of Tragedy,* published several years later, was his first and most ambitious effort in the field of classical studies. Unfortunately, it did not receive a warm and cordial reception in the academic world, and this fact had its own tragic influence upon the course of Nietzsche's later life and thought.[2] His view of scholarship and of science was that such learning is without aim and direction of itself, and that consequently it must be guided either by a theory of art or by the exigencies of life.[3] His small work *The Use and Abuse of History* makes clear enough his rejection of a detached scholarship which is without some clear relationship to the actual problems of human life. In accordance with this conviction it was impossible for him to pursue classical studies after the fashion of the reigning academic philology. A. H. J. Knight, in his instructive and measured work on Nietzsche, has expressed the point very well in saying, "It appears . . . that Nietzsche considered Greek literature, Greek life, and Greek thought from the unusual and unphilological standpoint of a Greek born out of time, not from the standpoint of a normal critic."[4] The curious fact is that what makes *The Birth of Tragedy* significant is the "unscholarly" and unusual thesis it contains concerning the

rise of the tragic art form as a means of expressing the pessimistic view of life, and the no less unexpected view that by
the Attic period tragedy had run its course, being finally laid
to rest by the approach of Euripides and the Socratic spirit.

It has often been pointed out, and with good reason, that in
The Birth of Tragedy Nietzsche's outlook was profoundly
under the influence of Schopenhauer, particularly his doctrine
of pessimism and his theory of music as the immediate language of the Will, the reality behind all phenomena. It would,
however, be an error to suppose that he had just taken over
Schopenhauer's philosophy, and thus to overlook the extent
to which Nietzsche believed that he had discovered tragic
pessimism for himself in his study of that portion of Greek
history that interested him most. And, since his unorthodox
interpretation of the Greek development was another instance
of Nietzsche the thinker "out of season," it is necessary for
us to turn to a brief consideration of the period he regarded
as the embodiment of the tragic sense of life.

II

Nietzsche's view of the origin of tragedy was not the only
novel result of his classical studies. Whereas most classical
scholars since Goethe had identified "the glory that was
Greece" with the achievements of the Attic period—the heart
of the fifth century—Nietzsche instead looked upon that
period as one of decadence and insisted that "the summit" of
Greek life was to be found in the preceding century and a
half, the period beginning after Hesiod and ending with
Aeschylus, which he called "the tragic age." For him this
was a time of profound participation in the mysterious depths
of life; he saw it as the great age of *lyric* or dithyrambic
poetry and, above all, as the time of Dionysus, the god after
whom Nietzsche named his philosophy.[5] His later attack upon

Euripides and Socrates as destroyers of tragedy through their optimism and rationalism must be understood against this background of the tragic age.[6] Nietzsche's characterization of the Greek attitude toward life as one of pessimism sounds strange if we are accustomed to deriving that outlook from the thinkers of the Socratic period, where all the emphasis falls upon rationality, optimism, and the moderation of the rational soul. But Nietzsche looked elsewhere for the foundation of his view, and consequently he emphasized the "dark side" of human existence in the period of the pre-Socratics. He was deeply impressed by the Greek's concern for the consequences of man's overstepping the limits set to his life—the consequences of *hybris*—and by his sensitivity to the pain in life which often amounted to a cosmic sense of guilt at being alive at all. Immediately prior to the writing of *The Birth of Tragedy*, he had been making a study of Theognis of Megara, the elegiac poet, and he was fond of his line, "For mortals not to be born is better than to be born." Nor was he any less attracted by the belief expressed by Sophocles in lines that might be duplicated from the works of many others, "Not to be born is the best fate: but, if a man be born, then it is much the next best thing that he should return whence he came as quickly as he can."

In addition to a grasp of the pessimistic outlook gained through his study of antiquity, Nietzsche, from the very outset, saw, in the speculations of the pre-Socratic philosophers, another idea, and it is one which stands in the center of his vision—the idea of the aesthetic man who has learned from the artist how to contemplate the plurality of human life and to envisage it as the *play* of a poet who has no other end in view but that of the play itself. This idea stands out clearly in his interpretation of the fragments of Heraclitus and Anaxagoras, and later on we shall have occasion to see the importance of the notion for the view expressed in *The Birth of Tragedy*, that man can triumph over pessimism only by capturing the standpoint of the creative artist.

III

It is now time to turn directly to Nietzsche's theory of tragedy as presented in *The Birth of Tragedy*,[7] and particularly to the philosophy of Dionysus and the redemption of the self through participation in the cosmic Will. Central to Nietzsche's interpretation is the initial contrast between Apollo and Dionysus and the two points of view which they symbolize, or the two forms of art over which they preside. For, from the contrast between the two, and their effective combination, comes the form of tragedy. Apollo, the god of plastic art, was, for Nietzsche, the symbol of rational form and moderation, of distance from the phenomenon such as characterizes the role of spectator or detached observer, and of high individualization of the self over against both society and the system of nature. Dionysus, on the other hand, was interpreted by Nietzsche as the god of music,[8] the symbol of enthusiasm and ecstasy, of participation by the self in an overwhelming unity having the power to destroy the isolation of individual life. It is important to notice that Nietzsche first presented the contrast as one between "formative forces arising directly from nature without the mediation of the human artist,"[9] and this would seem to suggest that he understood the two aspects in a metaphysical and not only in an aesthetic sense. This is true, but it is only part of the truth, since the impulses or forces of which he speaks are themselves taken as "artistic urges" on the part of nature.[10] Nietzsche offers illustrations for the two principles wherein the Apollonian is said to be represented by the *dream* and the Dionysiac by the state of *intoxication* or ecstasy, although, in his discussion, it is difficult to know where to draw the line between the two impulses, as belonging to life in a more extended sense or as belonging exclusively to art. One thing at least is clear: the Apollonian and Dionysiac are taken as expressing distinct attitudes toward life, and, as such, the contrast is revealing because it gives us an insight into Nietzsche's *Weltanschauung* at the time. In the dream, reality is endowed with the definiteness of form and the sharpness of individuality; the Apollonian man faces the world with the confidence that he is an individual capable of understanding both himself and that world by reference to a perfection not exhibited by the everyday world itself. Implicit in this interpretation is the idea that the followers of Apollo derive their security in life from a beauty, a wisdom, and a truth that have the status of "illusion," just because they are not exhibited in the world as it actually exists.[11]

At the other pole (and here we have Nietzsche's peculiar philosophy of power beginning to make itself felt) stands the Dionysiac rapture in which the self puts aside its ordinary hold upon both the world and itself—"the individual forgets himself completely"—and experiences the oneness of all things, and especially his bond with the life and power coursing through the whole of nature. The philosophy of Dionysus means the breaking through all that individuates a self and sets it off from other selves and from nature. Nietzsche's way of expressing this underlines the contrast between the Dionysiac principle and the Apollonian principle at the same time that it reveals the hand of Schopenhauer:

> each individual becomes not only reconciled to his fellow but actually at one with him—as though the veil of Maya had been torn apart and there remained only shreds floating before the vision of mystical Oneness.[12]

Nietzsche thus set himself at this time on the side of all those philosophers for whom the movement toward reality is a movement not toward individuality and specification but toward the ultimate unity of the undifferentiated. Consequently he always viewed the Dionysiac principle as involving direct participation by the self in the stuff of existence, as identification of the self with the "primal Unity" and as a sort of individual redemption from life through transcendence of the Apollonian individuality. Nietzsche was still thinking of Schopenhauer's idea that the aim of life is to transcend the will and to tranquilize desire through an identification of the self with the Oneness of things, but Nietzsche's own voluntarism and tragic sense stood in the way of his acceptance of Schopenhauer's quietistic solution. Nietzsche's view of the primordial unity is not of something static, but is the conception of *a surging power filled with pain and contradiction*, and yet also filled with a fierce joy in all the creativities of life. Dionysiac intoxication not only points the way to the conquest of tragic life, but it is also, in the first instance, an avenue of illumination and the means whereby the tragic character of life is disclosed.

Following another lead pointed out by Schopenhauer, Nietzsche took the ancient lyric, the Dionysiac art, as the one *direct* expression of the pain at the heart of things, and he contrasted it anew with the Apollonian expression of experience through images which, because they *reflect* reality as through a mirror, do not *immediately express* it. Music, on the other hand, is the very language of the Will or primordial power, and, in considering it, we come upon the clear idea behind the obscurity of Nietzsche's analysis. Tragedy was born from the Dionysiac lyric (Nietzsche identified the chorus with the followers of Dionysus), because music expresses directly the terrible truth about existence—that it is pain and sorrow—whereas the plastic arts always interpose between man and his life the images of form which lead to the contemplation of individuality and thus provide a place of standing that is safe from the ravages of existence. From this it is possible to see more clearly why Nietzsche was more inclined to describe the Apollonian world as one of "illusion" but not the Dionysiac. The lyrical poet does not project anything but rather participates directly in life and is expressive of the ultimate will. He writes:

> the lyrical poet . . . himself becomes his images, his images are objectified versions of *himself*. Being the active center of that world he may boldly speak in the first person, only his "I" is not that of the actual waking man, but the "I" dwelling, truly and eternally, in the ground of being.[13]

Yet, despite the priority given to the Dionysiac element in this account (even the full title asserts that tragedy is born from "the spirit of music"), we must not forget that only from the co-operation of *both* impulses can tragedy arise. Thus, for example, the tragedy of Aeschylus, so much admired by Nietzsche, would have been impossible without the utterly Apollonian metaphysical justice standing in the background.

We must add to this entire picture a further notion, the full import of which will be clarified in the succeeding section. In addition to his description of the Apollonian and Dionysiac as two forces in existence which later are expressed in art, Nietzsche also came to view the world including human beings as itself a great work of art; at this point insight into life and into the meaning of the aesthetic aspect of life become indistinguishable. In a comment more revealing of his ultimate position than he was perhaps aware of at the time, Nietzsche maintained that

> we have every right to view ourselves as esthetic projections of the veritable creator and derive such dignity as we possess from our status as art works. Only as an *esthetic product* can the world be *justified* to all eternity.[14]

Moreover, the discussion continues by emphasizing the idea that life and art are a "comedy" prepared by the "primordial artist" for his own "edification," and that only the creative artist himself—the man of genius—is really in a position to understand what this means.

The curious fact about Nietzsche's analysis is that he was so eager to grasp and to express the cosmic forces which spawned tragedy that he almost neglected to give a clear account of tragedy itself. The tragic material, the stuff of tragic existence, appeared to Nietzsche primarily as *destructiveness* and *divisiveness;* the world seemed to him a scene of strife leading to untimely death, a realm of loneliness and human isolation. In many ways the latter was more important because it pointed up Nietzsche's sense of the gulfs separating man and man in late nineteenth-century technical society, and, even more, the isolation of man from nature in a culture dominated by what he took to be the Socratic or rationalistic spirit. Tragedy, however, is a more complex and subtle affair in Nietzsche's thought than the mere description of these more or less prevalent evils of life. Tragedy was attached in his mind to a concept of sin and necessity in man's situation. Man must understand, he says, "that everything that is generated must be prepared to face its painful dissolution."[15] And this outcome is bound up with the conflict between different spheres of existence (for example, the human and the divine), each of which harbors a claim that cannot be set aside as long as the spheres maintain their separate natures.

His view can best be presented through the contrast between the Greek (he called it the "Aryan") and the Hebraic concepts of the tragic flaw or sin. He compared the classic myth of Prometheus (who was an eternal type for Nietzsche and not an "individual character" in a play) with the story of the Fall, and in the former he saw sin as *active,* as the transgression and guilt necessarily bound up with the fact that "man's highest good must be bought with a crime and paid for by the flood of grief and suffering which the offended divinities visit upon the human race in its noble ambition."[16] He took this myth and its power over the Greek imagination as evidence of the capacity of the Greeks to sense and to bear suffering in the world: to him it meant that the Greeks really felt the deep offense given by man to the gods. And from this offense *inexorable* punishment follows no less than the sense of guilt. Nietzsche was deeply attracted by the idea of an *active* sinning—that is, by the circumstance that in the exercise of his powers of art and artifice man should incur his guilt, and he even compares this Promethean view with the "passive" *hybris* of Oedipus who "unwittingly" brought about his downfall. Oedipus was regarded by Nietzsche as a genuinely tragic figure, but he was not as much attracted by him as by Prometheus, whose downfall was brought about through a tremendous display of power and daring adventure.

At the other extreme, in Nietzsche's description, stands the Hebraic conception of sin which he is content to characterize simply as weakness in the face of temptation. Concentrating all of his attention upon the motif of disobedience in the story, Nietzsche could see in it only "feminine frailties," and, consequently, he was unable to see the point of the myth as the misuse of freedom. No doubt it appeared as a moralistic conception to him, but it is ironic that, having always been a voluntarist at heart, he should have missed the fact that the biblical tradition found the flaw of man in the interiority of his will, understood as the seat of decision and of the self's basic orientation. Failure at this point may have been due to Nietzsche's different conception of the will, as power and as restless creativity, but the fact remains that the peculiar voluntarism of the Judeo-Christian tradition—as Augustine showed, without counterpart in the classical world—was lost upon him in its fundamental significance.

Nietzsche's choice of the downfall of Prometheus as the model of tragic existence enables us to see how the concept of individuation is related to suffering in the world and how Dionysiac art can provide a resolution. The heroically striving individual seeks to break through the limits of his individuality and to approach the universal unity,[17] but in so doing he commits the crime of injustice which leads to pain and suffering and ultimately to the tragic end. The Apollonian impulse, according to Nietzsche, does not fully comprehend the tragic necessity involved and is content to seek a resolution by drawing more sharply the lines of individual existence through self-knowledge and control. Nietzsche's solution is to condemn the individuality at the root of the problem by declaring it to be merely phenomenal—an appearance of separation which does not actually exist from the vantage point of the universal Will. Behind the phenomena of individual life stands the one primordial unity, ever self-sufficient and exulting in the production of the greatest spectacle of all—the cosmos and its raging life. The redemption of existence is the discovery, not as a piece of mere information or knowledge but in the form of ecstatic participation, that the real self is united with all selves and with the power of nature in the one genuine reality. The transitoriness of the phenomenal world of individuality revealed in the eternality of the world of Dionysus represents the triumph of that "eternal life" which, as Nietzsche says, tragedy affirms.[18] The manner in which Dionysus conquers tragedy can best be understood through two ideas, the "metaphysical comfort" provided by art and the *necessity* of suffering which is of the essence of the pessimistic outlook.

IV

There is implicit in both Nietzsche's view of the form of tragedy and of tragic existence itself a means of resolution or of overcoming the tragic dissonance. And the centrality of Dionysus appears most clearly in the fact that the god not only co-operates with the Apollonian principle in bringing about the birth of tragedy, but he points the way beyond tragedy at the same time. Through art and the aesthetic standpoint there comes what Nietzsche called a "metaphysical comfort," and it is this which justifies and redeems existence. The essence of this solace resides in the assurance that "life flows on, indestructibly, beneath the whirlpool of appearances."[19] Further clarification of the meaning of this function of art is to be found in the contrast drawn by Nietzsche between the Old tragedy and the New, or between the earlier "metaphysical" and the later "earthly" solution to the tragic problem. It must be noticed that The Birth of Tragedy contains, in addition to the theory announced in the title, a theory of the death of tragedy as well, and the opposition between the Old (Aeschylus) and the New (Euripides) tragedy is the best way of making clear what the metaphysical solution means.

Nietzsche found the purest example of tragedy in Aeschylean drama, in which problems of cosmic proportions are raised and in which an effort is made to resolve them against a metaphysical background.[20] He did not, however, believe that this original level had been sustained throughout the entire development of the form, and after Aeschylus he saw a steady decline. He traced the death—he called it the "suicide" —of tragedy to the two spirits represented by Socrates and Euripides. The former is said to have destroyed the world in which tragedy can exist by removing its mystery, by identifying virtue with knowledge (so that a morality of individual

reflection replaces the aesthetic standpoint), and by optim-
istically minimizing the darker side of human life. Euripides,
working within the tragic form itself, is accused of eliminating
Dionysiac music and of substituting the *deus ex machina* solution to tragedy—which is an earthly solution regarded by
Nietzsche as theatrically conceived and lacking in metaphysical explanatory power. The most serious aspect of the
charge is that the Euripidean answer no longer has "metaphysical" comfort in it; it no longer unites us with the primordial unity beyond the pain and loneliness of individual
existence, and it no longer makes us feel, as Nietzsche thought
genuine tragedy should, that we directly participate in "the
abiding phenomenon of Dionysiac art, which expresses the
omnipotent will behind individuation, eternal life continuing
beyond all appearance and in spite of destruction."[21] He
summed up his understanding of the type of tragedy in which
the form met its end in the following words:

> It opposes Dionysiac wisdom and art; tries to dissolve the
> power of myth; puts in place of metaphysical comfort a
> terrestrial consonance and a special *deus ex machina*—the god
> of engines and crucibles; forces of nature put in the service
> of a higher type of egotism. It believes that the world can be
> corrected through knowledge and that life should be guided
> by science; that it is actually in a position to confine man
> within the narrow circle of soluble tasks, where he can say
> cheerfully to life: "I want you. You are worth knowing."[22]

When it is said, however, that Old tragedy furnishes what
Nietzsche has been calling a metaphysical comfort or solace,
we must be careful not to mistake his solution for one of a
very different kind. It does not mean that in Old tragedy
there is a metaphysical theory which is presented in "artistic"
dress, for, were this the case, art would be merely a means for
the expression of knowledge. On the contrary, although there is

a theory behind the resolution (for the Apollonian principle also exists in genuine tragedy), the main point is that the self must *experience* and directly *participate* in the primal unity which knows no division and exults in its power to create; and only through tragic art can this be accomplished. In this Nietzsche is the true follower of Dionysus: experience and participation have the priority over comprehension at a distance. And this point is not at all undercut by his idea that tragedy incorporates *both* Dionysiac and Apollonian features. That is, the importance of direct participation is not lost just because the element of Apollonian "illusion" intervenes and transforms our participation into a vicarious experience.[23] The self, confronted with the drama of high tragedy, must directly experience the loss or exchange of itself in the state of ecstasy, and in so doing it finds a solace which is something more than the communication of an idea. It is thus that the resolution is presented as one that only art and the aesthetic viewpoint can achieve.[24]

V

Now, in order fully to grasp what is involved in Nietzsche's effort to conquer the tragic through art, we must be attentive to what is meant by the *necessity* of suffering and especially to the sense in which pessimism is said to express the truth about human existence. When he referred to all the terrors of human life as the "terrible truth" about the world, he meant, among other things, to attack the idea that there is a *moral* order behind the world or that there is a *divine* justice beyond the phenomena. Thus at the outset he set himself against both the classic Christian view and the moral idealism of Kant and Leibniz. He seems to have been obsessed with the belief that only if life is surveyed in the first instance without the "illusion" of morality is it possible to grasp its true character and to make this truth a starting point from which to cope with the human predicament. As a result both of his own experience and his study of the classical world, Nietzsche came to believe that the pessimistic view is the only true one and that life must be regarded as essentially pain and destruction and suffering. Yet, though he accepted this verdict as the initial truth about existence, he was very far from being content with it, and, in the end, he refused to admit pessimism as the final word about life. Indeed, even if we do not take without qualification his later description of *The Birth of Tragedy*,[25] it is still true that he was from the outset seeking some resolution of the problem presented by pessimism. And what most attracted Nietzsche in Aeschylean tragedy was its drive beyond the tragic facts themselves to the cosmic background of mystery. We long, he said, for something transcending the symbolic picture of the drama, for some transfiguration of tragic existence itself. And what, in fact, he intended to do was to conquer tragic pessimism by starting with it, by admitting its truth, and then by passing beyond it, all the while avoiding every solution that refused to begin with an acknowledgment of the tragic facts. The aesthetic expression of the pessimistic view in Aeschylean tragedy may, in other words, become the means whereby pessimism itself can be transcended, for, in providing us with an insight into the nature of tragic life, it helps us to admit it and to bear it without "being turned to stone" by the vision. But the question then is: How shall this be accomplished?

The key to Nietzsche's solution is to be found in the concept of *necessity*, for his contention is that, when the inevitability of suffering is grasped, the dark side of our life must appear to us as transfigured and permeated by a new meaning. He asks us to look upon the world as it might appear to a cosmic artist who expresses himself freely and creatively and, in so doing, produces just the world we see. Such an artist cannot but create, and he can do so, in satisfaction of his own unbounded will, only in superabundant fashion. For Nietzsche, we must remember, there is no transcendent idea of the good or of justice present to the artist: there is only the sense of restless power and joy in self-expression. It is clear from his early lectures on Greek philosophy that he was fascinated by the idea that a cosmic artist would *play* with the materials of creation[26]—and that the very superabundance of this creativity would *inevitably* lead to conflict and to suffering. And his point was that beings who owe their existence to such a creator must, in the very nature of the case, exceed their limits, this being a consequence of the creative abundance: as he says,

> For a brief moment we become, ourselves, the primal Being, and we experience its insatiable hunger for existence. Now we see the struggle, the pain, the destruction of appearances, as necessary, because of the constant proliferation of forms pushing into life, because of the extravagant fecundity of the world will.[27]

What is arresting in this theory is the peculiar manner in which man is made to know the truth through the medium of the art of tragedy. It is not presented merely as a theory to be understood and considered, but as direct participation and experience. The power of tragic myth is that it brings us, after the fashion of Dionysus, into the presence of the one Will expressing itself in the world, and it makes it possible for us to share in the joy of superabundant creation. From this vantage point we are to understand the whole spectacle of life as deriving its pattern from art. "At this point," said Nietzsche,

> we must take a leap into the metaphysics of art by reiterating our earlier contention that this world can be justified only as an aesthetic phenomenon. On this view, tragic myth has convinced us that even the ugly and discordant are merely an aesthetic game which the will, in its utter exuberance, plays with itself.[28]

Nor did he shrink from describing this view itself as a kind of "illusion" which makes life bearable for "nobler natures" who are more sensitive to the wounds inflicted by life. Such natures must, nevertheless, be strong and daring; they must not only accept the tragic facts, but they must also affirm life as it is and not merely after it has been coated over by a moral or religious ideal. Once the tragic truth has been admitted, however, only an aesthetic view of the world will suffice to conquer tragedy.

VI

With Nietzsche's view before us, we must now consider the relation of this essentially aesthetic solution to the religious and moral faith of the Christian tradition. It may seem strange to set his view in this comparison, for, after all, did he not crucify Christianity in virtually every writing and describe himself through the mask of Zarathustra as the anti-Christ? Moreover, is it not clear that the aesthetic orientation of his proposed solution of the tragic problem exists in another world from that of biblical religion? All this is true, but it does not alter the fact that he was endeavoring to find some interpretation of tragic existence, and his understanding of the human situation is sufficiently similar to that of Christianity to make comparison both possible and instructive.

An opening word about Nietzsche's personal relation to Christianity is not without its importance. Both his father and grandfather were Lutheran pastors, and he seems to have regarded himself as standing in some special, even if not very clear, relationship to the Christian faith. In *Zarathustra* Nietzsche said:

> Here are priests: but although they are mine enemies pass them quietly and with sleeping swords! . . . my blood is related to theirs; and I want withal to see my blood honored in theirs.[29]

This sense of not being entirely dissociated from Christianity, at the same time that he rejected it, helped to create in Nietzsche an attitude that can only be described as ambivalent. There are passages in his writings (and they are in the majority) in which Christianity is opposed with a savage violence, but here and there one can find a hint of the reformer who criticizes distortions and aberrations chiefly for the purpose of purifying and restoring. Underneath, however, there can be no doubt concerning Nietzsche's position: his is an aesthetic resolution, and he constantly opposed it to a moral and religious faith. This is not to say that art and religion are necessarily at war with one another or that they cannot dwell together in peace and harmony, but it does mean that they come to stand in opposition to each other in the moment when art is transformed into a substitute for religion. And this is exactly what art was made to be in Nietzsche's thought.

The first point to be noticed is that Nietzsche had no flat view of human life such as was characteristic of late nineteenth-century moralism, naturalism, and positivism. To be sure, he had his own type of genetic reductionism, as is shown by his interpretation of the "bad conscience" as a mere disease in *The Genealogy of Morals*, but this should not be allowed to obscure the fact that he did understand the meaning of tragedy and knew at the same time that no mere moralism would suffice to conquer it. It is most revealing in this connection that he should have grasped the religious significance of the concept of salvation, even if he rejected its specifically Christian form. Describing redemption in *The Genealogy of Morals*, Nietzsche wrote:

> Neither the Hindu nor the Christian believes that such redemption can be reached by the path of virtue, or moral improvement, no matter how highly both regard the hypnotic value of virtue. The fact that they have been staunchly realis-

tic in this regard is much to the credit of the three greatest religions, otherwise so thoroughly riddled with moralizing.[30]

It is clear, in other words, that, while Nietzsche sought for his own solution to the problem of salvation, he could not accept any of the solutions offered in the optimistic progressivism, the scientism, or the social meliorism of his age. And his rejection of later tragedy in favor of the metaphysical approach of Aeschylus shows the reason why. So there can be no question, then, that he knew the metaphysical, even if not the full religious, depth of man and of the cosmos in which he lives.

But since every solution should be internally related to the problem from which it emerges, it is necessary to recall Nietzsche's understanding of the circumstances that give rise to the tragic situation. As we have noted, suffering, in his view, stems from superabundance of life on the one hand, and from the crime committed by man in exceeding the limits of individual existence on the other. In both aspects, tragedy stems from the nature of existence itself and from the necessity of conflicting claims—between man and the gods and between man and man—neither of which can finally and simply be subordinated to the other. Part at least of the tragic conflict is to be attributed to the fact that the universe is the expression of no single plan or idea, with the result that the terrifying fruitfulness of the cosmic Will ultimately produces a chaos of incompatible claims. The superabundance alone, however, is not sufficient to explain tragic existence, because it leaves out Nietzsche's estimate of the status of individuality and of the tragic possibilities inherent in it. If we take his own interpretation of the Prometheus myth literally, we must suppose that *being individual* and thus limited *is itself the root of tragedy*. That is to say, Nietzsche saw in the *hybris* of Prometheus a move away from individuality itself and a symbol of man's inevitable exceeding of the bounds of individual existence in a drive "towards universality, de-individuation."[31]

This overstepping of the limits represents man's basic crime which, in its encroachment upon the legitimate claims of both the gods and other men, inevitably leads to the prevalence of pain and suffering in human life. And it is just here that we find a point of greatest contrast with Christianity and indeed with the whole of biblical religion. For Nietzsche found the flaw in individuality itself, whereas the Bible views it as bound up with the basic orientation of the self in relation to God. The idea of a rebellion against or a disobedience in the face of a divine command, while not itself excluding the notion of a limit overstepped, is not adequately interpreted in terms merely of a flaw in the nature of individuality. It posits instead the notion of the individual self making a particular decision, and this in turn involves not a movement away from individual existence but away from complete dependence upon God. The biblical story of the Fall of man, while not to be taken as an account of the origin of individual existence, must, nevertheless, be understood in terms of a drive from the side of man to enhance his status as an individual self. The separation from God occurs at the point where man wants to have his own individuality solely within his own hands and at the command of his own will.

Nietzsche, on the other hand, looked upon the individual character of things, the fact of their finitude and limitation, as itself the cause of tragedy. And this is precisely why he sought for a solution not in a higher type of individuality but in the transcendence of individual being.[32] Man is driven by his restless will to *create*—the artist was never far from the center of Nietzsche's thought—and in so doing he violates the rights of others. Such creativity is, however, a form of triumphant self-affirmation and, as Nietzsche frequently expressed it, it is at most a display of *folly* when it leads inevitably to tragic consequences. By contrast, Christianity understands man's tragic situation as related to something more internal to the center of the self; it is seen as bound up with man's will and purpose in life, and especially with his orientation as a total self. The cause of the tragic Fall is seen as coming from a decision within individuality and not from the fact of individuality itself. Moreover, in describing the tragic self-affirmation as *sin*, Christianity means to indicate the self-willed separation of man from God and not merely the defect of man as subject to folly and error. Nietzsche, at least in so far as he followed in the footsteps of Schopenhauer, had an essentially Buddhist conception of the resolution: since the suffering follows from separateness, the supreme aim of life must be to overcome such individual separation. This is achieved by an ecstatic and enthusiastic identification of the self with the source of life, the cosmic and creative Will. Lyrical poetry or music makes this identification possible, and in this sense his resolution is an aesthetic one. And Nietzsche was emphatic in his insistence that aesthetic values be recognized as such and that art not be taken merely as an external form in which doctrines either of ethics or theology are expressed. He was, in other words, most deeply earnest in his conviction that the function of art is a metaphysical one and that it is ultimately for the purpose of conquering tragedy.

Now, throughout our study, emphasis has been placed upon the importance of art as a means of overcoming tragic existence. But the question now is: How are we to assess this general approach from a Christian perspective? In Nietzsche's view, the aesthetic standpoint provides us not only with an insight into the necessity of suffering which makes life bearable, but it also holds forth the means of attaining a sense of oneness with and participation in the cosmic creativity behind the world of individual phenomena. The solution is essentially one in which the eye of the beholder is changed, and the manner in which the world is viewed or contemplated becomes uppermost in importance. The world that stands over against man is left exactly where it was before, only the light in which it is seen is now different. The solution is typically Oriental: change the eye, and the reality that is beheld is transformed. From a Christian standpoint there are at least two difficulties with this solution: first, in finding redemption only in the change of viewpoint, the moral and religious aspects of the self are neglected; and, secondly, the tragic character of reality is in no way affected beyond the change in the viewpoint of the beholder.

It is a far-reaching defect in Nietzsche's thought that his criticism of conventional morality and religion, incisive and justified as it was in many particulars, left him without a positive replacement for what he had destroyed. He could not hope to deal with the moral defects in the human will, because his transvaluation of values had gone so far in the elimination of the ethical dimension altogether. Nor is the case different with regard to religion: there the genetic reduction of religious concepts to the status of ideology made it impossible for him to consider man's religious problems except as manifesting a form of disease.

The second difficulty is more important. Christianity cannot find itself in accord with any view of tragic existence in which the proposed resolution leaves existence exactly where it was before, while merely changing the viewpoint of the self. For Christianity, something new must enter the objective situation as a leaven which must eventually transform the character of existence itself and not only the standpoint from which it is viewed. In a passage from *The Birth of Tragedy* which has not attracted much attention, Nietzsche saw a solution that he did not develop but which, ironically enough, is very close to the Christian view. "The gods," he said, speaking of Greek mythology, "justified human life by living it themselves—the only satisfactory theodicy ever invented."[33] And, indeed, for Christianity it is God himself who takes tragic existence upon himself in order to break through the tragic circle: man, being in need of wholeness, cannot, in virtue of that very need, perform the task of himself alone. The idea that tragedy can be conquered by a type of life willing and able to take suffering upon itself, without at the same time being destroyed by it, is implicit in Nietzsche's suggestive remark. But he had no genuinely transcendent element capable of assuming the tragic burden, and, consequently, he was forced to retreat to a solution essentially aesthetic and contemplative in character.

NOTES: Chapter 8

1. *Ecce Homo, The Complete Works of Friedrich Nietzsche,* O. Levy, ed. (New York: The Macmillan Co., 1924), Vol. 17, p. 69.
2. Nietzsche's creative and vigorous attempt to project himself into the life of classical Greece and to animate it through his own spirit was too much for the classical philologists of his time. Wilamovitz-Möllendorff, the authoritative classicist of the period, set out at once to destroy Nietzsche's speculative approach in a monograph, *Zukunftsphilologie!* (Berlin, 1872). He paid no attention whatever to Nietzsche's efforts to understand the philosophical and religious significance of the tragic form, and consequently he missed all that was important in the work; instead, he confined himself to historical details and inaccuracies of which there were admittedly many. E. Rohde, Nietzsche's lifelong friend and author of the brilliant work *Psyche,* came to his defense, only to be met with a second monograph of the same title further aimed at discrediting *The Birth of Tragedy.* It is not without significance, however, that, whereas we still discuss the ideas of Nietzsche and Rohde, Wilamovitz is all but forgotten.
3. *Vide,* for example, *The Genealogy of Morals,* trans. by F. Golffing (New York: Anchor Books, 1956), pp. 284–285.

4. A. H. J. Knight, *Some Aspects of the Life and Work of Nietzsche* (London: Cambridge University Press, 1933), p. 9.

5. *Vide* especially Section II of *The Birth of Tragedy*.

6. Of great importance for a fuller understanding of Nietzsche's outlook in *The Birth of Tragedy* are his lectures on the pre-Socratic philosophy, entitled, appropriately enough, "Philosophy during the Tragic Age of the Greeks" (1873), to be found in *The Complete Works of Friedrich Nietzsche*, O. Levy, ed., Vol. 2, pp. 71–170. *Vide* also Knight, *op. cit.*, pp. 22 ff., for the suggestive idea that Nietzsche viewed the history of Greece itself as a great tragic drama, once again reversing received opinion by regarding the triumph over the Persians in 470 B.C. not as the beginning of an ancient glory but as the start of the tragic decline.

7. Limitations of space preclude a treatment based upon all of Nietzsche's writings. It is true that in *Ecce Homo* and in the Preface added to *The Birth of Tragedy* in 1886 he tried to give a somewhat different emphasis to his earlier views (e.g., he later distinguished sharply between pessimism and tragedy and contended that, for the Greeks, the latter was the means of overcoming the former), but this need not destroy the authoritativeness of the position that he first expressed.

8. The clue to the importance attached by Nietzsche to the music of Wagner is to be found in Nietzsche's identification of Wagner's music with the spirit of Dionysus. *Vide* Knight, *op. cit.*, pp. 9–10.

9. *The Birth of Tragedy*, p. 11. All citations from this work are to be found in the new translation of *Die Geburt der Tragodie* by Francis Golffing, *The Birth of Tragedy and The Genealogy of Morals* (New York: Anchor Books, 1956).

10. *Ibid.*, p. 24. Unfortunately Golffing's translation misses this point and does not make clear that the "artistic urges" *belong to nature*, as the German text requires—"*ihre Kunsttriebe.*" We have here Nietzsche's idea that nature represents the free play of an artistic impulse.

11. *The Birth of Tragedy*, p. 22.

12. *Ibid.*, p. 26.

13. *Ibid.*, p. 39. "Himself" is italicized in the original.

14. *Ibid.*, pp. 41–42. Unfortunately, the translation misses the connective "because" between the last sentence and what precedes it; the italics are in the original.

15. *Ibid.*, p. 102.

16. *Ibid.*, pp. 63–64; cf. *The Genealogy of Morals*, p. 228, where Nietzsche holds that in Greek life it is *folly* which leads to suffering,

whereas in the Judeo-Christian tradition it is *sin*. Folly is, presumably, more admissable because it is not a "moral" category.

17. Nietzsche failed to see a matter of the greatest importance at precisely this point; since he had already given himself over to the influence of Schopenhauer, he was bound to regard the activity of Prometheus as a drive toward the universal Will and *away* from his limited individuality, and consequently he could not see that the activity of Prometheus is essentially *toward* and not away from higher and higher individualization. The more man has the conditions of existence at the command of his own will, the more is he individuated through high culture and the further is he removed from the source of his being. Nietzsche did not see Prometheus in this light, but instead saw in his heroic activity only an attempt to break through the narrow limits of his individuality.

18. *The Birth of Tragedy*, XVI. This entire section is essential.

19. *Ibid.*, p. 108.

20. *Vide* especially pp. 62–63.

21. *The Birth of Tragedy*, pp. 101–102; cf. pp. 108–109.

22. *Ibid.*, p. 108.

23. *Ibid.*, p. 140. It is important to notice that tragedy represents a genuine co-operation of both principles. In the earlier part of his theory where Nietzsche is intent on explaining the birth of the tragic form, there is an overemphasis upon the Dionysiac contribution, but in the latter part of the work (especially Section XXIV) the function of the Apollonian image is further explained. Tragedy, nevertheless, is impossible without both, and Nietzsche even asserted that the union of the two represents "the final consummation of both the Apollonian and Dionysiac tendencies."

24. When Nietzsche came to review his works in *Ecce Homo*, he had occasion to re-emphasize the fundamentally aesthetic standpoint of his first work. In criticizing Christianity, he said: "It denies all aesthetic values; which are the only values that *The Birth of Tragedy* recognizes." *The Complete Works of Friedrich Nietzsche*, O. Levy, ed., Vol. 17, p. 70.

25. *Ecce Homo*, 'The Birth of Tragedy': ". . . the book contains the first attempt to show how the Greeks succeeded in disposing of pessimism—how they overcame it." *The Complete Works of Friedrich Nietzsche*, O. Levy, ed., Vol. 17, p. 68. Nietzsche's account here makes a sharper distinction between the pessimistic outlook and tragedy as a solution to it than is made in the original discussion.

26. *Vide* the striking expression of this point in *The Genealogy of Morals*, pp. 218–219; man is said to be in the center of the spectacle which is the "game of dice" played by "Zeus or Chance."

27. *The Birth of Tragedy*, pp. 102–103.
28. *Ibid.*, p. 143.
29. *Thus Spake Zarathustra*, II, xxvi, *The Complete Works of Friedrich Nietzsche*, O. Levy, ed., Vol. II, pp. 105–106. *Vide* also the following from a letter to Peter Gast of July 21, 1881: "From childhood on I have pursued it [Christianity] into many corners, and I believe that I have never in my heart been disrespectful to it. After all I am the descendant of a whole tribe of Christian ministers . . ." *Friedrich Nietzsches Briefe an Peter Gast*, herausgegeben von Peter Gast (Leipzig: Insel, 1908), p. 69; no. 66 (Vol. 4 of *Gesammelte Briefe*).
30. *The Genealogy of Morals*, trans. by F. Golffing, p. 269.
31. *The Birth of Tragedy*, p. 64.
32. Nietzsche's later philosophy of the *Ubermensch* was, of course, quite different; it was a summons to the courageous *individual* to abandon conventional existence and heed the call of Zarathustra.
33. *The Birth of Tragedy*, p. 30.

The Vision of Evil in Hawthorne and Melville

HAWTHORNE AND MELVILLE are a great pair. In nine-teenth-century American literature, they stand opposed to an-other famous pair, Emerson and Whitman. The point of op-position is the question concerning the nature of man. If (to use T. E. Hulme's definition[1]) Romantics are those who deny the Fall of man, then Emerson and Whitman must be called Romantics, and Hawthorne and Melville by some such name as "Counter-Romantics." It is significant that Melville dedi-cated *Moby Dick* to Hawthorne. The Dedication seemed to cement an alliance, for Hawthorne and Melville were orthodox Christians, at least to this extent—they both believed in Original Sin.

There is a great deal of friendship and admiration for Haw-thorne in Melville's writings. To begin with, in Melville's great essay on Hawthorne, published pseudonymously in 1850,[2] the lines of agreement are emphatically laid down. Here, after speaking of the "blackness" in Hawthorne, he goes on to say:

> . . . this great power of blackness in him derives its force from its appeal to that Calvinistic sense of Innate Depravity and Original Sin, from whose visitations, in some shape or other, no deeply thinking mind is always and wholly free. For, in certain moods, no man can weigh this world without throw-ing in something, somehow like Original Sin, to strike the uneven balance. . . . Perhaps no writer has ever wielded this terrific thought with greater terror than . . . Hawthorne. Still

> more: this black conceit pervades him through and through.
> . . . It is that blackness in Hawthorne . . . that so fixes and
> fascinates me.

Melville goes on to find the same "blackness" in Shakespeare.
He hastens to add that he does not mean to imply that Hawthorne is as great as Shakespeare, but (writing in that nineteenth-century American atmosphere of all-is-good, all-is-well,
which Emerson had helped so much to create, and finding a
contrary view around him so rare, Edwards being a hundred
years dead, and having left no worthy successor, and under
such circumstances being perhaps all the more inclined to
exaggerate the merits—great though they were—of Nathaniel
Hawthorne) Melville ventures to declare that "the difference
between the two men is by no means immeasurable." Mrs.
Hawthorne was pleased with the comparison. Hawthorne
himself, always clearheaded, said, "The writer is no common
man, and, next to deserving his praise, it is good to have be-
guiled or bewitched such a man into praising me more than I
deserve."[3]

From May, 1850, until November, 1851, Hawthorne and
Melville were near neighbors, Hawthorne living in Lenox,
Massachusetts, in the red farmhouse overlooking the Stock-
bridge Bowl, and Melville living in Pittsfield, some six miles
distant. A remarkable friendship soon developed, perhaps the
most fruitful friendship in our literary history. Hawthorne had
published *The Scarlet Letter* in the spring of 1850, and was
therefore famous; he was soon busy with *The House of the
Seven Gables*, which appeared early in 1851. Melville was deep
in the throes of *Moby Dick*, which appeared, with the dedication to Hawthorne already noted, in the autumn of 1851. The
two men visited back and forth a good deal, talking far into
the night over gin and cigars (as Hawthorne said) "about time

and eternity, things of this world and of the next, and books, and publishers, and all possible and impossible matters."[4]

The spirit of these sessions is suggested in an eloquent passage in one of Melville's letters, where he imagines a meeting in the next world under conditions more ideal, but (one must believe) not, so far as personal relations go, essentially dissimilar. The passage reads:

> If ever, my dear Hawthorne, in the eternal times that are to come, you and I shall sit down in Paradise, in some little shady corner by ourselves; and if we shall by any means be able to smuggle a basket of champagne there (I won't believe in a Temperance Heaven), and if we shall then cross our celestial legs in the celestial grass that is forever tropical, and strike our glasses and our heads together, till both musically ring in concert,—then, O my dear fellow mortal, how shall we pleasantly discourse of all the things manifold which now so distress us,—when all the earth shall be but a reminiscence, yea, its final dissolution an antiquity.[5]

The meetings of these two—who were the greatest writers then living in America—were mutually stimulating. Each was to the other the best and most rewarding writer-friend whom he had known, or was ever to know.

Melville's letters to Hawthorne are among the most remarkable letters ever written. It is regrettable that none of Hawthorne's to Melville have survived. That Hawthorne wrote Melville is beyond doubt, because Melville refers to such letters (Hawthorne's letter written in acknowledgment of *Moby Dick* Melville called "joy-giving and exultation-breeding"). But we do have references to Melville in Hawthorne's *Notebooks*. In the notebook which he kept in the Berkshires (already quoted from), there are accounts of meetings, journeys taken together, conversations; and, in the English journal, there is this sad, moving account of the meeting in 1856 at

Liverpool (where Hawthorne was Consul), which proved to be their last:

> Melville stayed with us from Tuesday till Thursday; and, on the intervening day, we took a pretty long walk together, and sat down in a hollow among the sand hills (sheltering ourselves from the high, cool wind) and smoked a cigar. Melville, as he always does, began to reason of Providence and futurity, and of everything that lies beyond human ken, and informed me that he had "pretty much made up his mind to be annihilated"; but still he does not seem to rest in that anticipation; and, I think, will never rest until he gets hold of a definite belief. It is strange how he persists—and has persisted ever since I knew him, and probably long before—in wandering to-and-fro over these deserts, as dismal and monotonous as the sand hills amid which we were sitting. He can neither believe, nor be comfortable in his unbelief; and he is too honest and courageous not to try to do one or the other.[6]

This fine passage is, in truth, about equally applicable to Hawthorne himself. For Hawthorne, like Melville, had reasoned much concerning Providence and futurity and the things which lie beyond human ken. It was his dilemma, as well as Melville's, to find it difficult either to believe or to be comfortable in unbelief. "Lord, I believe; help thou mine unbelief" has been the prayer of many a good doubting Christian since it was first prayed (in Mark 9:24) by the father of the possessed child. There can, indeed, be no Christian faith worthy of the name (unless it be among the cherubim and seraphim) without this struggle between belief and unbelief; and there can be no true human sympathy without it.

II

The concept of Original Sin runs through all of Hawthorne. The story "The Birthmark" is one of his better illustrations of the idea.

Georgiana's otherwise perfect beauty is marred by a tiny blemish on her cheek which has the shape of a hand. Aylmer, her husband, who is a "scientist," is more and more disturbed by this blemish, for he is a perfectionist. He is also a man who is ambitious for success and fame in his profession. He feels that, if he could remove this one imperfection (and he thinks he can), several advantages would accrue to him: he would have made something new under the sun, namely, a perfect being; he would have satisfied his desire for perfection; and he would have satisfied his desire for power.

His wife submits to the trial. He brings to bear on the problem all of his experimental resources. He tries, and fails. For just as the hand fades away and at last completely disappears, Georgiana dies. The grief of Aylmer is equivocal: it is partly for the loss of his wife, and quite as much (one suspects a good deal more) for the failure of his experiment.

It is interesting that Aylmer was in the beginning the only one concerned about the mark. Georgiana herself was not unhappy about it—that is, until Aylmer became unhappy, and then her unhappiness was owing to his unhappiness rather than the mark itself. Her suitors had positively admired the mark. They thought it actually enhanced her beauty and would have been most happy for the privilege of kissing it. What wise, sensible lads *they* were!

But, you ask, is not Aylmer's pursuit of perfection worthy of all praise? Yes, and no. The admiration of perfection is praiseworthy, but Aylmer was trying to make over another human being. This was a presumptuous sin. It was a usurpation of the role of the Creator himself. Aylmer, moreover, sees imperfection in Georgiana, but not in himself. He richly deserves Jesus' rebuke, "Thou hypocrite, cast out first the beam out of thine own eye, and then shalt thou see clearly to pull out the mote that is in thy brother's eye" (Luke 6:42). Georgiana, in charity and love, does not blame Aylmer; she praises him, rather, with her last breath. "You have aimed loftily," she said. But Hawthorne judges differently. "Had Aylmer reached a profounder wisdom," he says, "he need not thus have flung away the happiness which would have woven his mortal life of the selfsame texture with the celestial."

What is this "profounder wisdom"? Well, for one thing, the acceptance, even the cherishing, of human imperfection. Georgiana's birthmark is a symbol of human imperfection: it is the mark of her humanity, it shows her to be human. It is a symbol, in theological language, of Original Sin. Not that Georgiana is guilty of any overt sinful acts; she is the soul of goodness and devotion. The term Original Sin does not refer primarily to overt sinful acts, as such acts are ordinarily understood. It means basic human nature—fallible, imperfect human nature; it means the state of being human; it reminds us that we live in an imperfect, non-ideal world.

If the question is asked as to wherein lay Georgiana's imperfection, the answer is not too difficult. Perhaps her "error" was putting her trust in a man unworthy of that trust, or putting in mortal man a trust which belongs to God alone. Possibly she succumbed too, the least bit, to vanity (she would hardly have been human if she hadn't), to the attractive thought of being the only "perfect" one. But the trust and the vanity endear her all the more to those who have a true appreciation of the fact that men and women were created a little *lower* than the angels.

The positive force of the evil principle is always at work in Hawthorne's fictions. The snake or serpent, symbolizing the Devil, is one of his central symbols. In Dr. Rappaccini's garden (in the story "Rappaccini's Daughter"), the luxurious plants extend themselves serpent-like along the ground. (There are no snakes in Emerson's "pleached garden.") The stranger in the tale "Young Goodman Brown" carries a walking stick which resembles a serpent, and this stranger turns out to be the Devil himself. Hawthorne takes over, in fact, the New Testament concept of diabolical possession; many of his characters are "possessed of the Devil." The young man in the tale "Egotism, or the Bosom Serpent" was "possessed" until the Devil was finally driven out, or exorcised. And Goodman Brown was "possessed," though in a somewhat different way.

Brown met up with the Devil, disguised as a kindly old man, at the edge of the forest at nightfall, and was persuaded to accompany the old man deep into the forest to attend a witch meeting. He was not too hard to persuade (man is prone to error); he had in fact planned to do this very thing. When he got to the witch meeting, which was a gaudy affair, he saw, or thought he saw, all the pious folk of the village, including his own wife Faith. It is never quite clear whether Brown takes the final vows of allegiance at the Devil's altar, nor does it much matter. He has had his vision of evil, and the experience has a permanent traumatic effect. Not all of Hawthorne's young men, however, are crushed by the knowledge of evil. Young Robin, for example, in "My Kinsman, Major Molineux," survives a somewhat similar experience and appears to be all the stronger for it.

What is the purpose of evil in the world? It is a question which Hawthorne asks over and over again, and with special emphasis in his last completed work. "Is sin then like sorrow," Kenyon asks in *The Marble Faun*, "an element of human education, through which we struggle to a higher and purer state than we could otherwise have attained? Did Adam fall, that we might ultimately rise to a far loftier paradise than his?" Milton raised the same question in the last book of *Paradise Lost*, where Adam speaks as follows, "full of doubt":

Full of doubt I stand
Whether I should repent me now of sin
By me done and occasioned, or rejoice
Much more that much more good thereof shall spring
To God more glory, more good-will to men
From God—and over wrath grace shall abound.

St. Paul had dealt with the same question. "Shall we continue in sin," he asks, "that grace may abound?" And he answers, "God forbid" (Romans 6:1). But he had previously observed that "where sin abounded, grace did much more abound" (Romans 5:20). Allied to this view is the doctrine of the *felix culpa*, the happy fault (or fortunate fall), which regards the fall of man as fortunate because, if he had not fallen, he would never have known the inestimable benefits of redemption. It is, of course, an old Catholic doctrine, and we have seen its elaboration by Milton and Hawthorne. If sin may seem to abound more than grace in Hawthorne, and the fall appear more often unhappy than happy, it must be borne in mind that we are not concerned with worldly criteria. If there is spiritual growth, however painfully attained (and spiritual growth is impossible of attainment without pain), grace can be said to "much more abound," and the fall can be said to have been fortunate. Grace much more abounds, for example, and the fall is fortunate, in *The Scarlet Letter*, though a worldly appraisal would point to a different view.

One of the chief thematic tensions in Hawthorne is the tension between his Puritan and his Romantic tendencies. His writings lean in the Puritan direction. But he lived in a Romantic age, and his work shows an awareness of the temper of that age. His work is, in a sense, a "criticism" of that temper, but it is not a criticism which is blind to the Romantic fascination, or which refuses it a sympathetic hearing.

In *The Scarlet Letter*, Hester is the spokesman for the

Romantic view, and her argument carries weight with the modern reader. Here is a woman—handsome, of a voluptuous beauty—who as a young girl was talked into marrying an old man, Roger Chillingworth, a medical doctor and a cold, intellectual scientist, who must have proved unsatisfactory as a husband. She came along to Boston (this was back in the 1630's) and fell in love with the brilliant, popular young clergyman, Arthur Dimmesdale. They had a love affair, the offspring of which was a baby girl whom her mother named Pearl (from the biblical "pearl of great price"). The stiff-necked Puritan community condemned Hester and required her to wear on the bosom of her dress at all times the red letter A, standing for Adulteress. Chillingworth arrived just after the birth of the child, to haunt Hester and persecute the minister, for he sensed infallibly that Dimmesdale was the child's father. Hester was a woman of great strength. She bore up well under her trials. She became a sister of mercy, and, eventually, a respected figure in this bigoted old town.

Meanwhile, the sensitive, conscientious minister was paying a high price for his secret. Chillingworth, whose identity as Hester's husband was not known to Dimmesdale for a long while, preyed upon the minister's mind and soul in sinister, insidious ways. And then, after seven long years (Hester serving, Arthur suffering), the lovers meet in the forest. Hester tells Arthur who Chillingworth is, and begs and wins Arthur's forgiveness for not having told him at the beginning (she had promised Chillingworth that she wouldn't tell, and had conspired with him all this time to keep the poor minister in the dark). And then she urges a course of immediate action: that the three of them embark on the ship at that moment in Boston harbor, and flee to Europe. The minister agrees, caught up in the old passion. But the story doesn't turn out that way. On the morrow, after preaching the "Election Sermon" before the Governor, the Magistrates, and the general populace, Arthur mounts the old scaffold where Hester was made to stand in ignominy seven years before, confesses his adultery to the breathless, incredulous multitude, and then dies.

This much of a synopsis has seemed necessary to remind the reader of the famous speech by Hester which I propose to call "Romantic." The occasion was the forest meeting just referred to, and the words spoken by Hester were these: "What we did had a consecration of its own. We felt it so! We said so to each other."

Hester never felt that she had sinned, and her speech is very appealing. Is not the book after all, some readers ask, an exposé of Puritan bigotry and intolerance? The answer is, Yes, to be sure: *The Scarlet Letter* is a criticism of Puritanism, as well as of Romanticism. But when the Romantic apologist goes on to insist that the book is a vindication of individual impulse, the right of the individual to "happiness," the sacredness of passion sincerely felt, it is necessary to demur.

The tension between the Puritan and the Romantic tendencies is especially emphasized in the forest scene. The symbolism is dualistic. The forest itself has a double significance: it stands for moral error, being the place where Hester and Arthur go astray; and it stands for natural innocence, for here little Pearl becomes a child of nature (in the Romantic sense) and is recognized as such by the creatures of the forest. Pearl herself has a double significance: not only is she an innocent child of nature, but she is at the same time an agent of retribution (she insists that Hester replace the scarlet letter on her dress after having cast it aside). Hester's casting of the letter aside was her "romantic revolt"; and her replacing of the letter is her outward compliance with (though not inward acceptance of) the Puritan law. Throughout the forest scene (perhaps the most richly symbolic scene in the book), Hester stands for Romantic individualism, and Arthur for the claims of law and conscience.

Although Arthur, stimulated by the excitement of the moment, agreed to Hester's plan of escape, his experiences after leaving Hester forced him back into the Puritan path. On re-entering the village, he was sorely tempted by the devil to say blasphemous things to the passers-by. On reaching his room, he destroyed the manuscript of the "Election Sermon" to be delivered on the following day and furiously set about writing a fresh sermon. The author does not tell us exactly what went on in Arthur's mind after his return to his study. To do so would be almost unavoidably to prepare us too well for the climactic scene of the public confession, and to sacrifice the element of legitimate surprise and shock. But though we are not told explicitly, we can be sure that there was a struggle, and that the minister trampled down Satan at last. It is axiomatic with Hawthorne that there can be no virtue without conflict and struggle. Only a great struggle can account for the minister's great heroism, and the greatness of the struggle came out of the greatness of his despair.

I have said that Arthur stood for the claims of the Puritan law. "Christian" can be used here interchangeably (as in so many places in a discussion of this kind) with "Puritan." The reader hardly needs to be told that the law broken by Hester and Arthur was the Seventh Commandment of the Decalogue, and that the Decalogue was not abrogated by the New Testament dispensation. The Puritans did not invent the Seventh Commandment, nor were they un-Christian in insisting upon its importance, though an uninformed reader might infer both of these notions from some of the commentaries on *The Scarlet Letter.* The Puritan community in Hawthorne's novel was un-Christian in its attitude and behavior—its bigotry and cruelty—but it was not un-Christian in its ethical doctrine.

Hester is a Romantic heroine, a splendid one. She has been much admired, and justifiably. The richly embroidered "A" has been called by one of her modern admirers "the red badge of courage." She was indeed courageous, and strong. Arthur, in comparison, has seemed pitiably weak; but justice, I believe, has not been done to Arthur.

Arthur's situation was much more difficult than Hester's. Her conflict was external. She was integrated within herself, and she set her solidly united self resolutely against that intolerant old community. A fight like this can be inspiriting; it is fortifying, it builds one up. But Arthur's fight was with himself. His was a state of civil war, not war with the outside world. The community idolized him, but he had his internal troubles, and these proved to be serious. (Psychiatrists who happen to read *The Scarlet Letter* often express surprise that Hawthorne, in 1850, should have understood how serious internal conflicts can be.) If heroism is measured in terms of the magnitude and severity of the struggle which is undergone, then Arthur must be adjudged the more heroic of the two, for Hester never did anything that cost a tithe of the sweat and the agony which Arthur's public confession cost him.

Hester is a noble, frustrated, pathetic figure, but she is not a tragic figure, because her mind is made up. My hat is off to her, as high as the highest. Wordsworth's wonderful words fit her perfectly—"A perfect Woman, nobly planned/To warn, to comfort, and command." But she is not the protagonist, the chief actor; and the tragedy of *The Scarlet Letter* is not her tragedy but Arthur's.

Arthur is the persecuted one, the tempted one. He it was whom the sorrows of death encompassed, whom the pains of Hell got hold upon. His public confession is one of the noblest climaxes of tragic literature. Poor, bedeviled Arthur Dimmesdale, the slave of passion and the servant of the Lord, brilliant of intellect, eloquent of voice, the darling of his congregation, the worst of hypocrites and the prey of endless rationalizations and sophistries! No veteran of the cavalry of woe was ever more battle-scarred or desperate than this man as he stood on the scaffold and began, "People of New England!"—"with a voice that rose over them, high, solemn, majestic."

The confession was decisive. Its function in the novel is to resolve the action. It turned the scales in the great debate, though Hester, romantic heretic to the last, remained unconvinced, impenitent, unredeemed. She had, at best, an imperfect understanding of Arthur's problem. As for Arthur, he saw the problem all too clearly. He must make a public confession: "Confess your faults one to another, that ye may be healed" (James 5:16). There could be no salvation without that. The confession brought about a reconciliation with God and man; and not least, with little Pearl, from whom there had been a complete estrangement. "Pearl kissed his lips. A spell was broken." Hester watched, wonderingly. "Thou lookest far into eternity with those bright eyes," she said; "Tell me what thou seest." What Arthur saw chiefly was God's mercy. "He is merciful," he said; "He hath proved His mercy most of all in my afflictions. . . . Praised be His name! His will be done!" Thus in his profoundest character-creation, and in the resolution of his greatest book, Hawthorne employed the Christian thesis, "Father, not my will, but thine be done."

III

The protagonist of Hawthorne's greatest book is redeemed at last; the protagonist of Melville's greatest is damned at last, utterly. Melville said to Hawthorne, after the completion of *Moby Dick*, "I have written a wicked book, and feel as spotless as the lamb." But if he felt justified in what he had written, why did he call *Moby Dick* "a wicked book"?

Perhaps because he had written a book with a wicked protagonist. The protagonist, to be sure, is punished for his wickedness. Still, what if he is presented sympathetically, admiringly, as a hero? Then perhaps the book becomes a "wicked book" in the eyes of its author. Melville's case recalls Milton's, in *Paradise Lost*, where Satan appears in a heroic light in the early part of the poem. Melville's description of Ahab, in fact, often seems reminiscent of Milton's description of Satan. Both are superheroes, archangelic though fallen, battle-scarred, vindictive, bent on revenge. Might not Milton have thought that *Paradise Lost* through Book II was a wicked book? Is not the treatment of Satan in those tremendous opening scenes too sympathetic to comport strictly with Christian piety? Possibly Melville felt this about his treatment of Ahab, the great difference being that Milton does get round, in due course, to debasing Satan, but Ahab, though defeated and destroyed at last, is never debased: his stature is of heroic proportions to the end.

What manner of man is this Ahab?

One of the best answers to this question is given in the remarks of Captain Peleg to Ishmael in Chapter XVI, before the start of the voyage, and before the *Pequod's* captain has appeared on the scene. "He's a queer man, Captain Ahab," says Peleg,

> He's a grand, ungodly, god-like man; doesn't speak much; but, when he does speak, then you may well listen. Mark ye, be forewarned; Ahab's above the common; Ahab's been in colleges, as well as 'mong cannibals; been used to deeper wonders than the waves; fixed his fiery lance in mightier, stranger foes than whales. . . . Ever since he lost his leg last voyage by that accursed whale, he's been desperate moody, and savage sometimes; but that will all pass off. . . . Besides, he has a wife—not three voyages wedded—a sweet resigned girl, and by that sweet girl, that old man has a child; hold ye then there can be

> any utter, hopeless harm in Ahab? No, no, my lad; stricken,
> blasted, if he be, Ahab has his humanities!

Ishmael's description of Ahab (in Chapter XXVIII), after his first sight of him, is even more powerful: "He looked like a man cut away from the stake, when the fire has overrunningly wasted all the limbs without consuming them, or taking away one particle from their compacted aged robustness." And Ishmael goes on to describe the livid white mark extending from his hair down his face and neck, resembling the seam made on a tree trunk by lightning. The scar may have been a birthmark, or it may have been received "in an elemental strife at sea." Regardless of its origin, it recalls Milton's Satan, who was scarred by God's thunderbolts.

Ahab's obsessive desire is for vengeance on Moby Dick, and he incites his crew to unite with him in this mad enterprise. No Hitler ever poured forth such hysterical, compelling eloquence. "And this is what ye have shipped for, men!" he shouts, "to chase that white whale on both sides of land, and over all sides of earth, till he spouts black blood and rolls fin out." When Starbuck, the only man on the *Pequod* who is not swept off his feet by Ahab's fury, remonstrates that "vengeance on a dumb brute . . . seems blasphemous," Ahab replies,

> . . . He tasks me, he heaps me. I see in him outrageous strength, with an inscrutable malice sinewing it. That inscrutable thing is chiefly what I hate, and . . . I will wreak that hate upon him. Talk not to me of blasphemy, man; I'd strike the sun if it insulted me.

One does not get very far into the book without having to face up, at least tentatively, to the question as to what the White Whale really stands for. It is a question which one should not be in too great a hurry to answer definitively (if, indeed, a definitive answer can be found), but it must be entertained, for the story soon takes on large symbolic dimensions. "Ever since that almost fatal encounter with Moby Dick," the narrator tells us,

> Ahab had cherished a wild vindictiveness against the whale, all the more fell for that in his frantic morbidness he at last came to identify with him, not only all his bodily woes, but all his intellectual and spiritual exasperations. The White Whale swam before him as the monomaniac incarnation of all those malicious agencies which some deep men feel eating in them, till they are left living on with half a heart and half a lung. . . . All that most maddens and torments; all that stirs up the lees of things; all truth with malice in it; all that cracks the sinews and cakes the brain; all the subtle demonisms of life and thought; all evil, to crazy Ahab, were visibly personified, and made practically assailable in Moby Dick.

The White Whale was all these things to Ahab.

But Ahab, we notice, is the victim of a "wild vindictiveness," a "frantic morbidness." He is, according to the narrator, a "monomaniac," and, indeed, "crazy." So the question may well be asked: Is what the White Whale stands for *to Ahab* what the White Whale *really* stands for? And to this question the answer must be, Yes, in part, certainly, despite Ahab's monomania and craziness. Much madness is divinest sense. But, to be sure, the meaning of the Whale is not necessarily identical with, or confined to, its meaning for Ahab. Still less, in discussions of this kind, should the author be identified with Ahab. Ahab is not Melville, or Melville's "spokesman." A dramatic, imaginative work has no "spokesman."

In that remarkable chapter on "The Whiteness of the Whale" (Chapter XLII), we have a discourse which sets forth with an amazing wealth of illustration the ambiguity of whiteness. One connotation of whiteness is benign: as in the bridal veil, the white hairs of old age, the ermine of the judge, the alb (from the Latin *alba*, white) of the Christian priest. But there are forms of whiteness which are sinister, and strike terror to the soul: as in the polar bear, the albatross (which Coleridge's poem made an omen of evil in the popular imagination), the albino man, the corpse, the shroud, the ghost.

Is reality, then, an ambiguity, a dualism? Is whiteness both benign and malignant? Must Ahab's report be corrected for astigmatism? Must Goodman Brown's in the tale by Hawthorne, where young Brown, after the traumatic experience of the witch meeting, could see nothing but evil around him? Ahab's encounter with the Whale was traumatic, too, and the two "meetings" are allegorically comparable, with the difference that Brown, finding no foe "visibly personified and practically assailable," succumbed to despair. The two fables indeed make an illuminating pair, and it is interesting to recall that Melville was strongly attracted to "Young Goodman Brown," saying in the essay already referred to that Hawthorne's tale is as "deep as Dante."

Ahab's moral character deteriorates in the course of the story. Progressively he stifles "his humanities." He rejects, one by one, the good influences: Starbuck, Pip, thoughts of home, wife, and child. He comes progressively under the domination of Fedellah, the Parsee, who is the Devil, or the Devil's efficient emissary.

Chapter CXIII, "The Forge," is a scene of powerful diabolism. As the Parsee looks on, the blacksmith forges a new harpoon for Ahab, who then anoints the barb with the blood of the "heathen" harpooners Tashtego, Queequeg, and Daggoo. And, "as the malignant iron scorchingly devours the baptismal blood," Ahab "deliriously howls" the wicked words, "*Ego non baptizo te in nomine patris, sed in nomine diaboli*" ("I baptize you not in the name of the father but in the name of the devil"). One recalls the devil's baptismal service in "Young Goodman Brown."

Shortly afterwards, the *Pequod* is surrounded by a great electrical storm, and the yardarms are alive with St. Elmo's fire. While each yardarm blazes with a "tri-pointed trinity of flames" (as if to mock the Holy Trinity), Ahab puts his foot upon the Parsee (as if to defy even the Devil), and speaks these blasphemous words:

> Oh! thou clear spirit of clear fire . . . of thy fire thou madest me, and like a true child of fire, I breathe it back to thee. . . . Leap! leap up, and lick the sky! I leap with thee; I burn with thee; would fain be welded with thee; defyingly I worship thee!

In the summer of 1851, while Melville was writing *Moby Dick*, he read Hawthorne's "Ethan Brand," the story of a man who had brought about such an imbalance in his own nature by cultivating the "head" (he became a great "philosopher") to the neglect of the "heart" that he at length committed suicide by jumping into a flaming limekiln. As Brand stood poised above the fiery furnace of the kiln, he spoke a speech somewhat like the one by Ahab just quoted. "Come, deadly element of Fire, henceforth my familiar friend!" he cried. "Embrace me, as I do thee!"

Melville may have been influenced by Hawthorne's story. The two characters are dissimilar in some respects, but basically similar. Brand does not have Ahab's defiance, and Ahab is not intellectually cold like Brand—he is the most impassioned of men. But both are fire-worshipers, Devil-worshipers. As Brand spoke, "blue flames played upon his face, and imparted a wild and ghastly light," recalling the St. Elmo phosphorescence on board the *Pequod*. Both Ahab and Brand made, in effect, a Faustian pact; they exchanged their souls for the Devil's help. Both are monomaniacs—Ahab ravingly so, while Brand is cold, impassive, uncommunicative. Both are suicides, for Ahab's last assault on the Whale is made with suicidal recklessness. Ahab is the more "sympathetic" of the two, the more heroic, the more admirable (we admire or sympathize with Brand scarcely at all), and Ahab's imbalance is owing not to the lack of passion, as in Brand's case, but to the excess of it. But both are colossal egotists, full of pride, and both are guilty (though Ahab is not destitute of "feeling," as Brand was) of what Hawthorne called "the unpardonable sin," the severance of all human ties.

We need not suppose that Melville "approved" of Ahab. He undoubtedly "admired" this hero, this Titan of men, but he did not necessarily approve of him, any more than Shakespeare approved of Macbeth, or Milton of Satan. Ahab is diabolical, and, like Macbeth and Satan, he has a hellish fall. From the moral standpoint, he is not an example but a warning: he illustrates both man's powers and their misuse: he is Romantic individualism carried to the last absurd degree.

One remembers, upon reaching the end of the book, Father Mapple's sermon (in Chapter IX), and, looking back, one sees its importance more clearly than before. For Father Mapple's sermon about Jonah gives us a yardstick by which to measure the sin of Ahab. The preacher recapitulated the biblical story as "a story of the sin, hard-heartedness, suddenly awakened fears, the swift punishment, repentance, prayers, and finally the deliverance and joy of Jonah." It is, of course, the latter part of this sequence which has no parallel in the story of Ahab: Ahab did not repent, he did not pray (to God), he was not redeemed. Father Mapple put the difficulty as follows: "If we obey God, we must disobey ourselves; and it is in this disobeying ourselves, wherein the hardness of obeying God consists." Ahab could not obey God because he could not disobey himself.

And what of the Whale? The Whale may be, of course, a

number of things. It may be, I suppose, some kind of obstacle to man's fulfillment. It is no mere physical obstacle, but possibly one of our own monomaniacal creation. Or perhaps the Whale stands for the inscrutable, the last mystery which man unsuccessfully strives to wring from the heart of the Universe, and, in so doing, like Marlowe's Dr. Faustus, attempts "more than Heavenly power permits." Or possibly the Whale stands not so much for an unachievable or impossible aim as for one which is not achieved because the protagonist goes about the business in the wrong way. Faulkner's "The Bear" tells of a *successful* hunt which is conducted in a very different spirit from Ahab's "fiery" one—with decorum, reverence, humility. The Bear, like the Whale, is a great mythical creature; both are given an aura of the supernatural. The difference between the two stories is in the spirit of the pursuit: it is the difference between anarchistic individualism and tradition, vengeance and respect, defiance and acceptance, blasphemy and piety.

Moby Dick is the greatest classic in the American tradition of man's defiance. Man is prone to defiance; it is another manifestation, and a chief one, of Original Sin. Paradoxically, though, man's great heroisms and his great crimes spring from the same source. Melville's concept of human nature (like Shakespeare's) is a heroic one, and he reminds us that man is capable of great heights and of great depths, and that he could not be capable of one without being capable of the other also.

These extremes, of height and depth, are illustrated again, but in a different way, in *Billy Budd*, a work perhaps as great as *Moby Dick*, written nearly forty years after *Moby Dick*, in the last years of Melville's life, and published posthumously.

Billy Budd was a handsome young sailor on board His Majesty's ship *Indomitable* during the Napoleonic Wars. Billy was accused falsely by the Master-at-Arms, Claggart, of plotting a mutiny, whereupon Billy instinctively struck Claggart a fatal blow. In the trial which followed, Captain Vere, though sympathetic with Billy, and certain that Claggart had lied, felt compelled to insist upon the death penalty, and Billy was hanged.

In the creation of Billy, Melville appears to have been influenced by Hawthorne's "The Birthmark," for, in the story, he writes:

> Though our Handsome Sailor had as much masculine beauty as one can expect anywhere to see; nevertheless, like the beautiful woman in one of Hawthorne's minor tales, there was just one thing amiss in him. No visible blemish, indeed, as with the lady; no, but an occasional liability to a vocal defect.

In short, in moments of emotional stress, Billy stuttered.

It might be interesting to explore a bit the parallel which Melville here suggests. A physical defect, in each case, is a symbol of human imperfection, of one's being human. Without the flaw, the person would be inhumanly perfect. The flaw, therefore, becomes a symbol of Original Sin. Both Georgiana and Billy, to be sure, are "innocent," apparently without guile, but the very guilelessness may lead to complicity. If Georgiana had not had the tiny hand on her cheek, she would not have conspired in its removal; if Billy had not been a stutterer, he would not have struck Claggart, for the vocal block seemed to trigger the blow. The flaw in each case closely concerns one's *amour propre*, one's vanity. Neither Georgiana nor Billy, though guileless, is quite unself-conscious, and in self-conscious moments the physical defect becomes more prominent: the red hand shows forth more boldly against the surrounding paleness, the speech impediment becomes an out-and-out stutter, or worse. Might these marks symbolize an irreducible vanity, the more insidious for its unobtrusiveness?

If these marks are emblematical of Original Sin, their possessors become particularly useful in showing how such a concept can comport with "innocence," as innocence is judged by worldly standards. We do not blame Georgiana for submitting to the experiment; we do not blame Billy for striking the Master-at-Arms. Original Sin means limitation, a failure somewhere along the line, a lack or shortcoming in no sense criminal, although a criminal act may possibly spring from such a lack or shortcoming, as happened in Billy's case.

At the same time, both stories seem to convey the idea that human perfection is not for this world. At the moment when the crimson hand entirely disappeared from Georgiana's cheek, she died, being translated, as it were, to a Heaven where perfection is at home. And, similarly, when Billy, the trap being about to be sprung, and the moment of "translation" being at hand, called out "God bless Captain Vere," he spoke the words without the slightest trace of impediment. There is a hint, perhaps in both stories, and certainly in *Billy Budd*, of an analogy with Christ, whose perfection made him unsuited to an imperfect world. Melville's inspiring account of Billy's last moments carries overtones of Christ's death and ascension:

> Billy stood facing aft. At the penultimate moment, his words, his only ones, words wholly unobstructed in the utterance, were these—"God bless Captain Vere!" . . . syllables delivered in the clear melody of a singing-bird on the point of launching from the twig. . . . At the same moment, it chanced that the vapory fleece, hanging low in the East, was shot through with a soft glory as of the fleece of the Lamb of God seen in mystical vision, and simultaneously therewith, watched by the wedged mass of upturned faces, Billy ascended; and, ascending, took the full rose of the dawn.

If Billy is innocence, though not perfection, Claggart is depravity of the blackest sort. But how do we account for

Claggart's depravity? Melville calls it "natural depravity, a depravity according to nature." He also calls such depravity a "mystery," and quotes St. Paul (II Thessalonians 2:7) on "the mystery of iniquity." But how do we account for Claggart's antipathy to Billy? Again, an unfathomable mystery. "For what," asks Melville, "can more partake of the mysterious than an antipathy spontaneous and profound such as is evoked in certain exceptional mortals by the mere aspect of some other mortal, however harmless he may be? if not called for by this very harmlessness itself?" Shakespeare had on his hands a somewhat similar question in the motivation of Iago. Coleridge said that Iago's villainy came from "a motiveless malignity." Iago said of Cassio, "He has a daily beauty in his life which makes mine ugly." Possibly Claggart felt shamed by Billy's innocence and beauty.

Captain Vere was confident of Billy's innocence of Claggart's charge and felt that the fatal blow struck by Billy was an act of divine justice: "It is the divine judgment of Ananias," he said; "Struck dead by an angel of God." And he added ironically, "Yet the angel must hang." For the Captain is the custodian of the law, "Caesar's" law, and the law must be enforced. Billy will certainly be acquitted, he believes, "at the last assizes," but "here," he says, "we must proceed under the law of the Mutiny Act." Captain Vere is sympathetically drawn. He is a practical man, making such compromises as he must, in an imperfect world, between the theoretically desirable and the practically attainable.

Claggart is unrelieved evil, and is destroyed. For, though the world contains much evil, the good principle strives against it (A. C. Bradley once made this point about *King Lear*[7]) and often succeeds in expelling embodiments of unmitigated evil, like Claggart. But just as that evil ship, the *Pequod*, the skyhawk's wing being nailed to the mast, "would not sink to hell till she had dragged a living part of heaven along with her," so Claggart (though not dragging Billy to *Hell*, unless perchance to *harry* it) brought to an end the earthly life of Billy Budd.

Do the good and evil forces, then, merely cancel each other out? No, there is a residue of good. There is the memory of Billy. The sailors revered Billy's memory. To them, a chip of the spar from which he was hanged "was as a piece of the Cross." Even Captain Vere reverenced the memory of Billy, the Captain most of all. On his deathbed, he was heard to murmur, "Billy Budd, Billy Budd." It was as if, Billy being a type of the Christ, faith in Billy and his atoning death were the power of God unto salvation to everyone that believeth.

Ahab's last words before he was jerked out of his boat by the harpoon rope were words of defiance. "From hell's heart I stab at thee," he yelled at the White Whale, "for hate's sake I spit my last breath at thee." Forty years later, Melville wrote a story with a very different kind of ending. Just as Christ answered "never a word" to the accusations made against him before Pilate, so Billy could say nothing against Claggart's charges when brought before Captain Vere. And just as Christ blessed his enemies ("Father, forgive them, for they know not what they do"), so Billy blessed Captain Vere.

Some have regarded *Billy Budd* as Melville's own personal testament of acceptance, and have reasoned that, as *Moby Dick* reflects the rebellion of Melville's youth, *Billy Budd* shows the reconcilement of his old age. This view is open to the objection that it identifies rather too closely the author with his characters, thereby reducing the work to mere autobiography. It is well not to confuse the critical question with the biographical question. At the same time, both Ahab and Billy are portrayed sympathetically, and it is reasonable to suppose that each character, in his respective period, reflects something of the mood of his creator. *Billy Budd* is certainly a brilliant and moving statement of the ultimate Christian wisdom of resignation to God's overruling Providence, and it is pleasant, as well as reasonable, to think that Melville in his last years felt the truth of this view. Perhaps he could not have written a book like *Billy Budd* without feeling it.

IV

Hawthorne and Melville were not satisfied with the prevailing Romanticism of their century in America, which inflated the individual and produced an extravagant individualism. Hawthorne's wonderful stories illustrated the perils of "self-trust," and *The Scarlet Letter* showed the hard road to redemption. Melville showed in *Moby Dick* the catastrophic end of Devil-inspired Ahab, and in *Billy Budd* the "victory" (through "defeat") of the Christlike Billy. Hawthorne and Melville take the Christian view that human life is a battleground. For man embodies both good and evil. God and the Devil are active in the world, and man's spiritual victories are won with God's help, and in Hell's despite.

Man is a wayward creature, but his state, unless by his own perverse willfulness, is never beyond the reach of God's redeeming grace. This is the essence of the human condition, and the essence of the Christian hope. And this is the meaning of the dramatizations of human experience by these two greatest of American writers.

NOTES: Chapter 9

1. *Vide* T. E. Hulme, *Speculations,* Herbert Read, ed. (London: Kegan Paul, Trench, Trubner & Co., Ltd., 1936), chap. III ("Romanticism and Classicism").
2. In *The Literary World* for August 17 and 24. This essay is reprinted in *Selections from Melville,* Willard Thorp, ed. (New York: American Book Company, 1938).

3. Quoted in Randall Stewart, *Nathaniel Hawthorne: A Biography* (New Haven: Yale University Press, 1948), p. 108.
4. *The American Notebooks by Nathaniel Hawthorne*, Randall Stewart, ed. (New Haven: Yale University Press, 1932), p. 220.
5. Willard Thorp, *op. cit.*, p. 391.
6. *The English Notebooks by Nathaniel Hawthorne*, Randall Stewart, ed. (New York: Modern Language Association of America, 1941), pp. 432–433.
7. A. C. Bradley, *Shakespearean Tragedy* (New York: Meridian Books, 1955; first edition: 1904), "Lecture I."

Freud and the Domestication of Tragedy

IN THE CLASSICAL TRADITION, tragedy is a vision of greatness in a man caught up in a contention for his destiny. The tragic hero (Oedipus, Hamlet, Captain Ahab) is touched with glory in his unequal struggle with fate. He achieves a certain grandeur and distinction from his courage to risk and to accept his doom. His death does not efface his dignity. Indeed, the tragic ruin becomes an uplifting and cathartic experience to all who look upon it with discerning eyes.

Tragedy springs from man's determination to express *himself*, regardless of consequence. It shows us the noble end of a man who dares to defy high heaven in a secret cause. The tragic hero becomes an extraordinary individual, standing out above the mass, affording the sensitive observer with a new perspective on the drama of existence. Tragedy, thus construed, becomes a power to help us "bear the burden of life, to sustain its battle."

The modern climate of tragedy is, of course, noticeably different from all this. Our representative dramatists (O'Neill, Anderson, Miller) and novelists (Lawrence, Hemingway, Faulkner) have accustomed us to see the human quandary in less exalted terms. With them, we take for granted the ambiguity of all human action, and especially action with any pretense to conventional virtue. We have come to expect man's doom at his own hands and to regard it as his own affair. To be sure, we are acutely aware of the suffering, the estrangement, the untowardness of life. And yet it seems all so familiar, commonplace, domesticated. When, in the heartbreaking "Requiem" of Arthur Miller's *Death of a Salesman*, Biff Loman says of his dead father Willy, "He had the wrong dreams . . . . He never knew who he was," it sounds now almost trite.

Now the question may be raised as to whether this *is* tragedy, in any proper sense. As long ago as 1929, Joseph Wood Krutch argued in his famous book, *The Modern Temper*, that modern man's disenchantment with himself and that the modern artist's misdoubt of human greatness had diminished the tragic element in literature and had flattened out the dimensions of the human struggle. There are others also who hold that the portrayal of "life with the lid off" does not of itself evoke the tragic vision. Man in the toils of his own nature, in the grim tides of flux and extinction, exposed to anxiety, suffering, and death, is not yet a tragic figure. "There is no tragedy without transcendence."[1]

We are not here called upon, however, to debate the question as to whether or not domesticated tragedy *is* authentic tragedy.[2] It is enough for our purposes simply to recognize the difference between the new atmosphere and the old. Then, if we ask how this difference has come about, one part of the answer leaps to mind as obvious: it is the influence of Sigmund Freud and the psychoanalytic view of human behavior. In the past half-century the basic Freudian motifs have become pervasive in modern literature, art, and social science. We need only to set down a list of them to see that this is so: the unconscious as the wellspring of motivation, the primacy of sex among the instincts, the critical importance of child-parent relations (the Oedipal situation), the governance of life by the pleasure-principle, the irrepressible conflict between man's primitive nature and human culture, the import of dreams and symbols as outcroppings of the unconscious, religion as wishful thinking, freedom as self-knowledge rather than choice, transience and death as life's final verities, science as its only hope. Freud invented none of these notions; he insisted, for example, that the *poets* "discovered" the unconscious. But he put them all together in a distinctive pattern, and he became the great explorer of this dark underworld of the human spirit. There is scarcely an artist of stature in our time who has not at least consulted the Freudian map as a guide to the human interior. And Lionel Trilling has observed that "if we want the sense of the human mystery, of tragedy truly conceived in the great terms of free will, necessity and hope, surely we do far better to seek it directly in Freud himself than in these three literary men [O'Neill, Dos Passos, Wolfe]."[3]

But we must be prepared for a lowered plane of tragic action. For, on Freud's construction of the human problem, it is only an illusion to project the conflict of man at the limits of his being against some cosmic screen. The human quandary is wholly immanent, set inside man himself. If the human spirit is broken or misshapen in its struggle for self-realization, there is no proper appeal to the gods or to fate. Tragedy is the miscarriage of our own resident forces: it is a purely domestic affair, shared by all men. Heroic or craven, "normal" or neurotic, we are all involved—one way or another—in the suffering, privation, transience, and death which make up the human lot.

Freud's influence in the arts was only a by-product of what he regarded as his proper business. His own self-image was that of a scientist—the topographer of the unconscious, the creator of psychoanalysis. At the age of seventy, he declared: "My life has been aimed at one goal only: to infer or to guess how the mental apparatus is constructed and what forces interplay and counteract in it."[4] And he never doubted the epoch-making character of his work, that it placed him amongst those great reflective geniuses like Goethe, Kant, Voltaire, and Nietzsche, whom he so much admired. He once compared himself to Columbus, and added:

> Great discoverers are not necessarily great minds (*grosse Geister*). Who changed the world more than Columbus? And what was he? An adventurer. He had character, it is true, but he was not a great mind.[5]

Freud saw himself, in other words, as a scientific *conquistador*.

It was this stubborn, adventurous spirit which sustained him through the long years of obscurity and the barren harvest of his early neurological work. It drove him beyond the first frontier of psychoanalysis which he and Breuer discovered in their *Studies in Hysteria* (1895). It led him to his most fundamental discoveries: the mechanism of repression and the efficacy of abreaction (free association and dream-interpretation) as a mode of access to the unconscious. It was this same undaunted self-correcting spirit that prompted him to revise his own first theories of sexuality, and to launch into a *self-analysis*, the most momentous undertaking of his career.[6] And all of this, to Freud, was a *scientific* enterprise—although, with his conception of science, he took for granted its wide impact on life in general.

But there was another Freud, a tragic hero with a secret cause, an Oedipean figure ready to risk his doom in the interest of self-knowledge. As a young student at the University of Vienna, he once had a vivid daydream of seeing his own bust among the others of famous professors there in the great arcaded court. It bore a revealing inscription—a line from the closing chorus of *Oedipus Rex:* "He who solved the famous riddle [of the Sphinx] and was a mighty man."[7] There was more to this than daydreaming, however; for there was a strong identification in Freud with Oedipus, the man who *had* to know the dangerous truth about *himself* ("I must. I cannot leave the truth unknown.")!

In Freud's *Letters to Fliess* (1887–1902), we see the emerging self-portrait of the tragic hero—burning with ambition, sure of the rightness of his cause, resentful of slights and rejections, discouraged but indomitable, confident of posterity's verdict. On even wider evidence, Ernest Jones's monumental biography confirms this image. In his account of the anxieties and distresses which beset Freud in the crucial years, Dr. Jones offers his own comment:

> It was as if he divined all along that the path he was treading would sooner or later lead to terrible secrets, the revealing of which he dreaded, but on which he was nevertheless as determined as Oedipus himself.[8]

Even after success and fame had come, this image still dominated Freud's memory:

> When I look back upon those lonely years [1890–1901] from the confusion and harassment of the present [1914] it seems to me to have been a beautiful heroic era.[9]

In his old age, Freud also came to identify himself in some degree with Moses, who had risked *his* doom on behalf of oppressed humanity.[10]

But whether scientist or tragic hero—or blend of both— Freud's chief significance for the modern world lies in his analysis of the human quandary. The gist of this quandary, in Freud's own italics, is that *"the ego is not master in its own house."*[11] Every man lives in basic, inescapable conflict *within* himself. Human society, at best, is a compromise between man's desire for pleasure and his need of others. The most primitive and perduring level of human impulse (the *id*) is purely appetitive, sheerly irrational, starkly amoral.[12] "The power of the id expresses the true purpose of the individual organism's life. This consists in the satisfaction of its innate [i.e., biological] needs."[13] Over against the amoral id stands the hypermoral *superego*, or ego-ideal. This represents the interiorized repressive power of society (especially one's parents), which cannot tolerate the id's unchecked expression.[14] In between these two arbitrary and irrational forces stands the *ego*, the level of adaptive intelligence and self-control. "The ego tries to mediate between the world and the id, to make the id comply with the world's demands . . ., to accommodate the world to the id's desires."[15]

Freud never meant, of course, for this trichotomy of the unconscious to be taken literally; it was, for him, an illuminating myth (in the Platonic sense of "a likely tale"). But his clinical evidence convinced him that man's turmoil springs from dynamic forces within his own mind. The conflict with culture reaches into the depths of human nature. The pleasure-principle "draws up the programme of life's purpose"[16]—and we have no other option. But this program brings us into tension with our human environment. From this strife come the psychological casualties that we know all too well. Freud comments dryly that "the intention that man should be 'happy' [i.e., success for the pleasure-principle] is not included in the scheme of 'creation.' "[17] "Men become neurotic because they cannot tolerate the degree of privation that society imposes on them."[18] Yet the "state of nature" is unendurable; men cannot be "happy" just by escaping social constraint. Nature has no place in itself for man as a unique, self-conscious organism: "It mocks at human control and buries man and all his works."[19] Men choose the curbs of culture, then, to defend themselves against nature—and to afford themselves compensatory values. This is a hard choice, for neither option is really satisfactory. We can never do better than the lesser of two "evils."

The deepest and most powerful "instinctual wishes" in us all are incest, cannibalism, and murder. Since these are inadmissible in society, they are universally repressed. Indeed, civilization consists very largely in maintaining their repression, in providing sublimations and substitutes, and in persuading men to endure the compromises involved.[20] But repression does not eliminate the impulse: the enmity between the individual and culture is held in uneasy equilibrium rather than overcome.[21] "We spring from an endless ancestry of murderers, with whom the lust for killing was in the blood, as it possibly is to this day with ourselves."[22] "*Homo homini lupus*, who has the courage to dispute it in the face of all the evidence in his own life and in history?"[23]

From time to time, in individuals and in groups, the level of social control falters, the veneer of civilization cracks, and we see before our eyes—in mob-action, mass-hysteria, totalitarian violence, and war—the seething, heartless cauldron *within us all*. Small wonder, then, that an artist with this perspective on man finds it natural to fix on life's ambivalence as the principle of his aesthetic projection.

Contrary to some of his popularizers and critics, Freud never advocated the uninhibited expression of human impulse. Although he thought it impossible "for the claims of the sexual instinct to be reconciled with the demands of culture,"[24] he steadfastly maintained the claims of culture, rejecting only authoritarian force and hypocrisy. Culture is much too valuable to be abandoned. Even if its best goods are obtained at the price of privation, they are worth it—for any other alternative is far worse."[25] Moreover, if given a chance, the ego can fashion intelligent life patterns which reduce tension and anxiety to tolerable levels, and which supply significant meaning and dignity to a man's life. But we must know what is going on inside ourselves and others—and we must not expect too much from creatures such as ourselves.

Freud knew that some will not readily

> abandon our belief that in man there dwells an impulse toward perfection which has brought him to his present heights of intellectual prowess and ethical sublimation and from which it might be expected that his development into superman will be ensured.[26]

But this is only "a pleasing illusion." The best controls falter. Our instincts, which never cease to strive for their own goals, have their way in the end. But their final triumph is our final end, the return to the inanimate from whence we sprang.

The deepest need of man is love, and the instinct which corresponds to this need is the most powerful and persistent drive in human nature. Freud refused to separate love, in any spiritual sense, from sex in its ordinary sense. But he did widen the notion of sex to include an immense repertory of acts and experiences which afford erotic pleasure. His interest in doing so was to be able to differentiate *mature* love from its inferior forms and to supply a norm of healthy love which could guide the course of therapy. Thus, he could trace all manner of ills and misery to immature or unhealthy love—and he established Eros as one of the two polar instincts which govern life.

But Freud felt driven beyond the pleasure-principle, to posit an antithesis to Eros. The basic aim of the organism is twofold: to enjoy—and to die! There is "*a tendency innate in living organic matter impelling it towards the reinstatement of an earlier condition.*"[27] "*The goal of all life is death, for the inanimate was there before the animate.*"[28] It is interesting to observe that this Thanatos-instinct of Freud's has been the least readily accepted of all his notions, among the psychotherapists.[29] We will not tarry here to argue its scientific rigor or its place in a system of depth-psychology. Our interest is in Freud's tragic vision—and it cannot be denied that the Thanatos-instinct belongs *there!* For man's lot is that he must live in this tension between instinct and social control —and, that he must die, thus concluding a transient episode in nature.

But in neither life nor death is man's struggle with any order *beyond* or *over against* nature. There can be no serious question about God or his design for human living. The human drama is played out on an interior stage, with society for its theater. When we fall into wishing for outside help against our helplessness, we fall into illusion. This is the essence of *religion,* "a longing for the strong father and the friendly gods."[30] The aims of religious wishful-thinking are threefold: to exorcise the terrors of nature, to reconcile us to the cruelties of our fate, and to make amends for our sufferings and privations. But there is no warrant for these wishes, in theory or in fact.[31] Religion, says Freud, is a universal obsessional neurosis of humanity. It originates in the Oedipus complex. Moreover, just as most children grow out of their childishness, so mankind can be expected to outgrow religion and be the more mature and rational for having done so.[32]

A man who knows the radical ambiguity of his life will learn "to confess his utter helplessness and his insignificant part in the working of the universe. He will confess that he is no longer the center of creation [i.e., his infantile delusion], no longer the object of the tender care of a benevolent providence."[33]

In short, man is on his own. He must learn to live in an inhospitable world with what intelligence he can muster, with an earnest faith in science and in his own untrammeled dignity. And at this point it is clear that Freud tends himself to provide an example of wishful-thinking (i.e., of "religion"), for he supposes that men of reason and of such a faith as his "will probably attain to a state of things in which life will be tolerable for all."[34]

Freud was conscious of having wrought a revolution in man's understanding of himself. From time immemorial, men had tended to think of themselves as the center of creation, the principal concern of Providence. And he calls this attitude "the general narcissism, the self-love of humanity."[35] But in modern times it has been thrice severely wounded. The first was the Copernican revolution which reduced man's place in the *cosmos*. The second was the Darwinian revolution, which domesticated man in the *animal kingdom*. The third revolution is the Freudian, a sharp *"psychological* blow to men's narcissism."[36] And all this is tragic news to the hero who "feels himself to be supreme in his own soul."[37]

The result is the domestication of tragedy within the human self—with psychoanalysis to supply the map of the battlefield. Man's tragic plight flows from this undeclinable contest —a contention never fully reconciled and, in the nature of the case, interminable.[38]

Space forbids illustration of the ways in which modern literature and art have appropriated these Freudian perspectives.[39] Every reader will have already thought of countless instances—and will have recognized some of the new dimensions of artistic creativity which they have reinforced: interior dialogue, dream sequences and free association, Oedipal conflicts and the perversion of love, sexual symbols masked and proliferated, hypocrisy exposed and pretensions deflated, the fumbling quest for self-knowledge, the sad spectacle of brave starts and sorry endings. The modern hero, as seen in the literature of both drama and fiction, is a man in the grip of dark and murky powers which well up from within, and he often proves himself to be capable of horrors hitherto ascribed to demonry and witchcraft. Here is man the murderer, the cannibal, the lecher at heart; man the incorrigible dreamer, whose dreams bespeak the truth in grotesque forms. The Freudian account of the raw stuff of human nature has become an aesthetic commonplace. And so has death. The scientists may have their doubts about the Thanatos-instinct. The artists have none.

There is, of course, another side to Freud, a positive and optimistic side, which has not deeply touched the modern artist. For, though fiercely scornful of "positive thinking" and all cheap reassurances for the anxious, his whole genius was dedicated to the amelioration of the human condition. He held it a worthy cause to do what he could to make life tolerable! His gospel was summed up in his famous text: "Where id was, there let ego be."

Indeed, a principal working assumption of modern psychotherapy is that behavior which appears irrational and bizarre is never wholly so. The disordered mind has good "reasons" for its disarray. It is the business of analysis to make sense out of apparent nonsense and to bolster the ego in its control and direction of life.[40]

> The voice of the intellect is a soft one, but it does not rest until it has gained a bearing. Ultimately, after endlessly repeated rebuffs, it succeeds. This is one of the few points in which one may be optimistic about the future of mankind, but in itself it signifies not a little.[41]

In his own life and career, Freud was on the side of the moralists—although he shunned any authoritarian basis for morality.[42] He counted himself in the great tradition of the European humanists and the Enlightenment philosophers— although he took a dim view of their utopian enthusiasm about man's prospects on earth. And when it came to science, he was a true believer, for he assumed that men can hope for knowledge or wisdom from *no other source*. Despite the disconcerting truth about man which he had discovered, Freud's aim was to put this truth to humane service. He might even have concurred—in spite of the professional acrimony between them—in Karl Jaspers' "vision of a great and noble life: to endure ambiguity in the movement of truth and to make light shine through it; to stand fast in uncertainty; to prove capable of unlimited love and hope."[43] And save for "unlimited love and hope"—for he was a man of harsh prejudices and many a brusque dogmatism—Freud was himself something of an exemplar of this ideal.

He has taught us to peer into the human abyss with seeing eyes—and has taught us also that it is a *human* abyss. Having learned this lesson, the literary artist can lay before us, in myriad forms, the human quandary of estrangement and ambiguity, the primacy of vitality over reason, the tissue of illusions by which we deceive and hoodwink ourselves. And his characters will evoke in us a sense of candor and deep unease, of pity and disgust, of fortitude and anxiety. But grandeur and glory seem generally to be beyond him, save in curiously devaluated forms. For the climate of domesticated tragedy turns man's vision inward, exposes the crack in our being, points us to the pathos of transience and death. But it *cannot* set man over against the Eternal—for this way lies illusion.

No small part of Freud's influence has been due to the aegis of science affixed to his views. There is, of course, no denying that they still carry a considerable weight of scientific authority. But, as with all scientific enterprises, the Freudian psychology has been greatly altered from the original model and will continue to undergo further correction and change. The number of "orthodox" Freudians at the present time is

quite small in comparison to other psychiatrists and psychotherapists who share the Freudian heritage but who have
struck out in new directions.[44]

But science and wisdom are not identical and, especially in
Freud's case, there is good ground for differentiating his "science" from his "wisdom" and preferring the former to the
latter. For Freud grew up in an atmosphere of dogmatic ma-
terialism.[45] And, although he insisted that psychoanalysis de-
pended on no philosophy whatever for its world-picture, the
fact remains that he and his followers (with J. J. Putnam and
Pfister the only exceptions) were thoroughly committed to
reductive naturalism as a philosophy and to "Science" as a
personal faith.[46]

Moreover, in Freud's "wisdom" there are patent flaws,
which are not derivatives of his scientific method—his unin-
spected prejudice against all serious and high religion, his own
unscientific gullibility at many points, his biased views on
political and social questions, his own death-haunted life.[47]
These suggest that the Freudian "wisdom" was never as con-
sequential as his "metapsychology." Whence it follows that
the Freudian wisdom may be appraised by the canons of philosophy, ethics, and religion—without appeal to the authority
of his scientific genius. In such an appraisal, it would turn out
that some of the alternatives which Freud rejected out of hand
still deserve to be seriously considered.

There is, of course, no way back to a *pre*-Freudian conception of human motivation. Any view of man that assumes that
he is primarily a rational being, crowned with sweetness and
light, is bound to seem absurd to all but the worst senti-
mentalists. Modern psychology and art, morality and religion,
must all take into account this new perspective upon the
depths and demonry of human nature. Freud has, in Hebbel's

phrase, "troubled the sleep of the world"—and we shall not sleep again without dreaming Freudian dreams.

But it is equally certain that Freud's answers no longer seem as clear or profound as his questions. There are other wisdoms fully as realistic as Freud's about the human quandary, with an equal vision of the depths to which man sinks and the heights to which he is raised. We may see this in his own Jewish tradition, for example, which Freud never troubled really to comprehend. There are wisdoms which take full account of the ambiguity and estrangement of existence but which match this dark knowledge with a redemptive vision of the Encompassing Mystery, "in knowledge of whom standeth our eternal life." And this is most clearly apparent in the Christian message—which Freud never troubled to submit to any serious inspection.[48]

The domestication of tragedy, then, has its uses, but the "ceiling" of its vision is too low. Man's destiny *is* wrought out in the depths of his inner being—but the outreach of his being meets the Infinite, the really Real "in whom we live and move and have our being." Men may not name the Real aright, and they may not trust in God for their salvation. Yet, for all that, our lives *are* shaped by power and love beyond our managing or merit: our plight *is* matched by a possibility given us from beyond ourselves. The round of human misery and shipwreck are tragic primarily because they are the signs of estrangement from our true life—a life made possible for us by God's victory in and over tragedy.

So tragedy, then, is *not* enough. The "bare truth" about ourselves is not the whole truth about our destiny. The faith of high religion must illuminate our lot before the grandeur and misery of man can be seen in their true proportions—where tragedy is crowned with glory and redeemed by grace.

NOTES: Chapter 10

1. Karl Jaspers, *Tragedy Is Not Enough*, trans. by H. A. T. Reiche, H. T. Moore, and K. W. Deutsch (Boston: The Beacon Press, 1952), p. 41.
2. For a vigorous argument in behalf of the affirmative, *vide* Mark Harris, *The Case for Tragedy* (New York: G. P. Putnam's Sons, 1932).
3. Lionel Trilling, *The Liberal Imagination* (New York: The Viking Press, 1950), p. 295.
4. Quoted in Ernest Jones, *The Life and Work of Sigmund Freud*, Vol. I (New York: Basic Books, 1953), p. 45.
5. Quoted in Ernest Jones, *op. cit.*, Vol. II, p. 415. *Vide* also the self-characterization in Freud's early *Secret Record* which Jones quotes in his first volume, p. 18.
6. *Vide* Jones, *op. cit.*, Vol. I, pp. 319-324.
7. Cf. Jones, *op. cit.*, Vol. II, pp. 11–12, for an account of how this dream finally came true!
8. Jones, *op. cit.*, Vol. I, p. 307.
9. Jones, *op. cit.*, Vol. II, p. 6.
10. *Ibid.*, p. 33.
11. Sigmund Freud, *Collected Papers*, Ernest Jones, ed. (London: Hogarth Press and the Institute of Psycho-analysis, 1950), Vol. IV, xx, p. 355.
12. For a summary account of "The Psychical Apparatus," *vide* Freud, *An Outline of Psychoanalysis* (New York: W. W. Norton & Company, 1949), pp. 13–24.
13. *Ibid.*, p. 19.
14. *The Ego and the Id* (London: Hogarth Press and the Institute of Psycho-analysis, 1927), pp. 44–53.
15. *Ibid.*, p. 83; cf. *An Outline of Psychoanalysis*, p. 62.
16. *Civilization and Its Discontents* (London: Hogarth Press and the Institute of Psycho-analysis, 1930), p. 27.
17. *Ibid.*
18. *Ibid.*, p. 46.
19. *The Future of an Illusion* (London: Hogarth Press and the Institute of Psycho-analysis, 1928), p. 26.
20. *Ibid.*, p. 17.
21. *Ibid.*, p. 9.
22. *Collected Papers*, Vol. IV, xvii, p. 312; *vide* also p. 308 and p. 316.
23. *Civilization and Its Discontents*, p. 85.

24. *Collected Papers*, Vol. IV, xii, pp. 215–216.

25. *Beyond the Pleasure-Principle* (London: Hogarth Press and the Institute of Psycho-analysis, 1922), p. 52; cf. *An Outline of Psycho-analysis*, p. 85.

26. *Beyond the Pleasure-Principle*, p. 52.

27. *Ibid.*, p. 44; italics in the original.

28. *Ibid.*, p. 47; italics in the original.

29. Cf. Clara M. Thompson, *Psychoanalysis, Evolution and Development: A Review of Theory and Therapy* (New York: Hermitage Press, 1950), pp. 50 ff.

30. *The Future of an Illusion*, p. 30.

31. *Ibid.*, p. 30 and p. 32.

32. *Ibid.*, p. 76.

33. *Ibid.*, pp. 94–95. This attitude, which Freud commends, he calls "*irreligion* in the truest sense of the word" (*Ibid.*, p. 57).

34. *Ibid.*, p. 86.

35. *Collected Papers*, Vol. IV, xx, p. 350.

36. *Collected Papers*, Vol. V, xiv, p. 173.

37. *Collected Papers*, Vol. IV, xx, p. 352.

38. *Vide* one of Freud's last essays, "Analysis Terminable or Interminable?" in *Collected Papers*, Vol. V, xxx, pp. 316–357.

39. *Vide* Frederick J. Hoffman, *Freudianism and the Literary Mind* (Baton Rouge: Louisiana State University Press, 1945).

40. *Vide* Jones, *op. cit.*, Vol. I, p. 282.

41. *The Future of an Illusion*, p. 93.

42. *Vide* Jones, *op. cit.*, Vol. I, p. 271.

43. Jaspers, *op. cit.*, p. 105.

44. *Vide* Clara M. Thompson, *op. cit.*; Patrick Mullahy, *Oedipus: Myth and Complex, A Review of Psychoanalytic Theory* (New York: Hermitage Press, 1948); Frieda Fromm-Reichmann, *Principles of Intensive Psychotherapy* (Chicago: University of Chicago Press, 1950); Harry Stack Sullivan, *Conceptions of Modern Psychiatry* (New York: William Alanson White Psychiatric Foundation, 1947); Franz Alexander and Helen Ross, eds., *Dynamic Psychiatry* (Chicago: University of Chicago Press, 1952).

45. *Vide* Jones, *op. cit.*, Vol. I, pp. 41–45.

46. *Vide ibid.*, pp. 19–20; also p. 40.

47. For Freud's preoccupation with death, *vide* Jones, *ibid.*, Vol. I, p. 16; Vol. II, pp. 21, 184, 188, 362, 392; *vide* also "Thoughts on War and Death" in *Collected Papers*, Vol. IV, xvii, pp. 288–317. *Vide* also the *Letters to Fliess* and Jones, *passim*: the references are too numerous to list here.

48. *Vide* my *Psychotherapy and the Christian Message* (New York: Harper & Brothers, 1954) for an appraisal of Freud in the light of Christian faith and an attempt to distinguish his scientific contributions which Christian faith can readily appropriate from his reductive naturalism which faith firmly declines.

Franz Kafka and the
Metaphysics of Alienation

Had one to name the artist who comes nearest to bearing the same kind of relation to our age that Dante, Shakespeare and Goethe bore to theirs, Kafka is the first we would think of.

—W. H. Auden

There is a goal, but no way; what we call the way is only wavering.

—Kafka

Franz kafka, from the very beginning of his life, was chained forever in the place of exile: "It seems to me as if I had not come by myself but had been pushed here as a child and then chained to this spot; the consciousness of my misfortune only gradually dawned on me, my misfortune itself was already complete."[1] Outside of the human world, outside of God's law, he felt condemned to wander forever in the wilderness outside of Canaan. This wandering is identical with being chained in one spot, for every place in the desert is identical with every other place, and they are all equally at an infinite distance from the goal: "Why did I want to quit the world? Because 'he' would not let me live in it, in his world. Though indeed I should not judge the matter so precisely, for I am now a citizen of this other world, whose relationship to the ordinary one is the relationship of the wilderness to cultivated land (I have been forty years wander-

281

ing from Canaan). . . . It is indeed a kind of Wandering in the Wilderness in reverse that I am undergoing."[2]

Doubtless it is Kafka's acute consciousness of his irrevocable alienation, and the incomparably subtle analysis of it presented in his works, that earn him his place as the most representative figure in twentieth-century literature. For our time is, even more than the time of Hölderlin (it is only an extension of his), the time of distress, the time when the link between God and man is broken, the time when God is no more present and is not yet again present, the time when he can only be experienced negatively, as a terrifying absence.

But the full consciousness of his plight only "gradually" dawns on the exiled one, and, besides, "the attraction of the human world is so immense, in an instant it can make one forget everything."[3] "I think," says Kafka, "that I am continually skirting the wilderness and am full of childish hopes . . . that 'perhaps I shall keep in Canaan after all.' "[4] Accordingly, the first act in the Kafkan drama is a frantic attempt to keep within the ordinary human world. At all costs he must believe that he is a perfectly normal person, that he is linked by a thousand ties to the tightly knit circle of the human community, that he has a justified and meaningful existence there, and that, above all, the established human world forms for him an avenue of approach to God. For is not the true way to God through the traditional institutions of the community? And if one does not belong to God, if one is not within the law, one does not exist, one is, literally, nothing: "The word 'sein' signifies in German both things: to be and to belong to Him."[5]

It is quite clear what Kafka meant by belonging to the human world. It meant, perhaps most of all in Kafka's Jewish tradition, being a good son, and, later, having a wife and children. Thus he writes in his journal: "The Talmud too says:

A man without a woman is no person."[6] And he expresses
again and again his horror of the bachelor's "ill-luck" and his
painful longing for a wife and children. For children are a
sign that one is in the right with God, that one has a meaningful part in history, in the temporal fulfillment of God's law on
earth.

But belonging to the human world also meant for Kafka
having a job and a profession. Only these would give one the
strength to act decisively: "For without a center, without a
profession, a love, a family, an income; i.e., without holding
one's own against the world in the big things . . . one cannot
protect oneself from losses that momentarily destroy one."[7]
Thus the hero of *Amerika*, the shy and diffident Karl Rossmann,
becomes aggressive and competent when he thinks he is established in the community, even at its lowest level: "He marched
up to the counter and rapped on it with his knuckles until
someone came; . . . he shouted across high walls of human
beings; he went up to people without hesitation. . . . He did
all this not out of arrogance, nor from any lack of respect
for difficulties, but because he felt himself in a secure position
which gave him certain rights."[8] To possess all these things—
a family, a job, and a secured place in the general human
family—would be, in other words, to enjoy the sense of well-
being which K. in *The Castle* momentarily (and falsely) experiences. And it would be to feel, as K. does, that his position allows him an avenue of approach to the divine power,
here present in Klamm, the Castle official: "Yet I have already
a home, a position and real work to do, I have a promised wife
who takes her share of my professional duties when I have
other business, I'm going to marry her and become a member
of the community, and besides my official connection I have
also a personal connection with Klamm, although as yet I
haven't been able to make use of it. That's surely quite a lot."[9]

So, then, a number of Kafka's stories, especially the early ones, can be interpreted as continuing that tradition which goes back through Dickens (whom he consciously imitated in *Amerika*) to the eighteenth-century novel. That is, they are stories about people who begin in estrangement from the human community, and who attempt through a series of adventures to find a stable place in society, and through that a meaningful identity. Kafka's most elaborate version of this traditional theme is *Amerika:* no other work expresses more clearly the opposition between the terrible freedom of having no connection with the human world and the longed-for security of a permanent place in the social order. But this same opposition between freedom and status is also central in other stories—in, for example, "A Report to an Academy," the disquieting story of an ape who, after being captured, escapes from his cage by finding "a special way" out, "the way of humanity": "With an effort which up till now has never been repeated," says the ape, "I managed to reach the cultural level of an average European. . . . There is an excellent idiom: to fight one's way through the thick of things: that is what I have done, I have fought through the thick of things. There was nothing else for me to do, provided always that freedom was not to be my choice."[10]

It is a choice, then, between "dreadful freedom" outside the human world and meaningful existence within it. But in Kafka's later writings there is a strange transformation of the value of belonging to the human world. Now, instead of being identified with obedience to God's law, it is opposed to it. The choice now seems to be between fulfilling God's law in isolation and evading its imperatives through self-immersion in the human collective. Thus, in a bitterly ironic journal note of 1917, Kafka asserts that his real aim is not to obey God but to escape into the human world where he can sin with impunity: "If I closely examine what is my ultimate aim, it turns out that I am not really striving to be good and to fulfill the demands of a Supreme Judgment, but rather very much the contrary: I strive to know the whole human and animal community, to recognize their basic predilections, desires, moral ideals, to reduce these to simple rules and as quickly as possible to trim my behavior to these rules in order that I may find favor in the whole world's eyes; and, indeed (this is the inconsistency), so much favor that in the end I could openly perpetrate the iniquities within me without alienating the universal love in which I am held—the only sinner who won't be roasted."[11]

What has happened to bring about this reversal? The answer is that Kafka has come to recognize that everybody, without exception, is outside the law. The entire human community is in the desert, attempting to build an impious tower of Babel to scale heaven, but really cutting itself off more and more from God and creating a self-enclosed structure of purely human values and institutions. Kafka's judgment of our urban, technological, industrial, bureaucratic world is unequivocal. Once, long ago, as Kafka says in one of his very last stories, the Word was close to man, and interpenetrated his world, but now it has withdrawn altogether, and all mankind is lost: "Even in those days wonders did not openly walk the streets for any one to seize; but all the same dogs [for "dogs" we are, of course, to understand: "men"]—I cannot put it in any other way—had not yet become so doggish as to-day, the edifice of dogdom was still loosely put together, the true Word could still have intervened, planning or replanning the structure, changing it at will, transforming it into its opposite; the Word was there, was very near at least, on the tip of everybody's tongue, any one might have hit upon it. And what has become of it to-day? To-day one may pluck out one's very heart and not find it."[12] To live within the human community is no longer to live in a world which is transparent to God, but is to "hasten in almost guiltless silence towards death in a world *darkened by others.*"[13] In other words, the true reason Kafka is impelled to reject the way to God that lies through the human world, through a family or a profession or religious observances, is not, it seems, that he is exiled by that community, but that the community is itself no longer a way to God. One *is* lost, but then one *must* be lost. For the entire human community is lost, though this is not generally known. Each of us has taken a wrong turning, and we wander in endless aberration: "Every person is lost in himself beyond hope of rescue."[14] The only difference in Kafka's case is that he knows he is lost, and this is his chance. The discovery of alienation is, perhaps, the only remaining possibility of salvation. For the spiritual state of Kafka's heroes is not extraordinary. Rather it is the true state of us all, whether we know it or not. It is not only Kafka who wanders farther and farther into the desert, but all of us, together, and yet separated infinitely by our mutual silence: "When our first fathers strayed they had doubtless scarcely any notion that their aberration was to be an endless one, they could still literally see the cross-roads, it seemed an easy matter to turn back whenever they pleased, and if they hesitated to turn back it was merely because they wanted to enjoy a dog's life for a little while longer; it was not yet a genuine dog's life, and already it seemed intoxicatingly beautiful to them . . . and so they strayed farther."[15]

II

The Kafkan man, then, is in exile, and he must *wish* to be in exile, must constantly reaffirm and choose his exile as the only possibility left open to him. Kafka's stories and his personal writings, in spite of the recurrent "attraction of the human world," and in spite of his momentary feelings that the human world is good and that he belongs to it, are, for the most part, a long, patient, and exhaustive analysis of what it means to be outside of everything, even outside of oneself.

To be outside of everything means, first of all, to be unable to reach and touch anything outside of one's own narrow limits: "I am divided from all things by a hollow space,"[16] says Kafka, "I am too far away, am banished."[17] One remains *here*, and everyone and everything else is *out there*, seen coldly across a gap, as a mere phenomenal spectacle. Moreover, one is also separated from the past and from the future. A really meaningful human life, of course, possesses its past and its future, and they eventually form a full circle, a totality of homogeneous existence supporting one in a fullness of being: "We . . . are held in our past and future. . . . Whatever advantage the future has in size, the past compensates for in weight, and at the end the two are indeed no longer distinguishable, earliest youth later becomes distinct, as the future is, and the end of the future is really already experienced in all our sighs, and thus becomes the past. So this circle along whose rim we move almost closes."[18] But the exiled one "has only the moment, the everlasting moment of torment which is followed by no glimpse of a moment of recovery."[19] Kafka's stories and journals are perfect expressions of this double isolation in the moment, isolation not only from all past and future moments, but also from what is seen and experienced in the moment itself. His heroes are, like Kafka himself, passive and cold, incapable of the least motion of human warmth which might extend outwards to embrace the world and other people: "A sad but calm astonishment at my lack of feeling often grips me"[20]; "It is as if I were made of stone";[21] "I have become cold again, and insensible."[22] And the world seen from the point of view of cold, detached passivity is a long succession of disconnected appearances. One "isolated momentary observation"[23] follows another. Each appears suddenly before the field of vision, swells up to fill the whole, and is seen vividly in microscopic detail for a moment: "observations of the moment, mostly only indoors, where certain people suddenly and hugely bubble up before one's eyes."[24] Then, what had absorbed all of one's attention dissolves, disappears, to be forgotten and replaced by something else.

To begin to read one of Kafka's stories is to enter a space where one is always *indoors*, where there are always limits to one's vision. Even if one is in the midst of a trackless desert, one's vision is soon stopped by the indeterminate horizon of sand and sky, or by a thick murk of fog, or by the dazzling brilliance of sunlight itself. But most often one finds oneself in a dreamlike interior, a realm of theatrical hallucination. (Kafka was fascinated by the theater, and many of his own dreams took place in a theater.) There is nothing behind the insubstantial backdrops of these stage sets, solid though they seem—nothing but the discarded bric-a-brac of unused props and ropes, or, as it may be, simply another room just like the first. The world of Kafka's stories is a world without depth, a world of sheer surface, a world of continual movement, in which one is condemned to explore, one after another, indefinitely multiplied chambers which replace one another and which are all the equivalents of one another. The scene is always changing, but it never really changes. It is a universe of pure spectacle. And in such a universe all things are traps which fascinate our attention. The people are as depthless as the walls: we see their gestures and expressions with extraordinary distinctness, but the meaning of these gestures and these glances is precisely that they have no meaning. They are simply there before us. They connect with nothing before or after, and they contain no significance hidden in their depths:

"Miserable observation," says Kafka, "which again is certainly the result of something artificially constructed whose lower end is swinging in emptiness somewhere."[25]

The world of *Amerika*, of *The Trial*, and *The Castle*, then, is a *labyrinth*. In this labyrinth, one moves constantly from place to place without ever getting anywhere, or reaching anything conclusive, or even knowing whether there is a goal to be reached: "The truly terrible paths between freedom and slavery cross each other with no guide to the way ahead and accompanied by an immediate obliterating of the paths already traversed. There are a countless number of such paths, or only one, it cannot be determined, for there is no vantage ground from which to observe. There am I. I cannot leave."[26] Thus, not one of Kafka's longer works is really finished. They could not, on principle, reach their end, since the very nature of the experience they describe is to be endless, or, rather, to be the "eternal recapitulation"[27] of the same experience. These novels, at best, can only jump over an infinite number of intermediate stages, and reach, as in the case of *The Trial*, their inevitable end. But, most often, that end is never reached: "A life like this could last forever and still be nothing but a moment. Moses fails to enter Canaan not because his life is too short but because it is a human life."[28]

In the end, however, Kafka's universe, for the very reason that it is so completely without depth, comes to seem very deep indeed. For the least gesture or glance from another person, the most insignificant detail observed in an inanimate object, precisely because they can be given no comforting human meaning, seem to put us in touch immediately with some unfathomable meaning from beyond the human world. They seem radiant with an ominous significance which transcends their immediate reality. The most we can hope is that this meaning has nothing directly to do with us: "The most appropriate situation for me: To listen to a conversation between two people who are discussing a matter that concerns them closely while I have only a remote interest in it which is in addition completely selfless."[29]

But, alas, such is not the case. The conversation *does* concern me. My guilt is being decided, and the moment of my execution set. All Kafka's stories about persons who wander within the labyrinth of the human world approach closer and closer to the same ending: the death of the hero, which is only the fulfillment of a spiritual death that precedes the beginning of the story. This is the central action of *The Trial:* Joseph K.'s slow recognition that he cannot ignore his trial, that he no longer belongs to the human world, that he is guilty, that his fate is to be executed. To yield oneself to the human world, to leave one's safe enclosure, is to put oneself at the mercy of judges who are infinitely powerful and infinitely merciless, and whether one is "guilty" or "innocent" (that is, whether one knows or does not know that one is guilty), the end is the same: "Rossmann and K., the innocent and the guilty, both executed without distinction in the end, the guilty one with a gentler hand, more pushed aside than struck down."[30]

Only one escape seems to remain: to withdraw altogether from the human world, to surround oneself with impenetrable walls and to live safely in complete isolation within one's own private enclosure: "I'll shut myself off from everyone to the point of insensibility. Make an enemy of everyone, speak to no one."[31] "Two tasks on the threshold of life: To narrow your circle more and more, and constantly to make certain that you have not hidden yourself somewhere outside it."[32]

The quality of life within the pure circle of complete isolation is brilliantly dramatized in the story called "The Burrow." The interior world too, we discover, is a labyrinth, a labyrinth one has made for oneself. But this labyrinth does not even have the multiplicity and changefulness of the exterior one. Each chamber and each passageway is exactly like all the others, and reflects back only the absolute blandness and indeterminacy of one's own inner life. Where there is nothing but oneself, there is nothing. In isolation, there is a rapid exhaustion of one's forces, an evaporation of the self. In a moment, all thoughts, all emotions, all one's powers, are dissipated, and there is nothing left but a complete void. Kafka's diaries are full of descriptions of the absolute inner emptiness resulting from this disastrous withdrawal into one's own center: "My inner emptiness, an emptiness that replaces everything else is not even very great."[33] "Completely indifferent and apathetic. A well gone dry, water at an unattainable depth and no certainty it is there. Nothing, nothing."[34] It is as though one had, deliberately or by inadvertence, stepped off the rim of one's circle into a bottomless abyss: "This circle indeed belongs to us, but belongs to us only so long as we keep to it, if we move to the side just once, in any chance forgetting of self, in some distraction, some fright, some astonishment, some fatigue, we have already lost it into space, until now we had our noses stuck into the tide of the times, now we step back, former swimmers, present walkers, and are lost."[35]

By enclosing oneself in a narrow circle of isolation, one has indeed stepped into a place of complete nullity. This nullity is not death, it is something worse, it is "the eternal torment of dying."[36] Gregor Samsa, for example, in "The Metamorphosis," after his horrible transformation into a cockroach, becomes more and more dry and empty within his carapace of solitude, but he is liberated, finally, by death. Gregor's end, however, like the death at the end of "The Judgment," or the execution at the end of *The Trial*, is as much wish-fulfillment as a possibility in which Kafka really believes. The true plight of Kafka's heroes is to be unable to die, to remain forever, like the hunter Gracchus, hovering between this world and the world of death, to remain in a prolonged emptiness which is neither death nor life: "In a certain sense I am alive too. My death ship lost its way; a wrong turn of the wheel, a moment's absence of mind on the pilot's part. . . . I am forever . . . on the great stair that leads up to [the other world]. On that infinitely wide and spacious stair I clamber about, sometimes up, sometimes down, sometimes on the right, sometimes on the left, always in motion. . . . My ship has no rudder, and it is driven by the wind that blows in the undermost regions of death."[37]

The ultimate fate of Kafka's heroes, then, and of Kafka himself, is to reach a frightening state of being neither alive nor dead, in which one can only live by endlessly falling into the void. The Kafkan man is drawn relentlessly toward a supreme moment, a moment as long as eternity itself, a moment in which he is pure negative consciousness speeding with infinite acceleration toward an incomprehensible transcendent power which he can never reach or escape from, however far or fast he goes: "To die would mean nothing else than to surrender a nothing to the nothing, but that would be impossible to conceive, for how could a person, even only as a nothing, consciously surrender himself to the nothing, and not merely to an empty nothing but rather to a roaring nothing whose nothingness consists only in its incomprehensibility."[38]

III

Again encouragement. Again I catch hold of myself, as one catches hold of a ball in its fall. Tomorrow, today, I'll begin an extensive work. . . .[39]

Now one final possibility remains, and it is literature itself, the rescue of oneself through writing. Writing, it may be, is the one action which, depending on nothing outside the self, and deriving from a voluntary and autonomous exercise of the power to transform things into words, can stop the endless fall into the abyss. The self will seize the self, as one catches hold of a ball in mid-air, and give to itself an indestructible solidity. The crucial importance of Kafka for twentieth-century thought lies not only in his extreme experience of the loss of selfhood, but also in his deep exploration of the tangled relations between writing and salvation. For Kafka, as does the thought of our century in general, pursues to its end the attempt, begun by the Romantics, to find in literature itself a means of salvation. Abandoned to utter dereliction by the collapse of every other hope, Kafka turns to writing as the sole possibility remaining. And it was no light burden he put upon words: it was, indeed, a burden no less heavy than the weight of his entire life and destiny: *"I am more and more unable to think, to observe, to determine the truth of things, to remember, to speak, to share an experience; I am turning to stone, this is the truth. . . .* If I can't take refuge in some work, I am lost."[40] "But I will write in spite of everything, absolutely; it is my struggle for self-preservation."[41] "I am nothing but literature."[42]

Kafka's notion of the process by which literature would bring him salvation was precise and definite: the words would not merely be put down on the paper to exist independently of their creator. They would be a kind of magical incantation which would replace the inner emptiness with solidity and firmness: they would summon "life's splendour" which "forever lies in wait about each of us in all its fulness, but veiled from view, deep down, invisible, far off."[43] "The firmness . . . which the most insignificant writing brings about in me is beyond doubt and wonderful."[44] "If you summon it by the right word, by its right name, it will come. This is the essence of magic, which does not create but summons."[45] "I have now . . . a great yearning to write all my anxiety out of me, write it into the depths of the paper just as it comes out of the depths of me, or write it down in such a way that I could draw what I had written into me completely."[46]

But at first Kafka's relation to writing remains, precisely, a *striving*, a *yearning*. The transformation of his inner life through writing is something he believes in but has not experienced. For, though all his inner forces rushed toward writing, Kafka was, for long months and years, unable to achieve a definitive experience of the power of words. What he lacked was time, for writing is "a task that can never succeed except all at once."[47] His job, his family, all the connections he had with the normal world, left him only the night for writing, and the night was not long enough. Kafka's early diaries are full of laments over his lack of time for writing, and full, too, of fragmentary stories, stories which start off strongly, create their own world in a few powerful sentences, and then suddenly and abruptly stop, like meteors which glow brightly in rarefied air, but are burnt up in a moment by the lower atmosphere and return to darkness. For Kafka cannot remain long enough in the upper air. He must sink back to his quotidian indigence, and leave his story behind to dissipate itself into the inarticulate chaos from which it came. This chaos is within him, and yet painfully separated from him. Only a complete story could bring the two together and give form and expression simultaneously both to the chaos of inner forces and to his consciousness itself: "I really don't have time for a story, time to expand myself in every direction in the world, as I should have to do";[48] "I have too little time to draw out of me all the possibilities of my talent. For that reason it is only disconnected starts that always make an appearance. . . . If I were ever able to write something large and whole, well-shaped from beginning to end, then in the end the story would never be able to detach itself from me and it would be possible for me calmly and with open eyes, as a blood relation of a healthy story, to hear it read, but as it is, every little piece of the story runs around homeless and drives me away from it in the opposite direction."[49]

Far from being able to escape out of his own inner emptiness into the solidity and coherence of a story, Kafka is repulsed by the broken fragments of incomplete ones, and kept outside in the void, hanging on, as it were, with both hands. And, worse yet, within this void, he is conscious of immense unused forces which circle in uncontrollable violence, which permit him no rest or sleep, and, far from holding him together, tear him apart: "Then, already boiling, I went home, I couldn't withstand one of my ideas, disordered, pregnant, disheveled, swollen, amidst my furniture which was rolling about me; overwhelmed by my pains and worries, taking up as much space as possible."[50]

"The tremendous world I have in my head. But how free myself and free it without being torn to pieces."[51] This is indeed the question: burnt up by "the unhappy sense of a consuming fire inside [him] that [is] not allowed to break out,"[52] tormented by "mysterious powers"[53] which have been unleashed within him and are tearing him to pieces, and prevented by external circumstances from directing them to a single continuous work, Kafka is driven toward a state even worse than those times when his mind is a "thoughtless vacuum." Indeed, he is driven, as he often feared, toward madness. In this dangerous condition, he is sustained only by an unproved conviction that this seeming chaos is really a harmony, a harmony which, if it were liberated, would not only fill up all the interior space of his consciousness, but would permit an expansion of that space toward unheard-of limits: "In the end this uproar is only a suppressed, restrained harmony, which, left free, would fill me completely, which would even widen me and yet still fill me."[54] "I have . . . experienced states (not many) . . . in which I completely dwelt in every idea, but also filled every idea, and in which I not only felt myself at my boundary, but at the boundary of the human in general."[55]

It is clear now what form Kafka's stories must take, if they are to be successful. They must be a perfect continuity, sweeping smoothly from beginning to end, with no scission or interstice, and they must be an expression, not of some limited action in the external world, but, precisely, of the *totality* of his inner world. In the words of the story, the emptiness of consciousness and the shapeless storms of unused forces must come together and fuse in the concrete particularity of narrative or image. We can see here why it is incorrect to speak of Kafka's stories as "symbolic," as if their mysterious images, descriptions, and actions *stood for* something other than themselves. They are not symbolic, but perfectly literal embodiments of his inner life. They are the very form his consciousness takes when it has any form at all, when it ceases to be a hollow shell filled with indeterminate energies careening in the void.

Kafka's definitive experience of the power of writing came on the night of September 22, 1912, when he wrote, in a single unbroken flow of inspiration, the short story called "The Judgment." That night he discovered that his literary powers were real, but he also discovered the true extent of those powers. He discovered that an authentic piece of writing would not simply give cohesion and firmness to his own narrow interior space, but would cause that interior space to expand and grow until it filled the entire universe. Or, rather, he discovered that the interior regions of his consciousness could, through the magic of words, become the entire universe turned inside out.

Every person and thing, without exception, everything real or imaginable, could be transformed into words and placed there within himself in an immutable form. Literature was not simply the salvation of his own poor identity; it was also the salvation of the world itself. It was, necessarily, both at once, for so long as any particle or fragment of the world remained unchanged into words, into image, that fragment would remain other than the self and constitute a deadly threat to it. Writing, in other words, he discovered to be " 'an assault on the last earthly frontier,' an assault, moreover, launched from below, from mankind."[56] "The strange, mysterious, perhaps dangerous, perhaps saving comfort that there is in writing: it is a leap out of murderer's row; it is a seeing of what is really taking place. This occurs by a higher type of observation, a higher, not a keener type, and the higher it is, and the less within reach of the 'row,' the more independent it becomes, the more obedient to its own laws of motion, the more incalculable, the more joyful, the more ascendant its course."[57]

Kafka, it seems, has escaped at last, though only by arrogating to himself almost divine powers. If narrowing oneself concentrically to even smaller and smaller dimensions provides no escape from the inexorable power of the world and of God, the other extreme alternative seems to work. By expanding his inner world even further and further outwards until it includes in a new form everything that is, Kafka liberates himself at last from the annihilating pressures which initially surround him. He makes of his nothing, everything.

IV

But what is this "new form"? What are the characteristics of this realm in which Kafka places all his hopes? Slowly, bit by bit, in the form that his writings force themselves to take, and in the recognition of his own inner experiences while writing, Kafka comes to make the terrifying discovery that the space of literature is identical with the place of exile where he first began. At first, seemingly an infinitely complex assembly of integrated parts, like the machine of execution in the story called "In the Penal Colony," the world of words in Kafka undergoes a hideous process of disintegration in which piece after piece, driven by some irresistible internal compulsion, bursts out of its place, and rolls senselessly away, until finally the entire structure is reduced to dispersed and meaningless fragments.[58] This inexorable disaggregation of the literary construct is proof that, far from escaping the conditions of estrangement through writing, Kafka has merely reaffirmed them in exacerbated form. The central tragedy of his spiritual adventure is thus the collapse of the attempt to identify literature and salvation, and his lasting significance as a writer consists in large part in the example that his career provides of a writer who had the courage to explore that collapse to the bitter end.

Kafka learned by experience that writing is not a smooth continuous movement which changes the world altogether and flies off with it to the free upper air. His experiences within the literary space were exactly like those he had had in the desert of exile: an endless wavering which rose up only to fall back again, which never reached and possessed the goal. He found writing, like human life itself, to be an interminably prolonged death: "What will be my fate as a writer is very simple. . . . I waver, continually fly to the summit of the mountain, but then fall back in a moment. Others waver too, but in lower regions, with greater strength; if they are in danger of falling, they are caught up by the kinsman who walks beside them for that very purpose. But I waver on the heights; it is not death, alas, but the eternal torments of dying."[58a]

Kafka recognized in the end that the attempt to reach the goal through writing "is not a task at all, not even an impossible one, it is not even impossibility itself, it is nothing."[59] This task is even worse than impossible, because the space of literature is, *par excellence*, the place of separation. It is the place of separation, because it is the place where everything is transformed into image. To make an image of something makes that thing at once attainable and unattainable. An image makes what it represents simultaneously present and absent. It makes it available *as image*, therefore unavailable. When we reach out to touch it, it changes again, recedes, and hovers there before us just beyond our grasp. By the very fact that something is described, is turned into image, it becomes illusion, and therefore false, separated from the truth. It becomes the mediate symbol of the goal rather than the goal itself. Far from giving immutable truth to things, Kafka, this "man with the too great shadow,"[60] destroys all things he approaches. He destroys them by transforming them into the shadow of themselves, by transposing them from the tangibility and closeness of the physical world into the strange inner world where nothing can ever be possessed: "For all things outside the physical world language can be employed only as a sort of adumbration, but never with even approximate exactitude, since in accordance with the physical world it treats only of possession and its connotations."[61]

The realm of literature, then, delivers Kafka over to an endless sterile vacillation between the sin of *impatience* and the sin of *laziness*.[62] On the one hand, Kafka is driven by impatience, by the desire to reach the goal immediately. But to do this means to commit the fatal mistake of taking the mediate for the immediate, of confusing an image of the goal with the goal itself. No, one is condemned to play out the game to the end, without any premature renunciation of method, going with infinite slowness from one stage of the way to the next: "The road is endless, there is nothing that can be subtracted from it or added to it, and yet everyone insists on applying his own childish measuring yard. 'Yes, you will have to go the length of that measuring yard as well; it will not be forgiven you.' "[63] But, on the other hand, to become absorbed in the stages of the way is laziness, the negligence which ignores the goal for something less. For each stage is only a delusive mirroring of the goal. One must go directly toward the goal without intermediary. But this is impossible. Between these two requirements Kafka and all his heroes waver endlessly. He must continuously reject all immanence for the sake of a transcendence. But what is transcendent remains, by definition, out of reach, and Kafka's experience of immanence is not of possession or closeness, but of distance, lack. Belonging to society, an intimate relation to another person, writing, all these forms of life reduce themselves in the end to the same universal mode of existence, and we recognize at last that Kafka can, by no expedient, whether lawful or unlawful, escape from the realm of errancy to which he has been condemned.

The fullest expression of the movement by which every step toward the goal is a step away from it is, however, Kafka's masterpiece, *The Castle*. This novel is Kafka's fullest expression of his sense of human existence, and, at the same time, of his experience as a writer. The two are here identified as the same eternal wandering this side of the goal. K., the hero of *The Castle*, is the most conscious of all Kafka's heroes. True to the lot he has chosen, K. rejects every place or advantage he wins in the village beneath the Castle: Frieda, his room in the inn, his job in the school; and, when at last he has an interview with a secretary from the Castle, he falls asleep! He rejects all things he attains, because, by the very fact that he reaches them, they all become only images of his goal. K. is driven, always, to go beyond whatever he has, to go beyond even Klamm, who belongs to the Castle: "It was not Klamm's environment in itself that seemed to him worth striving for, but rather that he, K., he only and no one else, should attain to Klamm, and should attain to him not to rest with him, but to go on beyond him, farther yet, into the Castle."[64] One can see clearly that *The Castle*, like Kafka's other novels, was interminable, or could only end, as Max Brod has told us it was meant to end, with the death, by utter exhaustion, of the hero (though it is significant that Kafka never wrote the ending). The rejection of what one has reached for the sake of a goal which can never be reached can be repeated, must be repeated, again and again, forever.

Kafka remains, then, until the end, within an inner space which may expand indefinitely, or contract to nothing, but always remains the place of solitude, at the same distance from the unattainable paradise of possession. His plight is perpetual dying. It is exile in the desert, without the possibility of ever approaching closer to the goal. His fate might be defined as that of the Protestant who, having pushed to its extreme point the rejection of all mediation as idolatry, goes on to reject even the possibility of a Christ as Mediator: for Kafka believed that the coming of the Messiah would always remain an event to be expected in the future, that Christ would always come a day later than any day which might be named. "The Messiah will only come when he is no longer necessary, he will only come a day after his arrival, he won't come on the last day, but on the last day of all."[65]

Kafka could, in other words, never make the leap from tragic vision to Christian faith, or even to the point at which the possibility of Christian faith might be entertained. His closest approach to Christianity is probably to be found in an important chapter of *The Trial,* "In the Cathedral." In this chapter, a priest tells Joseph K. a parable about what is involved in reaching (or, perhaps, in never reaching) heaven, and this parable is the nearest thing to an explanation of his situation that Joseph K. ever receives. Earlier, he had seen on the cathedral wall a picture of Christ being lowered into the tomb, with a knight in attendance—that is, he had seen a representation of the most dreadful moment in the Christian story, the time when Christ, the God-Man, the Mediator, is dead, and the link between the fallen human world and the divine world is broken. This is the time which Hölderlin's poems describe, the hard time, when the gods are no longer present and are not yet again present to man. And this is Kafka's time too. For it is as though not only Joseph K. but all his characters had been condemned to endure permanently the terrible time between the death of Christ and his resurrection. This is the time when, as in the priest's parable to Joseph K., one stands forever at the door which is the beginning of the way to the Law, the promised land, and yet forever put off by the statement that this is indeed one's very own door, but that one may not yet enter it.

One may compare Kafka, then, with Pascal, for whom the mystery of the Incarnation, the joining of the two worlds through the God-Man, alone could provide an escape from the contradictions of the two. Only Christ, the *deus absconditus* made present and manifest, could, for Pascal, provide an avenue from the world of *divertissement* and ambiguity to the higher realm which is the simultaneous affirmation of the yes and the no. But for Kafka, obeying to the end the interdiction against idolatry, against the acceptance of any manifest Mediator, there was no way out of the world of endless wandering and contradiction. For Kafka there was a goal but no way, only endless wavering, and he chose to remain true to the wavering, to his "deeper, uneasier skepticism": with infinite patience, he pushed on, ever farther and farther into the desert with each work, until, paradoxically, his work became the falsehood which testifies to the truth, the wavering that reveals the goal, even though the goal is never reached. For Kafka God remained *"absconditus,"* yet, in making this testimony, he did, in a way, testify to God's presence. And it is in this testimony to God in a time when he is absent that Kafka fulfills Auden's description of him as the most truly *exemplary* figure of our time.

NOTES: CHAPTER 11

1. Franz Kafka, *Diaries: 1914–1923*, Max Brod, ed., trans. by Martin Greenberg and Hannah Arendt (New York: Schocken Books, 1949), p. 211.
2. *Ibid.,* p. 213.
3. *Ibid.,* p. 215.
4. *Ibid.,* p. 214.
5. Franz Kafka, *The Great Wall of China*, trans. by Willa and Edwin Muir (New York: Schocken Books, 1946), p. 288.
6. *Diaries: 1910–1913*, Max Brod, ed., trans. by Joseph Kresh (New York: Schocken Books, 1948), p. 162.
7. *Ibid.,* p. 24.
8. *Amerika*, trans. by Edwin Muir (New York: New Directions, 1946), p. 138.
9. *The Castle*, trans. by Edwin and Willa Muir (New York: Alfred A. Knopf, 1951), p. 256.
10. *Selected Short Stories*, trans. by Willa and Edwin Muir (New York: Modern Library, 1952), p. 179.
11. *Diaries: 1914–1923*, pp. 187–188.
12. "Investigations of a Dog," *The Great Wall of China*, pp. 46–47.
13. *Ibid.,* p. 47; my italics.
14. *Diaries: 1914–1923*, p. 10.
15. "Investigations of a Dog," *The Great Wall of China*, pp. 47–48.
16. *Diaries: 1914–1923*, p. 180.
17. *Ibid.,* p. 215.
18. *Diaries: 1910–1913*, p. 27.

19. *Ibid.*, p. 26.
20. *Ibid.*, p. 180.
21. *Ibid.*, p. 33.
22. *Diaries: 1914–1923*, p. 98.
23. *Diaries: 1910–1913*, p. 73.
24. *Ibid.*, p. 69.
25. *Ibid.*, p. 310.
26. *Ibid.*, p. 324.
27. *The Great Wall of China*, p. 293.
28. *Diaries: 1914–1923*, p. 196.
29. *Diaries: 1910–1913*, p. 305.
30. *Diaries: 1914–1923*, p. 132.
31. *Diaries: 1910–1913*, p. 297.
32. *The Great Wall of China*, p. 302.
33. *Diaries: 1910–1913*, p. 323.
34. *Diaries: 1914–1923*, p. 126.
35. *Diaries: 1910–1913*, p. 27.
36. *Diaries: 1914–1923*, p. 77.
37. "The Hunter Gracchus," *The Great Wall of China*, pp. 210, 214.
38. *Diaries: 1910–1913*, p. 316.
39. *Ibid.*, p. 254.
40. *Diaries: 1914–1923*, p. 68; italics in the original.
41. *Ibid.*, p. 75.
42. *Diaries: 1910–1913*, p. 299.
43. *Diaries: 1914–1923*, p. 195.
44. *Ibid.*, p. 314.
45. *Ibid.*, p. 195.
46. *Diaries: 1910–1913*, p. 173.
47. *Ibid.*, p. 248.
48. *Ibid.*, p. 61.
49. *Ibid.*, p. 134.
50. *Ibid.*, p. 101.
51. *Ibid.*, p. 288.
52. *Diaries: 1914–1923*, p. 142.
53. *Diaries: 1910–1913*, p. 76.
54. *Ibid.*, pp. 74–75.
55. *Ibid.*, p. 58.
56. *Diaries: 1914–1923*, p. 202.
57. *Ibid.*, p. 212.
58. *Vide Selected Stories*, p. 124.
58a. *Diaries: 1914–1923*, p. 77.
59. *Diaries: 1910–1913*, p. 206.
60. *Diaries: 1914–1923*, p. 214.

61. *The Great Wall of China*, p. 292.
62. *Vide The Great Wall of China*, p. 278.
63. *Ibid.*, p. 287.
64. *The Castle*, p. 146.
65. *Hochzeitsvorbereitungen auf dem Lande* (New York: Schocken Books, 1953), p. 90; my translation.

William Faulkner's
Passion Week of the Heart

WILLIAM FAULKNER's first novel, *Soldier's Pay*, closes
with what is almost an announcement of the subjects that were
to be central in the works of the next thirty years of his
career: "sex and death and damnation." The cover of his
recent book, *A Fable*, is lavishly decorated with crosses, apparently designed by his publishers at once to call attention
to the fact that this work is a retelling and reinterpretation
of the Gospel story of Passion Week and to draw into an
already large public the great numbers of church people who
read only, or chiefly, religious or "inspirational" novels. Faced
with these suggestive facts, the reader is likely to conclude that
the pattern of Faulkner's development is clear: from violence
and sensationalism and "lost generation" despair to religious
affirmation. One more novelist, it would seem, has completed
the pilgrimage so common in our time.

Unfortunately for the possibility of quick and easy gen-
eralization, there is just enough truth in this view to undercut
any sweeping rejection of it. There *is* a difference in tone and
mood between Faulkner's early and later works, and one way
of pointing to that difference is to say that in the books of
approximately the last fifteen years one often feels the effort
to affirm some kind of faith, though the precise nature of this
faith very often remains unclear. It is also true to say that
Faulkner the man, when he speaks as prophet and moralist,
as he did most notably from the platform afforded him by his

reception of the Nobel Prize, has in recent years consistently urged us to have faith in man and his destiny; though, again, precisely what this means, precisely what obligations and commitments it involves, is far from clear, when we inspect the pronouncements themselves. Yet it was at the very beginning of his career, in his second novel, *Mosquitoes*, in what has been thought of as his "lost generation" period, that he had a character who is clearly a spokesman for the artist announce as the highest mark of genius in the arts the creation of a "Passion Week of the heart." But, though Faulkner's mood has changed over the years, and though the relative proportions in his work of denial and affirmation have shifted, Christians who would claim him for one of their own had best proceed cautiously.

Faulkner is, of course, a highly complex man whose vision and faith are full of paradox and ambivalence. But, if any one thing begins now clearly to emerge, it is that, whatever the relationship between his work and creedal Christianity—a sort of fellow-traveling, perhaps—a crucial factor in that relationship, the element indeed without which there would almost certainly be no relationship of similarity, is the tragic vision. Though there are undoubtedly several useful and suggestive ways of labeling his position, there is one conjunction of terms that obviously cannot be invoked for its description: however else it be defined, it, clearly, cannot be regarded as "optimistic-liberal-secularist," or "pragmatic-positivistic-modernist."

II

At this point it would be pleasant to assume that we are done with the tortuous qualifications and solemn warnings against glibness, and that we may now proceed to align Faulkner's work with the neo-Christianity of our time (as, surely, we must eventually do in some way or other). But we are not yet through with our *caveats* and our paradoxes. Simplicity is always desirable but not always attainable; and, in any effort to understand Faulkner's relation to the Christian faith and the tragic vision, it will be attainable, if at all, only late, not early.

We may begin to overcome the glibness of popular generalizations by turning our attention once again to the first novel. *Soldier's Pay* not only closes with what hindsight now sees as a kind of program-note for future novels—"sex and death and damnation"; it also closes with a complex image that has been hovering in the background of the work since the opening of the second chapter, when it was first introduced: an image of a falling church spire. The canting spire of the shabby little Negro church where Gilligan and the unbelieving Episcopal rector hear Negroes singing hymns is at least as revealing in its foreshadowing of the books to come as the stated list of subjects. Much of the best of Faulkner's fiction between *Soldier's Pay* and *A Fable* amounts to a kind of continuous running commentary on the situation of man in a world in which the spire is falling and no adequate substitute has been found for the faith which the spire symbolizes. *Soldier's Pay* is Faulkner's "lost generation" novel; and the lost generation was lost precisely because it had become acutely aware that the faith which had supplied a center of meaning for earlier generations was no longer available to it. Despite the popular opinion, the fiction of the first half of Faulkner's career was as "religious" in theme and mood as the later work.

And one could very well argue, further, that *A Fable,* far from being the most orthodoxly Christian of the novels, is the least Christian, despite its elaborately allegorical retelling of the events of Passion Week. I could be quite wrong—there is no general agreement yet on how one should finally interpret the work—but when I read *A Fable* I think of Robert Graves's *Nazarene Gospel Restored,* restored, that is, to its supposedly original humanistic and naturalistic purity from the distortions and deliberately dishonest perversions of it by St. Paul and his followers in the early church. There is something very reminiscent of nineteenth-century rationalism in this recent book of Faulkner's: it would almost seem to be trying to take us back to "the simple gospel of Jesus," who was a sweet, idealistic, inspiring young man who, unfortunately, was crucified before he could complete his work of bringing an end to war and human strife. This may not be a proper reading of *A Fable*, but it is certainly a justifiable interpretation of that trend in nineteenth-century liberal Christianity with which the book seems to have a connection. And, as this version of things went, Jesus' simple ethical message got terribly distorted by the supernaturalistic Hebraizers, and we are only now recovering his teaching in its purity—the simple injunction of the second great commandment, love thy neighbor. The world then, so the argument goes, was not ready for Jesus, and he came to a pathetic end; but we can appreciate him more fully, now that we are free from the long dominance of Pauline doctrine and institutional distortions.

If this is anything at all like what the theme of *A Fable* finally comes to—and I think it is, though it is certainly not *all* that it comes to, and perhaps not even the major part— then it fits in very well with the views on the nature of Christ that Faulkner expressed many years ago, at the very beginning of his career. Among the early sketches—now collected as *Mirrors of Chartres Street*—in which he characterized Christianity as "a fairy tale that has conquered the whole Western earth," there was one, "Out of Nazareth," which was devoted to a modern Jesus: a fine, sympathetic, young dreamer-idealist, doomed to be defeated, who carries around with him a battered copy of *A Shropshire Lad*. And there was another, "The Kingdom of God," in which there occurs the first use of the flower-splinting image that was later to become so suggestive a part of *The Sound and the Fury:* the idiot with the flower is a Christ-image, implicitly, as Benjy in *The Sound and the Fury* was later to be, even more explicitly. We are here in the world of Melville, the Melville of *The Confidence Man*— not at all in that of Kierkegaard or Niebuhr or others who put us in mind of the close affinity between Christianity and the tragic vision.

The idiot as the Christ-figure splinting the broken stem of the flower prepares us for a number of Faulkner's most recent pronouncements outside his fiction, as well as for some of the rhetoric in the novels. We may think particularly, for example, of the recent *Harper's Magazine* fulmination[1] against those who are betraying our American heritage, an essay in which he concluded that, if our way is to be saved, it will not be by the publishers, the politicians, or the churchmen, but by "the humanitarian in science and the scientist in the humanity of man." Or we may even think of the Nobel Prize acceptance speech, despite the fact that it was generally welcomed as a religious affirmation from an author whose works were popularly supposed to be wholly negative and despairing in their impact. For, despite the biblical tone of that address, despite even the fact that its central affirmation (that man will "prevail") can be interpreted in the terms of biblical faith, there still remains what is to me a crucial ambiguity in it all. And one wonders if the rhetoric is so tortured and forced because the underlying convictions are so insecurely held. What will man prevail over, and how? Over the world, himself, his machines, his folly, his death? And by virtue of the Atonement? Or by the efforts of "the humanitarian in science and the scientist in the humanity of man"? When the Bible uses the word *prevail,* as it so often does, the meaning is generally quite clear. Always the frame of reference is theistic in a fully supernaturalist sense. Man's hope rests in a transcendent God. In the Old Testament man will prevail because God keeps his promises, despite the faithlessness of man; in the New, man will prevail by virtue of Christ's victory over sin and death on the cross, which was precisely God's way of keeping his promise. But when Faulkner says man will "prevail," it is by no means easily possible to find out what he means.

III

I venture the opinion that a close study of the various religious pronouncements that have come over the years from Faulkner the moralist and prophet, and a comparison of these with the themes of the fiction, would indicate that the fiction is much more susceptible of interpretation in terms of classic Christianity than are the utterances of the man. We are brought, of course, at this point to another paradox. For the common view that the fiction is a kind of personal testament, firmly grounded in immediate knowledge and experience—springing, as it were, straight from the soil of Yoknapatawpha County—is undoubtedly, in some sense, justified. Yet, if the personal and subjective character of the fiction were the whole truth, we should be at a loss to explain the very apparent difference between the fictional themes and the nonfictional pronouncements. Why novels that often seem quite orthodox from a man whose opinions, when they are not clearly humanistic to a degree that places them quite outside any of the several emphases of classic Christianity, are at least heterodox?

The problem is insoluble only if we hold to the romantic notion of art as exclusively and distinctively self-expression. If we recall T. S. Eliot's reminder of many years ago that there is a sense in which the greatest art is always impersonal, we may see that the paradox here need not bring analysis to an abrupt halt. For, as Faulkner implied in the interview reported recently in *The Paris Review*,[2] he is primarily an artist, not primarily a prophet or moralist; and the artist uses the materials available to him, including the myths he finds ready at hand, and uses them without necessarily implying personal commitment to them as a man.

Mr. Eliot long ago, in his review of James Joyce's *Ulysses*, hailed Joyce's discovery or creation of a new method for the artist, a method of which he felt *Ulysses* was a perfect expression. He called it the "mythological method" and implied that, with its discovery, a new epoch in literature was beginning. And history has borne him out. For the fiction of William Faulkner springs not only from the soil of Yoknapatawpha, the sociology of which it reports with such amazing and wonderful verisimilitude; it springs equally, and more significantly as far as the problem before us is concerned, from the soil prepared by Eliot and Joyce and the others who were initiating the "mythological method" in the years just before Faulkner was beginning to write.

Faulkner *uses* Christian myth (I mean *myth* here in a purely neutral sense, implying no judgment of the degree of its ultimate truth, or of the kind of truth it may contain; I do not mean "mere myth," myth as contrasted either with history or with "truth")—Faulkner, I say, uses Christian myth in his stories to deepen and enrich them, to give them meaning and form. And to those who are committed to the "art as expression" approach to fiction, there may seem to be something irresponsible in the kind of relation that he enters into with Christianity. But, to the rest of us, Faulkner's procedure in this matter may seem to illustrate both the "irresponsibility"— "impersonality" is perhaps the better word—of any artist whose primary dedication is to his art, and the limited usefulness of the genetic approach to fiction. Indeed, the fact of the matter seems to be that Faulkner's incorporation of Christian myth into his work is no more "irresponsible" than the use to which he has put the myths of more primitive religions in "The Bear" and elsewhere. Benjy in *The Sound and the Fury* is, indeed, and beyond dispute, a Christ-image, whether or not his creator is, or wants to be called, or should be called, a Christian in the classic, creedal, historic sense. And the effect of this kind of perception is to send us from the man to his works, from an attempt (unlikely to be successful, and involving even what is perhaps a certain impertinence) to untangle the threads of Faulkner's personal religion to an attempt to find out what the novels and stories themselves mean.

IV

A great deal of Faulkner's work is interpretable in Christian terms, and some of it seems impossible to interpret rightly in any other terms. In *Requiem for a Nun*, for example, I do not see how it would be possible to argue convincingly that Nancy is not intended (to judge intention here both by the structure of the work itself and its relation to the other fictions) to be a sympathetic character, perhaps *the* sympathetic character— one of the redeemed, and redeemed precisely because, as "negro, dopefiend, whore," she has suffered and learned her need to be saved. Her message to Temple and Lawyer Stevens is simple, yet enigmatic: "Believe." And when she is asked what is to be the object of belief, she is sufficiently articulate to make her meaning quite clear: "Just believe": accept Him, she explains, not for what He taught but for what He is, "Trust in Him." So far as Nancy expresses the theme of the work, the meaning of the novel is radically Christian.

Which is not to say that Nancy is here to be taken as Faulkner's spokesman, enunciating his "message." For, if Faulkner is in the work at all, he is there as Lawyer Stevens, who visits

Nancy in jail not only to comfort her but also to discover her secret, who listens with respect to her ruminations upon the necessity of belief, but who never says that he too "believes." One judges that he would like to believe, as she does, but that in fact he doesn't—not yet, at any rate.

But Nancy, with her formula of simple faith in Him, is not the only clue to the achieved theme of *Requiem for a Nun*. In the end Temple and Stevens come very close to acknowledging that Nancy's is the only way that offers any hope. In the final scene Temple says, in effect, that she cannot save herself, that she is totally and irrevocably lost unless there is someone to save her soul: "Anyone to save it. Anyone who wants it. If there is none, I'm sunk. We all are. Doomed. Damned." Stevens answers, "'Of course we are. Hasn't He been telling us that for going on two thousand years?'"

Requiem for a Nun, in short, seems to me to have for its *achieved* meaning a powerful statement of the need for redemption from sin, of the necessity for the acknowledgment and confession of sin, and of the redemptive power resident in Christ. If, as I assume, it is open to interpretations with somewhat different emphases, it is certainly open to this one; and the others, if they are true to all the evidence, will not invalidate this one.

This is, of course, a late novel in the Faulkner canon, and it has sometimes been taken as evidence for that spiritual journey toward orthodoxy that has been posited for Faulkner and that I warned earlier against accepting too simply. But, if we turn back to the beginning of Faulkner's career, to *The Sound and the Fury*, we find a very similar situation and a very similar achieved meaning. It may be, in fact, that we should think of *The Sound and the Fury* not as Faulkner's statement of despair but as his most effective artistic statement of "the case for Christianity." It is, indeed, Dilsey's book, and Dilsey is a greater, more sympathetic, and aesthetically more rounded and convincing Nancy.

For Dilsey, life is not a tale told by an idiot, full of sound and fury, and signifying nothing. She believes and is saved— saved at least from futility and despair in this life, if not in some eternal dimension. The idiot Benjy cannot judge the tale he "tells," he can only present it for our judgment. Quentin judges it and finds that it signifies nothing: so he takes what seems to him the only way out. And the reader judges Jason, placing him surely among the damned and the doomed. Dilsey emerges as the only redeemed and redemptive character; she wins the reader's heart, whether or not she is able, by her example, to win his mind as well. She takes Benjy to church on Easter morning, and they listen to one of the great sermons in literature. And the meaning of the work emerges from this conjunction of Benjy, whose thirty-third birthday is being celebrated (but only by Dilsey); of Dilsey, who lives in two worlds at once and knows a time not our time, whatever the broken clock in the kitchen may say; of Quentin, the Prufrockian character who is searching for significance but knows too much to find it; and of Jason, the pragmatist in action who judges all things by their results and accepts nothing on faith.

Like Eliot's "The Waste Land," which also used to be taken as a personal credo of despair, *The Sound and the Fury* makes more sense when it is taken as a portrayal, diagnosis, and judgment of an age than it does when taken as a simple confession of despair by its author. It is related to "The Waste Land" in many ways, and in this most of all: that it springs from a conception of the impersonality of the work of art and proceeds by the "mythological method." Its complex transposition into modern terms of the events of Holy Week puts it into a rather small category, the class of great Christian novels.

V

The theology implied in the fiction strikes us as orthodox or heterodox not only according to the novels we have in mind but also according to the position from which we view it. If we are thinking primarily of the main currents of thought expressed in American literature in the last hundred and fifty years or so, we shall be likely to see Faulkner as one of the party of Hawthorne, Melville, the elder James, Eliot: the ironists with a vision of the possibility of tragedy and an unwillingness or inability to ignore the presence of evil in the world. This is the "conservative" party, the party that, with whatever necessary qualifications, and many *are* necessary, can be labeled the Christian party, not in some absolute sense but in contrast to the party of Emerson, who was hopeful that we should soon simply forget historic Christianity, and Whitman, who conceived his mission as helping to usher out the era of priests and creeds and to assist at the birth of the brave new world of science and humanity.

From this perspective we can see that Faulkner is profoundly akin to Hawthorne, and even more so to Melville. Like them he is concerned with the "truths of the heart." Like them he emphasizes both the fact and the ideal of community—Hawthorne's "magnetic chain of humanity" and Melville's "monkey rope." Like them also he refuses to settle for a simple solution to the problem: neither Whitman's two poles (the "simple, separate person" and the "mass"), nor even a conjunction of the two; neither Emerson's self-reliant isolated man nor the pre-Emersonian, "European" submergence of the individual in an authoritative institution: none of these may be read out of Faulkner's fiction. Instead, his characters, like Hawthorne's, are constantly in danger of isolation, and they need always to face the necessity of individual, and often lonely and unpopular, decision. And we are also put in mind of Melville, for Hightower in *Light in August* is another Pierre, starting out from innocence to do battle with the world and being overwhelmed by its evil—though, unlike Pierre, Hightower, before his final act of engagement, is judged in negative terms by his creator, for he is found to be guilty of a false romantic idealism. Little Ahabs also abound in Faulkner, and we may see in them precisely the ambivalence we find in Melville's portrait of Ahab—namely, satanic monomania combined with an appealing heroism. Faulkner's kinship with Hawthorne and Melville is, in other words, deep and far-reaching—and largely unexplored. He belongs in *their* party.

The parallels between Faulkner and Eliot are just as remarkable. The fiction up to and including *Pylon* in the later thirties is full of Eliot echoes, allusions, and parallels. The reporter in *Pylon* is explicitly related to Prufrock, but there are many other Prufrocks in Faulkner, prominent amongst whom is Quentin of *The Sound and the Fury*, who suffers "death by water." *Sartoris*, the book in which Faulkner really found himself as an artist, marks the beginning of a relationship that becomes less obvious after 1940 but that has not ended yet. Faulkner is of Eliot's party too, as that party is defined by its difference from the party of scientism and the pragmatic hope.

In short, from any perspective established chiefly from a view of American literature, Faulkner belongs with those who, whatever the ambiguities of their own position, have felt and expressed a kinship with the historic Christian view of the human situation. He belongs with those who have felt that the past is not without value or instruction for us, with those who have extended their sense of community to include the past, with those, like Hawthorne and Melville and Eliot, who, even against the high tide of nineteenth-century humanistic optimism, have kept alive the Christian tradition in the realm of thought. In common with these writers, and with the long tradition which they continue and develop, Faulkner assumes in his fiction that man is "fallen"—that is, that he is neither perfect, nor indeed perfectible, by purely rational, scientific, educational methods; that he can only be redeemed by an inner change, a drastic reorientation and movement of reversal.

The Faulknerian universe, then, is a universe in which sin and suffering, redemption and damnation, the way of faith and the way of faithlessness, are the really decisive categories. At the risk of oversimplifying a highly complex book, we may say, for example, that what *Absalom, Absalom!* finally comes to is the perception that only by the way of faith and compassion, and the creative imagination, can we either understand the past or free ourselves from it sufficiently to act redemptively in the present. Or, again, the really redemptive characters in *Light in August* are Lena Grove and Byron Bunch, and they are so because she exemplifies St. Paul's three theological virtues, and because he teaches Hightower that passive charity is not enough, that one must run the risks of engagement. And, of all the great figures in Faulkner, Ike McCaslin, who is a central character in the stories collected in *Go Down, Moses*, is perhaps most wonderfully endowed with the charismata of redemption. He faces the evil and the guilt in the past and present of his region and his family, and he attempts to atone for them so far as he is able. A childless carpenter, he initiates others into the mysteries into which he was himself initiated as a boy. And natural piety and compassion are at the bottom of what he has to teach.

The burden of Faulkner's fiction as a whole is compassion. When it has its effect on us, it leads us to include within our love even—or rather especially—the Joe Christmases and the

Nancys of the world: yes, even the Popeyes. It constantly reminds us of the injunction, "Judge not"; Popeye, we come to see, is as much a victim as a perpetrator of evil, and Joe Christmas, for all his malevolence, not only suffers a Christlike fate but is himself, we must finally believe, a Christlike figure. What think ye of Joe Christmas, who was, surely, "one of the least of these"? By our attitude toward him, we ourselves, the novel implies, are judged. Unlike Christ though he is in character, Joe Christmas is like him in situation and function: he sits in judgment on the world by forcing it to judge him.

VI

But, if the meanings of Faulkner's work may be seen as for the most part basically consistent with the broad outlines of the classic Christian view of man and the world as expressed in American literature, yet it remains true that, when viewed in relation to a tradition older than American literature, when viewed as a part of the Christian literature of two thousand years, the meanings of Faulkner's books may come to seem Christian only in a very much more partial and restricted sense. It is not simply that Faulkner is not Dante or Milton or Bunyan: neither is Eliot. It is, rather, that in Faulkner's work the Crucifixion is central and paradigmatic and the Resurrection might never have occurred. Grant all objections that may reasonably be made at this point, grant the difficulty of defining not only "orthodoxy" but "belief" of any sort in the religious area, grant all this and more, and it still remains true that the common core of belief that has united Christians of all persuasions in all ages has been belief in, acceptance of, the great miracle of that first Easter. Without it the early church would have had no gospel, no "good news"; without it, there would be no radical distinction between Christianity and other theistic religions. And the Crucifixion without the Resurrection is pure tragedy. Christianity has room for, indeed has usually tended to insist upon, the tragic vision—but not final and unqualified tragedy. Unlike Whitmanic optimism, Christianity does not bypass or deny tragedy, but neither does it rest in the final tragic dilemma: it holds that "in the end," when all things are made manifest, it will become apparent that perfect power and perfect love are one. Tragedy has been once and will be again transcended: it is, as it were, an *interim* condition—perhaps better, the purely *human* condition.

In Faulkner's work, however, the tragedy seems final, unrelieved, and unescapable in any dimension—which is very nearly to say that in his books we may find all the categories of Christian thought and feeling except faith and hope, in the classic, and Pauline, sense. The works, that is to say, are built out of blocks of Christian thought and feeling, shaped by Christian images and symbols, and deepened by biblical allusions; but behind or within all this is a core of what we may call (though not in a derogatory sense) old-fashioned deism, tinctured with romantic nature mysticism. We are back again, in other words, with the Melvillean element in Faulkner, and there is, indeed, as much reason for looking into "Faulkner's Quarrel with God" as there is into Melville's.

In a time when the reaction against secular optimism has made it almost fashionable to rediscover Original Sin, it is easy to conclude that Faulkner's tragic vision is sufficient to make his work Christian. But this approach is too easy and is not finally defensible. As Hawthorne told us long ago in his story "Young Goodman Brown," it is not enough for a Christian to discover the universality of guilt. If to deny the radical nature of evil is to make Christianity seem irrelevant, as it came to seem to the believers in the "religion of humanity" and the followers of the gospel of Progress in the nineteenth and early twentieth centuries, for a Christian to affirm evil without also affirming the effectiveness of the Atonement is for him to stop in a position that St. Paul characterizes as pre-Christian and conducive to despair. And, indeed, despair is never far from the surface of many of Faulkner's earlier works. Surely it would not be unfair, for example, to call *Sanctuary* a despairing novel. And when, in some of his more recent things, Faulkner attempts to convey a more hopeful view, we often feel a sense of strain, of effort: the dramatizing sometimes stops, and the rhetorician takes over to tell us to do God's work and save the Republic. The result is both less great as art and less convincing as argument.

Despair and the tragic vision are not, of course, the same thing at all, but they are related in at least one way: a denial of the contradictions, ironies, and tensions of experience, a denial of the effectiveness of intelligence and action—and a denial which would, if it could really be maintained, cut any objective ground out from under the sense of despair, and which would also make tragedy itself impossible, or, rather, pointless. Emerson assumed that there is no tragedy in the world: he had, as he said, never been able really to accept the reality of evil. But if *only* evil is really real, then there is no meaningful principle in terms of which we may protest against it, and the appropriate attitude, therefore, becomes that of nihilism.

Hope can only subsist where there is faith, faith in God or in man or in both. Some of Faulkner's works, like *Sanctuary* and *Pylon*, remain close to despair at all times; others, like *The Sound and the Fury* and *Intruder in the Dust*, include a movement toward faith, and consequently a note of hope. But the object of the faith, whether in man or in God, is either left undefined or, when it is defined as God, is so defined by our identification with simple believers like Dilsey and Nancy. In the former case we have Christian terms without, necessarily, Christian meanings; in the latter, Quentin's problem is still with us, for, however strong our sympathy for the Dilseys of this world may be, we cannot, merely by an act of will, attain to their simple faith. So let us say, then, that the earlier works hover between present despair and the memory of a lost faith, and that the later works seem to be bidding us to repent and believe in God and man, as we wish, or can, or must. Faulkner's entire achievement, in other words, demands ultimately to be construed in religious terms. But, as we have observed, when his work seems most obviously Christian, it is often least so; and when it does not seem Christian at all, or seems even explicitly non-Christian (as is the case with *The Sound and the Fury*, if we identify with Quentin), then Christian meanings often emerge most powerfully. Or, if that should seem too positive a way of putting it, we may say that the terms in which experience is analyzed are such as to make the historic Christian answers to the questions implicitly raised seem pertinent and natural. I take it, for example, that in *As I Lay Dying* the intended meaning is that it is Addie, violent, bitter, in a religious sense almost nihilistic, who is the "saved" and saving character, not Cora Tull with her conventional piety. Though the book is replete with biblical echoes and Christian symbols, and even parallels at one crucial point the service of Holy Communion in the Anglican Prayerbook, the theme of it would seem to be that it is deeds and not words (or doctrines, or faith) that save. But, if we push this interpretation, we may come out with a reading reminiscent of the readings of *Moby Dick* that resulted from identifying completely with Ahab and forgetting Ishmael. *Absalom, Absalom!* on the other hand, which does not have the problem of belief at its center, contains nothing that would contradict a Christian interpretation and much that would support it.

VII

In conclusion it should be remarked how profoundly and centrally existentialist is Faulkner's fiction, and to say this is not to change the subject. It is existentialist as the paintings—some of them—of Picasso are existentialist, and the fiction of Kafka, and the earlier poetry of Eliot, and the theology of Paul Tillich. For, as Tillich himself has recently said, existentialist art rediscovers "the basic questions to which the Christian symbols are the answers in a way which is understandable to our time."[3] Faulkner's fiction breaks up and reconstitutes the conventional patterns of experience, imposing on us the burden of painfully fresh perception. From its sometimes violent dislocations of the familiar, the old questions of man's nature and destiny emerge with new and unsuspected urgency. And one of the chief results of this process is very relevant to the whole question involving the relation of Faulkner's work to Christianity and the tragic vision: for our secularist culture has tended to forget not just the Christian answers but the questions that must be put before the answers can seem meaningful. Faulkner's Passion Week, in short, may only be "of the heart," obscurely and ambiguously related to history, but it is well to remember that in a wholly pragmatic and positivistic culture there would be no Passion Week at all.

NOTES: CHAPTER 12

1. William Faulkner, "On Privacy . . . The American Dream: What Happened to It," *Harper's Magazine*, July, 1955, pp. 33–38.
2. *The Paris Review*, Spring 1956, pp. 28–52.
3. Paul Tillich, "Existentialist Aspects of Modern Art," in *Christianity and the Existentialists*, Carl Michalson, ed. (New York: Charles Scribner's Sons, 1956), p. 147.

About the Contributors

EDMOND LAB. CHERBONNIER, Associate Professor of Religion and Head of the Department of Religion, Trinity College, Hartford 6, Connecticut; previously taught on the faculties of Vassar College, Barnard College, and Union Theological Seminary; b. 1918; married; Harvard University, B.A., 1939; Union Theological Seminary, B.D., 1947; Cambridge University, B.A., 1948; Columbia University, Ph.D., 1951; also studied at the Universities of Zurich and Paris and Strasbourg; Fellow of the National Council on Religion in Higher Education; author of *Hardness of Heart: A Contemporary Interpretation of the Doctrine of Sin* (Doubleday, 1955) and contributor of articles to *Theology Today*, *The Journal of Religion*, *The Anglican Theological Review*, and *The Christian Scholar*.

ROY W. BATTENHOUSE, Professor of English, Indiana University, Bloomington, Indiana; previously taught on the faculties of Ohio State University, Vanderbilt University, and the Episcopal Theological School (Cambridge, Mass.); b. 1912 in Nevinville, Iowa; married; Albion College, B.A., 1933; the Yale Divinity School, B.D., 1936; Yale University, Ph.D., 1938; Fellow of the National Council on Religion in Higher Education; author of *Marlowe's Tamburlaine: A Study in Renaissance Moral Philosophy* (Vanderbilt University Press, 1941); editor of *A Companion to the Study of St. Augustine* (Oxford University Press, 1955); contributor of articles to *PMLA*, *Studies in Philology*, *Journal of English Literary History*, *Church History*, *Journal of the History of Ideas*, *Theology Today*, and other journals.

T. S. K. SCOTT-CRAIG, Professor of Philosophy and Religion, Dartmouth College, Hanover, New Hampshire; previously taught on the faculties of Drew University, the General Theological Seminary, and Hobart and William Smith Colleges;

b. 1909 in Edinburgh, Scotland; married; University of Edinburgh, M.A., B.D., and Ph.D.; author of *Christian Attitudes to War and Peace* (Scribner's, 1938); contributor to *A Companion to the Study of St. Augustine*, Roy W. Battenhouse, ed. (Oxford University Press, 1955); contributor of articles to *Huntingdon Quarterly, Renaissance News,* and *The Living Church;* editor of *Faculty Papers* for The National Council of the Episcopal Church, 1951–55; author of forthcoming book on Milton.

ÉMILE CAILLIET, Stuart Professor of Christian Philosophy, Princeton Theological Seminary, Princeton, New Jersey; previously taught on the faculties of the University of Pennsylvania, Scripps College, and Wesleyan University; lectured at Davidson College and McGill University; b. 1894 in Dampierre, France; married; studied at College of Châlons, University of Nancy, University of Montpellier, and the University of Strasbourg; author of *Symbolisme et âmes primitives* (Paris, 1936), *La tradition littéraire des ideologues* (American Philosophical Society, 1943), *The Clue to Pascal* (Westminster Press, 1943), *Pascal: Genius in the Light of Scripture* (Westminster Press, 1945), *The Christian Approach to Culture* (Abingdon-Cokesbury, 1953), *The Dawn of Personality* (Bobbs-Merrill, 1955), and many other books; National Fellow of the French Academy of Colonial Sciences, 1932; Officier d'académie (France) for service in the field of letters, 1934.

RICHARD KRONER, Professor Emeritus of Philosophy, University of Kiel (Germany); Adjunct Professor Emeritus of the Philosophy of Religion, Union Theological Seminary; Permanent Visiting Professor at Temple University and at the University of Bern; previously taught on the faculties of the University of Freiburg, Dresden, and Oxford; delivered the Gifford Lectures at the University of St. Andrews (Scotland) in 1939–40; b. 1884 in Breslau, Silesia; studied at Universities of Breslau, Berlin, and Heidelberg; University of Freiburg, Ph.D., 1908; was for many years the editor of the distinguished German philosophical journal, *Logos;* author of many outstanding works in German—the monumental two-volume study of

German idealism, *Von Kant bis Hegel* (1921–24), *Logische und aesthetische Allgemeingültigkeit* (The Validity of Logical and Aesthetical Judgments, 1908), *Zweck und Gesetz in der Biologie* (Finality and Causality in Biological Thought, 1913), *Das Problem der historischen Biologie* (The Problem of Historical Biology, 1919), *Die Selbstverwirklichung des Geistes* (The Actuality of Mind, 1928), *Kulturphilosophische Grundlegung der Politik* (Fundamental Principles of Politics, 1931), and many others; in English, *The Primacy of Faith* (Macmillan, 1943), *How Do We Know God?* (Harper, 1943), *Culture and Faith* (University of Chicago Press, 1951), *Speculation in Pre-Christian Philosophy* (Westminster Press, 1956), and others.

PAUL L. HOLMER, Professor of Philosophy, University of Minnesota, Minneapolis, Minnesota; previously taught on the faculties of Yale University and Gustavus Adolphus College; b. 1916 in Minneapolis; married; University of Minnesota, B.A., 1940, M.A., 1942; Yale University, Ph.D., 1945; Fellow of the National Council on Religion in Higher Education; contributor of articles to *Ethics, Theology Today, Review of Religion, Cross Currents, Journal of Religion,* and other journals; author of forthcoming book on Kierkegaard.

NATHAN A. SCOTT, JR., Assistant Professor of Theology and Literature, The Federated Theological Faculty, University of Chicago, Chicago, Illinois; previously taught on the faculty of Howard University; Visiting Professor of Philosophy and English Literature, Gustavus Adolphus College, Spring 1954; b. 1925 in Cleveland, Ohio; married; University of Michigan, B.A., 1944; Union Theological Seminary, B.D., 1946; Columbia University, Ph.D., 1949; member of the Editorial Boards of *The Journal of Religion* and *The Christian Scholar;* Fellow of the National Council on Religion in Higher Education; author of *Rehearsals of Discomposure: Alienation and Reconciliation in Modern Literature* (King's Crown Press of Columbia University Press, 1952); contributor to the symposium *Religious Symbolism,* F. Ernest Johnson, ed. (Harper, 1955); contributor to the forthcoming symposium-volume *Theology and Literary*

Criticism, being edited by Preston T. Roberts, Jr.; contributor of articles to *Religion in Life, Christianity and Society, The Journal of Religious Thought, The Journal of Religion, The Christian Scholar, The Review of Metaphysics, Christianity and Crisis, Frontiers, The University of Kansas City Review, Motive, The Journal of Human Relations, The Christian Century, The Intercollegian, Cross Currents,* and other journals.

JOHN E. SMITH, Associate Professor of Philosophy, Yale University, New Haven, Connecticut; previously taught on the faculties of Vassar College and Barnard College; b. 1921; married; Columbia University, B.A., 1942; Union Theological Seminary, B.D., 1945; Columbia University, Ph.D., 1948; Secretary, Metaphysical Society of America, 1954–56; Executive Committee, Peirce Society, 1953–55; Fellow of the National Council on Religion in Higher Education; author of *Royce's Social Infinite* (Liberal Arts Press, 1950); translated and prepared the introduction to Richard Kroner's *Kant's Weltanschauung* (University of Chicago Press, 1956); contributor of chapters to several symposium-volumes, the most recent of which is an essay on Ibsen ("When Shall We Not Tell the Truth?") in the volume *Great Moral Dilemmas,* R. M. MacIver, ed. (Harper, 1955); contributor of articles to *The Journal of Philosophy, The Review of Metaphysics, The Journal of Religion, The Yale Review, Yale French Studies,* and other journals; author of forthcoming book, *Religion and Reality: A Dialectic Between Philosophy and Religion.*

RANDALL STEWART, Professor of English and Head of the Department of English, Vanderbilt University, Nashville, Tennessee; previously taught on the faculties of the University of Oklahoma, U.S. Naval Academy, University of Idaho, Yale University, and Brown University; b. 1896; married; Vanderbilt University, B.S., 1917; Harvard University, M.A., 1921; Yale University, Ph.D., 1930; edited *The American Notebooks of Nathaniel Hawthorne* (Yale University Press, 1932), *The English Notebooks of Nathaniel Hawthorne* (Modern Language Association of America, 1941); collaborated in the editing with others of *The Literature of the United States* (Scott,

Foresman, 1946), *Living Masterpieces of American Literature* (Scott, Foresman, 1954), *Living Masterpieces of English Literature* (Scott, Foresman, 1954); author of *Nathaniel Hawthorne: A Biography* (Yale University Press, 1948); contributed articles to *American Literature, The New England Quarterly, College English, The Yale Review, Philological Quarterly, The Virginia Quarterly Review, The University of Kansas City Review,* and other journals; author of forthcoming book on religious attitudes in American literature.

ALBERT C. OUTLER, Professor of Theology, Perkins School of Theology, Southern Methodist University, Dallas, Texas; previously taught on the faculties of Duke University and Yale University; Visiting Senior Fellow in the Council of the Humanities, Princeton University, 1956–57; b. 1908 in Thomasville, Georgia; married; Wofford College, B.A., 1928; Emory University, B.D., 1933; Yale University, Ph.D., 1938; Wofford College, D.D., 1952; Fellow of the National Council on Religion in Higher Education; author of *Psychotherapy and the Christian Faith* (Harper, 1953); editor and translator of *The Confessions and Enchiridion of St. Augustine* (Westminster Press, 1955); contributor to *A Companion to the Study of St. Augustine,* Roy W. Battenhouse, ed. (Oxford University Press, 1955); contributor of articles to *Church History, The Journal of Religion, Christendom, The Ecumenical Review, Religion in Life, The Harvard Theological Review, The Perkins Journal,* and other journals.

J. HILLIS MILLER, JR., Assistant Professor of English, Johns Hopkins University, Baltimore, Maryland; previously taught on the faculty of Williams College; b. 1928 in Williamsburg, Virginia; married; Oberlin College, B. A., 1948; Harvard University, M.A., 1949; Harvard University, Ph.D., 1952; Fellow of the National Council on Religion in Higher Education; member of the Editorial Boards of *Modern Language Notes* and *The Journal of English Literary History;* contributor of articles to *The Harvard Advocate, The Journal of English Literary History,* and *Modern Language Notes;* author of forthcoming book on Dickens; contributor of essay on Dylan Thomas to forthcoming symposium-volume on *Theology and Literary Criticism*, being edited by Preston Roberts.

HYATT H. WAGGONER, Professor of American Literature, Brown University, Providence, Rhode Island; previously taught on the faculties of the University of Omaha, New York University, Wayne University, and the University of Kansas City; b. 1913 in Pleasant Valley, Dutchess County, New York; married; Middlebury College, B.A., 1935; University of Chicago, M.A., 1936; Ohio State University, Ph.D., 1942; edited *Nathaniel Hawthorne: Selected Tales and Sketches* (Rinehart, 1950); author of *The Heel of Elohim: Science and Values in Modern American Poetry* (University of Oklahoma Press, 1950) and *Hawthorne: A Critical Study* (Belknap Press of Harvard University Press, 1955); contributor of articles to *American Literature, Beloit Poetry Journal, Chimera, College English, Explicator, The New England Quarterly, The Sewanee Review, South Atlantic Quarterly, The University of Kansas City Review, The Western Review,* and other journals.

Selected Bibliography

The following bibliographical notes and check lists are offered as guidance for the reader who wishes to pursue further one or another of the subjects treated in this book.

1. BIBLICAL FAITH AND THE IDEA OF TRAGEDY

THE BIBLICAL WORLD-VIEW

Bowman, John W., *Prophetic Realism and the Gospel.* Philadelphia: The Westminster Press, 1955.

Dix, Dom Gregory, *Jew and Greek.* New York: Harper & Brothers, 1953.

Dodd, Charles H., *History and the Gospel.* London: Nisbet and Co., Ltd., 1938.

Heschel, Abraham, *God in Search of Man.* New York: Farrar, Straus and Cudahy, 1955.

Niebuhr, Reinhold, *Beyond Tragedy.* New York: Charles Scribner's Sons, 1938.

Robinson, H. Wheeler, *The Religious Ideas of the Old Testament.* New York: Charles Scribner's Sons, 1913.

Tresmontant, Claude, *Essai sur la Pensée Hébraique.* Paris: Editions du Cerf, 1953.

———, *Études de Métaphysique Biblique.* Paris: J. Gabalda, 1955.

Wright, G. Ernest, *God Who Acts.* Chicago: Henry Regnery Co., 1952.

THE NATURE OF THE TRAGIC VISION

Berdyaev, Nicolas, *The Destiny of Man,* trans. by Natalie Duddington. London: Geoffrey Bles Ltd., 1948.

———, *Freedom and the Spirit,* trans. by Oliver F. Clarke. London: Geoffrey Bles Ltd., 1948.

Brooks, Cleanth, ed., *Tragic Themes in Western Literature.* New Haven: Yale University Press, 1955.

Dixon, W. Macneile, *Tragedy*. London: E. Arnold and Co., 1924.

Frye, Prosser Hall, *Romance and Tragedy*. Boston: Marshall Jones Company, 1922.

Greene, W. C., *Moira*. Cambridge: Harvard University Press, 1944.

Jaeger, Werner, *Paideia: The Ideals of Greek Culture*, Vol. I, Bk. Two; trans. by Gilbert Highet. New York: Oxford Univerity Press, 1945.

Jaspers, Karl, *Tragedy Is Not Enough*, trans. by H. A. T. Reiche, H. T. Moore, and K. W. Deutsch. Boston: Beacon Press, 1952.

Muller, Herbert J., *The Spirit of Tragedy*. New York: Alfred A. Knopf, 1956.

Myers, Henry A., *Tragedy*. Ithaca, N. Y.: Cornell University Press, 1956.

Nietzsche, Friedrich, *The Birth of Tragedy*, trans. by Francis Golffing, in *The Birth of Tragedy and The Genealogy of Morals* (Garden City, N. Y.: Doubleday Anchor Books, 1956).

O'Connor, William Van, *Climates of Tragedy*. Baton Rouge: Louisiana State University Press, 1943.

Roberts, Preston, "A Christian Theory of Dramatic Tragedy," *The Journal of Religion*, Vol. XXXI, No. 1 (January, 1951), pp. 1–20.

Unamuno, Miguel de, *The Tragic Sense of Life*, trans. by J. E. C. Flitch. New York: Dover Publications, 1954.

Weisinger, Herbert, *Tragedy and the Paradox of the Fortunate Fall*. London: Routledge & Kegan Paul Ltd., 1953.

Werblowsky, R. J. Z., *Lucifer and Prometheus*. London: Routledge & Kegan Paul Ltd., 1952.

2. SHAKESPEAREAN TRAGEDY

An excellent Shakespeare edition for nonspecialist readers is *Shakespeare: The Major Plays and the Sonnets*, edited by G. B. Harrison (New York: Harcourt, Brace & Co., 1948). Readers desiring more extensive scholarly editing and single-volume editions of the plays will use the volumes in the new

"Arden" edition, under the general editorship of Una M. Ellis-Fermor (London: Methuen and Co. Ltd., 1951 ——).

The following critical studies will be found useful:

Bethell, S. L., *Shakespeare and the Popular Dramatic Tradition.* London: King and Staples, 1944.

Campbell, Lily B., *Shakespeare's Histories.* San Marino, Calif.: The Huntington Library, 1947.

Curry, W. C., *Shakespeare's Philosophical Patterns.* Baton Rouge: Louisiana State University Press, 1937.

Farnham, Willard, *Shakespeare's Tragic Frontier.* Berkeley: University of California Press, 1950.

Goddard, H. C., *The Meaning of Shakespeare.* Chicago: University of Chicago Press, 1951.

Granville-Barker, Harley, *Prefaces to Shakespeare,* 2 vols. Princeton: Princeton University Press, 1946–47.

Knight, George Wilson, *The Wheel of Fire: Interpretations of Shakespearean Tragedy.* London: Methuen and Co. Ltd., 1949.

——, *The Imperial Theme.* London: Methuen and Co. Ltd., 1951.

Spencer, Theodore, *Shakespeare and the Nature of Man.* New York: The Macmillan Co., 1949.

Stauffer, Donald A., *Shakespeare's World of Images: The Development of His Moral Ideas.* New York: W. W. Norton & Company, 1949.

Traversi, D. A., *An Approach to Shakespeare.* Garden City, N. Y.: Doubleday Anchor Books, 1956.

Van Doren, Mark, *Shakespeare.* Garden City, N. Y.: Doubleday Anchor Books, 1953.

3. MILTON

The standard modern edition of Milton's works is that of the Columbia University Press, edited by Frank A. Patterson and others, in 18 volumes, 1931–38. The editions of *Paradise Lost* edited by A. W. Verity (Cambridge, Eng.: The University Press, 1910) and M. Y. Hughes (New York: The Odyssey

Press, 1935) are useful, as is also the volume *Paradise Regained, the Minor Poems, and Samson Agonistes*, edited by M. Y. Hughes (Garden City, N. Y.: Doubleday, Doran, and Co., 1937). *The Portable Milton*, edited by Douglas Bush (New York: The Viking Press, 1949), is an inexpensive and handy volume for nonspecialist readers.

Various aspects of the major texts and of the literary, philosophical, and religious background are illuminated by the following studies:

Bush, Douglas, *Paradise Lost in Our Time*. Ithaca, N. Y.: Cornell University Press, 1945.

——, *Mythology and the Renaissance Tradition in English Poetry*. Minneapolis: University of Minnesota Press, 1932.

——, *English Literature in the Earlier Seventeenth Century*. Oxford: The Clarendon Press, 1945.

Dorian, D. C., *The English Diodatis*. New Brunswick, N. J.: Rutgers University Press, 1950.

Eisler, R., *Man into Wolf*. London: Routledge & Kegan Paul Ltd., 1951.

Hanford, J. H., *John Milton, Englishman*. New York: Crown Publishers, 1949.

——, *A Milton Handbook*. New York: F. S. Crofts & Co., 1929.

Kelley, M., *This Great Argument*. Princeton: Princeton University Press, 1941.

Lewis, C. S., *A Preface to Paradise Lost*. London, New York: Oxford University Press, 1943.

Lovejoy, Arthur, "Milton and the Paradox of the Fortunate Fall," *Journal of English Literary History*, Vol. IV (1937), pp. 161–179.

McColley, Grant, *Paradise Lost: An Account of Its Growth and Major Origins*. Chicago: Packard and Co., 1940.

Parker, W. R., *Milton's Debt to Greek Tragedy in Samson Agonistes*. Baltimore: The Johns Hopkins Press, 1937.

Pope, Elizabeth Marie, *Paradise Regained: The Tradition and the Poem*. Baltimore: The Johns Hopkins Press, 1947.

Rajan, Balachandra, *Paradise Lost and the Seventeenth Century Reader*. London: Chatto and Windus, 1947.

Riecke, B., "The Knowledge Hidden in the Tree of Paradise," *Journal of Semitic Studies*, July, 1956.

Saurat, Denis, *Milton: Man and Thinker*. London: J. M. Dent and Sons, Ltd., 1944.

Scott-Craig, T. S. K., "Concerning Milton's Samson," *Renaissance News*, Autumn 1952.

Sewell, Arthur, *A Study of Milton's Christian Doctrine*. London: Oxford University Press, 1939.

Tillyard, E. M. W., *The Miltonic Setting: Past and Present*. Cambridge, Eng.: The University Press, 1938.

Waldock, Arthur, *Paradise Lost and Its Critics*. Cambridge, Eng.: The University Press, 1947.

Weisinger, Herbert, *Tragedy and the Paradox of the Fortunate Fall*. London: Routledge & Kegan Paul Ltd., 1953.

Woodhouse, A. S. P., "The Argument of Milton's *Comus*," *University of Toronto Quarterly*, Vol. XI (1941), pp. 46–71.

4. Pascal

The standard French edition of Pascal is the *Oeuvres de Blaise Pascal*, published according to *chronological* order with complementary documents, introductions, and notes by Léon Brunschvicg, Pierre Boutroux, and Félix Gazier, Paris: Hachette, 1904–14, 14 volumes. The *Pensées* and *The Provincial Letters* are readily available in English in a "Modern Library" volume (published by Random House). The *Pensées* may also be secured in English in an "Everyman's Library" volume (London: J. M. Dent and Sons Ltd.), and here the splendid companion-piece is T. S. Eliot's long and brilliant Introduction. See also *Great Shorter Works of Pascal*, translated with an introduction by Émile Cailliet and John C. Blankenagel (Philadelphia: The Westminster Press, 1948); and *Pascal's Short Life of Christ*, translated with an introduction by Émile Cailliet and John C. Blankenagle (Princeton Theological Seminary Pamphlets—No. 5, 1950). A convenient "bibliography on Blaise Pascal" has been compiled by Roger Hazelton in the *Bulletin of the General Theological Library*, Vol. XLVII, No. 4, July, 1955 (53 Mount Vernon St., Boston 8, Mass.).

The general reader will find the following biographical and critical studies helpful:

Bishop, Morris, *Pascal: The Life of Genius.* New York: Reynal and Hitchcock, 1936.

Cailliet, Émile, *The Clue to Pascal.* Philadelphia: The Westminster Press, 1943.

——, *Pascal: Genius in the Light of Scripture.* Philadelphia: The Westminster Press, 1945.

Mesnard, Jean, *Pascal: His Life and Works,* trans. by G. S. Fraser. London: Harvill Press, 1952.

Patrick, D. G. M., *Pascal and Kierkegaard,* Vol. I. London: Lutterworth Press, 1947.

Sainte-Beuve, C. A., *Port-Royal,* 7 vols. Paris: 1871–78.

Stewart, H. F., *The Holiness of Pascal.* Cambridge, Eng.: The University Press, 1915.

——, *The Secret of Pascal.* Cambridge, Eng.: The University Press, 1941.

5. GOETHE

The English translation of *Faust* most widely used in this country is still perhaps the old Bayard Taylor version from which the quotations in this book are drawn, and it is readily available in a "Modern Library" edition. The Taylor version is, however, by no means as readable as some of the more recent translations, the most attractive of which are C. F. MacIntyre's (New York: New Directions, 1941) and Philip Wayne's (Baltimore: Penguin Books, 1949). Unfortunately, however, the MacIntyre and Wayne versions consist merely of Part I. MacIntyre, in his appended Note to the New Directions edition, promised, at the time of its appearance in 1941, to give us also Part II, and it is to be hoped that this promise may soon be fulfilled. Parts I and II are, however, available in George Madison Priest's version (New York: Alfred A. Knopf, 1941), and many will doubtless find his Part II more imaginatively accessible than Taylor's. Also, an abridged translation of both Parts has been done by the English poet, Louis MacNeice (London: Faber and Faber, 1951). Those readers who have German will find the critical edition of *Faust* by Roe-Merrill Heffner, Helmut Rehder, and W. F. Twaddell (Boston: D. C. Heath & Company, 1954–55, 2 vols.) to be useful, and these editors have also prepared, as a companion-piece, a very helpful handbook, *Goethe's "Faust": A Complete German-English Vocabulary* (Boston: Heath, 1950).

The following biographical and critical studies are recommended:

Croce, Benedetto, *Goethe*. New York: Alfred A. Knopf, 1923.

Enright, D. J., *A Commentary on Goethe's Faust*. New York: New Directions, 1949.

Fairley, Barker, *Goethe as Revealed in His Poetry*. London: J. M. Dent and Sons Ltd., 1932.

———, *A Study of Goethe*. Oxford: The Clarendon Press, 1947.

Jantz, Harold S., *Goethe's Faust as a Renaissance Man*. Princeton: Princeton University Press, 1951.

Ludwig, Emil, *Goethe: The History of a Man*. New York: G. P. Putnam's Sons, 1928.

Mann, Thomas, *Freud, Goethe, Wagner*. New York: Alfred A. Knopf, 1937.

Miller, Ronald Duncan, *The Meaning of Goethe's "Faust"*. Cambridge, Eng.: W. Heffer and Sons Ltd., 1939.

Rose, William, ed., *Essays on Goethe*. London: Cassell & Co. Ltd., 1949.

Santayana, George, *Three Philosophical Poets*. Cambridge: Harvard University Press, 1910. Reprinted as an Anchor Book (Garden City, N. Y.: Doubleday, 1954).

Viëtor, Karl, *Goethe, the Poet*. Cambridge: Harvard University Press, 1949.

6. KIERKEGAARD

The following Kierkegaard texts are especially relevant to a consideration of his thought within the context established by this book:

The Concluding Unscientific Postcript, trans. by David F. Swenson; introduction and notes by Walter Lowrie. Princeton: Princeton University Press, 1941.

The Concept of Dread, trans. by Walter Lowrie. Princeton: Princeton University Press, 1944.

Fear and Trembling, trans. by Walter Lowrie. Princeton: Princeton University Press, 1941.

Either/Or: A Fragment of Life, trans. by David F. and Lillian M. Swenson. 2 vols. Princeton: Princeton University Press, 1944.

Stages on Life's Way, trans. by Walter Lowrie. Princeton: Princeton University Press, 1940.

The Sickness Unto Death, trans. by Walter Lowrie. Princeton: Princeton University Press, 1941.

Readers seeking further critical guidance in the Kierkegaardian literature will find the following studies helpful:

Collins, James D., *The Mind of Kierkegaard*. Chicago: Henry Regnery Co., 1953.

Croxall, T. H., *Kierkegaard Commentary*. London: James Nisbet and Co. Ltd., 1956.

Geismar, Eduard, *Lectures on the Religious Thought of Sören Kierkegaard*. Minneapolis: Augsburg Publishing House, 1937.

Lowrie, Walter, *Kierkegaard*. New York: Oxford University Press, 1938.

Patrick, D. G., *Pascal and Kierkegaard*. Vol. II. London: Lutterworth Press, 1948.

Swenson, David F., *Something About Kierkegaard*. Minneapolis: Augsburg Publishing House, 1941.

Thomte, Reidar, *Kierkegaard's Philosophy of Religion*. Princeton: Princeton University Press, 1948.

7. DOSTOEVSKI

The standard English translation of Dostoevski's work is that of Constance Garnett, available in this country in the twelve-volume Macmillan edition. Garnett versions of *Crime and Punishment, The Possessed, The Idiot,* and *The Brothers Karamazov* are also available in "Modern Library" editions. David Magarshack has produced new versions of *Crime and*

Punishment, The Idiot, and *The Possessed* (under the title *The Devils*) which are available in inexpensive editions published by Penguin Books (Baltimore). A new version of *Memoirs from the House of the Dead* has recently been produced by Jessie Coulson (New York: Oxford University Press, 1956). And readers who are undertaking to steer a course through the imaginative universe of Dostoevski will find enormously interesting his great book, *The Diary of a Writer,* translated and annotated by Boris Brasol (New York: George Braziller, 1954). There is also a convenient collection of *The Short Novels of Dostoevsky,* with an introduction by Thomas Mann (New York: The Dial Press, 1945).

The following biographical and critical studies are recommended:

Berdyaev, Nicolas, *Dostoievsky,* trans. by Donald Attwater. New York: Sheed & Ward, 1934.

Carr, Edward Hallett, *Dostoevsky.* Boston: Houghton Mifflin Co., 1931.

Gide, André, *Dostoevsky.* London: J. M. Dent and Sons., 1925.

Ivanov, Vyacheslav, *Freedom and the Tragic Life: A Study in Dostoevsky.* New York: Noonday Press, 1952.

Lavrin, Janko, *Dostoevsky and His Creation.* London: W. Collins and Co. Ltd., 1920.

Lloyd, J. A. T., *Fyodor Dostoevsky.* New York: Charles Scribner's Sons, 1947.

Murry, J. Middleton, *Fyodor Dostoevsky: A Critical Study.* New York: Dodd, Mead & Co., 1916.

Simmons, Ernest J., *Dostoevsky: The Making of a Novelist.* London: John Lehmann, 1950.

Zander, L. A., *Dostoevsky.* London: SCM Press Ltd., 1948.

Zernov, Nicolas, *Three Russian Prophets: Khomiakov, Dostoevsky, and Soloviev.* London: SCM Press Ltd., 1944.

8. NIETZSCHE

The standard English Nietzsche edition is *The Complete Works of Friedrich Nietzsche,* edited by Oscar Levy (New

York: The Macmillan Co., 1924). Five of the major works (*Thus Spake Zarathustra, Beyond Good and Evil, The Genealogy of Morals, Ecce Homo*, and *The Birth of Tragedy*) are also available in one volume, *The Philosophy of Nietzsche* (New York: Modern Library). New versions of *The Genealogy of Morals* and *The Birth of Tragedy* have recently been produced by Francis Golffing and are available in a Doubleday Anchor Book (Garden City, N. Y.: 1956).

The following critical studies are recommended:

Bonifazi, Conrad, *Christendom Attacked: A Comparison of Kierkegaard and Nietzsche*. London: Rockliff Publishing Corp. Ltd., 1953.

Copleston, Frederick, *Friedrich Nietzsche, Philosopher of Culture*. London: Burns, Oates and Washburne Ltd., 1942.

Heller, Erich, *The Disinherited Mind: Essays in Modern German Literature*. Philadelphia: Dufour and Saifer, 1952. Chapters III–V.

Kaufman, Walter A., *Nietzsche*. Princeton: Princeton University Press, 1950.

Knight, A. H. J., *Some Aspects of the Life and Work of Nietzsche*. Cambridge, Eng.: The University Press, 1933.

Lavrin, Janko, *Nietzsche: An Approach*. London: Methuen and Co. Ltd., 1948.

Reyburn, Hugh A., *Nietzsche*. London: Macmillan & Co., 1948.

9. HAWTHORNE AND MELVILLE

HAWTHORNE

The standard edition of Hawthorne is the Riverside edition, edited by George Parsons Lathrop in 15 volumes (*The Works of Nathaniel Hawthorne*, Boston: Houghton Mifflin Co., 1882–91). To this should be added the following modern texts which supersede the corresponding portions of Lathrop's edition: *The American Notebooks*, edited by Randall Stewart (New Haven: Yale University Press, 1932); *The English Notebooks*, also edited by Randall Stewart (New York: Modern Language Association of America, 1941); and *Dr.*

Grimshawe's Secret, edited by Edward H. Davidson (Cambridge: Harvard University Press, 1955). A convenient collection for nonspecialist readers is *The Complete Novels and Selected Tales of Nathaniel Hawthorne*, edited, with an introduction, by Norman Holmes Pearson (New York: Modern Library, 1937).

The following biographical and critical studies are recommended:

Arvin, Newton, *Hawthorne*. Boston: Little, Brown & Co., 1929.

Davidson, Edward H., *Hawthorne's Last Phase*. New Haven: Yale University Press, 1949.

Fogle, Richard H., *Hawthorne's Fiction: The Light and the Dark*. Norman: University of Oklahoma Press, 1952.

James, Henry, *Hawthorne*, reprinted in *The Shock of Recognition*, Edmund Wilson, ed. Garden City, N. Y.: Doubleday & Company, 1947.

Matthiessen, F. O., *American Renaissance*. New York: Oxford University Press, 1941.

Stein, William Bysshe, *Hawthorne's Faust: A Study of the Devil Archetype*. Gainesville: University of Florida Press, 1953.

Stewart, Randall, *Nathaniel Hawthorne: A Biography*. New Haven: Yale University Press, 1948.

Waggoner, Hyatt H., *Hawthorne: A Critical Study*. Cambridge: Belknap Press of Harvard University Press, 1955.

MELVILLE

The standard edition of Melville is still the Constable edition (London: Constable and Co. Ltd., 1922–24), published in 16 volumes. A fine modern edition of *Moby Dick* has been prepared by Luther S. Mansfield and Howard P. Vincent (New York: Hendricks House, 1952). And Dr. Henry A. Murray has edited a psychiatrically interesting edition of *Pierre* (New York: Hendricks House, 1949). F. Barron Freeman has prepared an excellent edition of *Billy Budd* (Cambridge: Harvard University Press, 1948). Jay Leyda has edited *The Complete Stories of Herman Melville* (New York: Random House, 1949), and Howard P. Vincent has prepared an edition of the *Collected Poems of Herman Melville* (Chicago: Packard and Co., 1947). Raymond Weaver's collection of the *Shorter Novels of Herman Melville* (New York: Liveright Publishing Corp., 1942) is also a convenient volume. And recently the Grove Press has issued, in its "Evergreen" series, an edition of *The Confidence Man* (New York, 1955).

The following biographical and critical studies are recommended:

Arvin, Newton, *Herman Melville*. New York: William Sloane Associates, 1950.

Chase, Richard, *Herman Melville: A Critical Study*. New York: The Macmillan Co., 1949.

Howard, Leon, *Herman Melville: A Biography*. Berkeley: University of California Press, 1951.

Mason, Ronald, *The Spirit Above the Dust*. London: John Lehmann, 1951.

Matthiessen, F. O., *American Renaissance*. New York: Oxford University Press, 1941.

Sedgwick, William Ellery, *Herman Melville: The Tragedy of Mind*. Cambridge: Harvard University Press, 1945.

Stone, Geoffrey, *Melville*. New York: Sheed & Ward, 1949.

Thompson, Lawrance R., *Melville's Quarrel With God*. Princeton: Princeton University Press, 1952.

Vincent, Howard P., *The Trying-Out of Moby Dick*. Boston: Houghton Mifflin Co., 1949.

Weaver, Raymond M., *Herman Melville: Mariner and Mystic*. New York: Geo. H. Doran Co., 1921.

10. FREUD

The Standard Edition of the Complete Psychological Works of Sigmund Freud, James Strachey, ed., 24 vols. London: Hogarth Press and the Institute of Psycho-analysis, 1953——.

Collected Papers, Ernst Jones, M.D., ed., 5 vols. London: Hogarth Press and the Institute of Psycho-analysis, 1950.

The Interpretation of Dreams, trans. by James Strachey. London: G. Allen, 1954.

The Origins of Psycho-analysis; Letters to Wilhelm Fliess, Drafts and Notes: 1887–1902 by Sigmund Freud, Marie Bonaparte, Anna Freud, Ernst Kris, eds. New York: Basic Books, 1954.

An Autobiographical Study. London: Hogarth Press and the Institute of Psycho-analysis, 1935.

New Introductory Lectures on Psycho-analysis. New York: W. W. Norton & Company, 1933.

Beyond the Pleasure Principle. London: Hogarth Press and the Institute of Psycho-analysis, 1922.

The Ego and the Id. London: Hogarth Press and the Institute of Psycho-analysis, 1927.

Civilization and Its Discontents. London: Hogarth Press and the Institute of Psycho-analysis, 1930.

An Outline of Psychoanalysis. New York: W. W. Norton & Company, 1949.

The following biographical and critical studies are recommended:

Jones, Ernest, *The Life and Work of Sigmund Freud*. New York: Basic Books. Volume I: The Formative Years and the Great Discoveries, 1953; Volume II: Years of Maturity, 1901–1919, 1955.

Mann, Thomas, *Freud, Goethe and Wagner*. New York: Alfred A. Knopf, 1937.

Marcuse, Herbert, *Eros and Civilization: A Philosophical Inquiry into Freud*. Boston: Beacon Press, 1955.

Outler, Albert C., *Psychotherapy and the Christian Message*. New York: Harper & Brothers, 1953.

Philip, Howard Littleton, *Freud and Religious Belief*. London: Rockliff Publishing Corp. Ltd., 1956.

Thompson, Clara, *Psychoanalysis, Evolution and Development: A Review of Theory and Therapy*. New York: Hermitage Press, 1950.

Trilling, Lionel, *The Liberal Imagination*. New York: The Viking Press, 1950. Chapter III.

———, *Freud and the Crisis of Our Culture*. Boston: Beacon Press, 1955.

11. KAFKA

The Castle, trans. by Edwin and Willa Muir. New York: Alfred A. Knopf, 1945.

The Trial, trans. by Edwin and Willa Muir. New York: Alfred A. Knopf, 1945.

Amerika, trans. by Edwin Muir. New York: New Directions, 1946.

The Country Doctor. A Collection of Short Stories translated by Vera Leslie. Oxford: Counterpoint Publications, 1946.

The Great Wall of China: Stories and Reflections, trans. by Edwin and Willa Muir. New York: Schocken Books, 1946.

The Penal Colony: Stories and Short Pieces, trans. by Edwin and Willa Muir. New York: Schocken Books, 1948.

Metamorphosis, trans. by A. L. Lloyd. New York: Vanguard Press, 1946.

Parables. New York: Schocken Books, 1947.

Diaries: 1910–1913, Max Brod, ed.; trans. by Joseph Kresh. New York: Schocken Books, 1948.

Diaries: 1914–1923, Max Brod, ed.; trans. by Martin Greenberg and Hannah Arendt. New York: Schocken Books, 1949.

"Dearest Father," trans. by Ernst Kaiser and Eithne Wilkins; with notes edited by Max Brod. New York: Schocken Books–Noonday Press, 1954.

Letters to Milena, trans. by Tania and James Stern; Willi Haas, ed. New York: Schocken Books–Noonday Press, 1954.

Selected Short Stories, trans. by Edwin and Willa Muir. New York: Modern Library, 1952.

The collected German edition of Kafka's works is published in this country by Schocken Books.

The following biographical and critical studies are recommended:

Auden, W. H., "K.'s Quest," in *The Kafka Problem*, Angel Flores, ed. New York: New Directions, 1946.

Brod, Max, *Franz Kafka: A Biography*. New York: Schocken Books, 1947.

Camus, Albert, "Hope and Absurdity," in *The Kafka Problem*, Angel Flores, ed. New York: New Directions, 1946.

Heller, Erich, *The Disinherited Mind*. Philadelphia: Dufour and Saifer, 1952. Chapter VII.

Savage, D. S., "F.K.: Faith and Vocation," in *Focus One*, A. Pearse and B. Rajan, eds. London: Dennis Dobson Ltd., 1945.

Scott, Nathan A., Jr., *Rehearsals of Discomposure: Alienation and Reconciliation in Modern Literature*. New York: King's Crown Press of Columbia University Press, 1952. Chapter II.

Tauber, Herbert, *Franz Kafka: An Interpretation of His Works*. New Haven: Yale University Press, 1948.

Vivas, Eliseo, *Creation and Discovery*. New York: Noonday Press, 1955. Chapter III.

Warren, Austin, "Kosmos Kafka," in *The Kafka Problem*, Angel Flores, ed. New York: New Directions, 1946.

12. FAULKNER

Though in the early forties much of Faulkner's best work was extremely difficult to come by, even on the used-book market, the enormous renascence of interest in his achievement during the past decade has happily resulted in all of his books coming back into print. In hard covers they are published by Random House; and many of them are today available in inexpensive paperback editions: *Intruder in the Dust, Knight's Gambit, Pylon, Sanctuary, Requiem for a Nun, Sartoris, Soldier's Pay, The Unvanquished, Wild Palms,* and *The Old Man* are published by the New American Library; *The Hamlet, The Sound and the Fury,* and *As I Lay Dying* are available in the Modern Library paperback series, and *Mosquitoes* is handled by Dell Books.

The following biographical and critical studies (which represent only an infinitesimal sampling of the enormous critical literature that has grown up about Faulkner's work in the last fifteen years) will be found useful by the general reader who wishes to test his own perceptions against those of some of the best contemporary students of Faulkner:

Brooks, Cleanth, "*Absalom, Absalom!:* The Definition of Innocence," *The Sewanee Review*, Vol. LIX (Autumn 1951), pp. 543–558.

Campbell, Harry M., and Foster, Ruel E., *William Faulkner: A Critical Appraisal*. Norman: University of Oklahoma Press, 1951.

Coughlan, Robert, *The Private World of William Faulkner*. New York: Harper & Brothers, 1954.

Cowley, Malcolm, "Introduction," *The Portable Faulkner*. New York: The Viking Press, 1946. Reprinted in *William Faulkner: Two Decades of Criticism*, Frederick J. Hoffman and Olga W. Vickery, eds. East Lansing: Michigan State College Press, 1951.

Frohock, W. M., *The Novel of Violence in America*. Dallas: Southern Methodist University Press, 1950.

Hoffman, Frederick J., "William Faulkner: An Introduction," in *William Faulkner: Two Decades of Criticism*, Hoffman and Vickery, eds.

Hopper, Vincent F., "Faulkner's Paradise Lost," *The Virginia Quarterly Review*, Vol. XXII (Summer 1947), pp. 405–420.

Howe, Irving, *William Faulkner: A Critical Study*. New York: Random House, 1952.

Jacobs, Robert D., "Faulkner's Tragedy of Isolation," *The Hopkins Review*, Vol. VI (Spring–Summer, 1953), pp. 162–163.

Kazin, Alfred, "Faulkner in His Fury," in *The Inmost Leaf*. New York: Harcourt, Brace & Co., 1955.

Lewis, R. W. B., "The Hero in the New World: William Faulkner's 'The Bear'," *The Kenyon Review*, Vol. XIII (Autumn 1951), pp. 641–660.

Lytle, Andrew Nelson, "The Son of Man: He Will Prevail," *The Sewanee Review*, Vol. LXIII (Winter 1955), pp. 114–137.

Miner, Ward L., *The World of William Faulkner*. Durham, N. C.: Duke University Press, 1952.

O'Conner, William Van, *The Tangled Fire of William Faulkner*. Minneapolis: University of Minnesota Press, 1954.

O'Donnell, George M., "Faulkner's Mythology," *The Kenyon Review*, Vol. I (Summer 1939), pp. 285–299. Reprinted in *William Faulkner: Two Decades of Criticism*, Hoffman and Vickery, eds.

Rice, Philip Blair, "Faulkner's Crucifixion," *The Kenyon Review*, Vol. XVI (Autumn 1954), pp. 661–670.

Sullivan, Walter, "The Tragic Design of *Absalom, Absalom!*," *The South Atlantic Quarterly*, Vol. L (October, 1951), pp. 552–566.

Warren, Robert Penn, "William Faulkner," in *Forms of Modern Fiction*, William Van O'Connor, ed. Minneapolis: University of Minnesota Press, 1948.

HADDAM HOUSE BOOKS

BEYOND THIS DARKNESS, *Roger L. Shinn*
CHRISTIAN FAITH AND MY JOB, *Alexander Miller*
PRIMER FOR PROTESTANTS, *James Hastings Nichols*
PREFACE TO ETHICAL LIVING, *Robert E. Fitch*
THE GRAND INQUISITOR, *Fyodor Dostoevsky*
CHRISTIANITY AND COMMUNISM, *John C. Bennett*
YOUTH ASKS ABOUT RELIGION, *Jack Finegan*
YOUNG LAYMEN—YOUNG CHURCH, *John Oliver Nelson*
THE HUMAN VENTURE IN SEX, LOVE, AND MARRIAGE,
Peter A. Bertocci
SCIENCE AND CHRISTIAN FAITH, *Edward LeRoy Long, Jr.*
A GOSPEL FOR THE SOCIAL AWAKENING, *Walter Rauschenbusch*
THE CHRISTIAN IN POLITICS, *Jerry Voorhis*
REDISCOVERING THE BIBLE, *Bernhard W. Anderson*
LIFE'S MEANING, *Henry P. Van Dusen*
THAT ALL MAY BE ONE, *James Edward Lesslie Newbigin*
THE QUEST FOR CHRISTIAN UNITY, *Robert S. Bilheimer*
THE CHRISTIAN STUDENT AND THE CHURCH, *J. Robert Nelson, Editor*
THE CHRISTIAN STUDENT AND THE WORLD STRUGGLE,
J. Robert Nelson, Editor
THE CHRISTIAN STUDENT AND THE UNIVERSITY,
J. Robert Nelson, Editor
THE UNFOLDING DRAMA OF THE BIBLE, *Bernhard W. Anderson*
THE STUDENT PRAYERBOOK, *John Oliver Nelson and Others, Editors*
RIVERSIDE POETRY
HOW TO MAKE FRIENDS ABROAD, *Robert Root*
COMMUNITY OF FAITH, *T. Ralph Morton*
ENCOUNTER WITH REVOLUTION, *M. Richard Shaull*
POLITICS FOR CHRISTIANS, *William Muehl*
THE PARADOXES OF DEMOCRACY, *Kermit Eby and June Greenlief*
THE TRAGIC VISION AND THE CHRISTIAN FAITH,
Nathan A. Scott, Jr., Editor

Twelve distinguished scholars in religion and the humanities here undertake to reassess the understanding of the human problem that emerges from some of the major writers in the intellectual and literary tradition who have comprehended the human story in terms of a tragic perspective.

After an initial chapter that relates the tragic vision to the perspectives of biblical faith, there follow essays on

Nietzsche

Hawthorne

Melville

Freud

Kafka

Faulkner

Shakespeare

Milton

Pascal

Goethe

Kierkegaard

Dostoevski

Though their primary concern is with problems that are ultimately of a religious order, the contributors do not approach the various artists and thinkers with whom they deal as if their books afforded any kind of direct guidance as to precisely how contemporary man might purchase his salvation. In each case, the intention